Using QuickBASIC

Don Inman
Bob Albrecht

Osborne **McGraw-Hill**
Berkeley, California

Osborne **McGraw-Hill**
2600 Tenth Street
Berkeley, California 94710
U.S.A.

For information on translations and book distributors outside of the U.S.A., please write to Osborne **McGraw-Hill** at the above address.

 A complete list of trademarks appears on page 425.

Using QuickBASIC

1234567890 DODO 898

ISBN 0-07-881274-7

Contents

Preface

BASIC has long been the language most used for personal programming. Most personal computer users have learned to program in BASIC because it is easy to learn and use. Over the years, many BASIC dialects have emerged from the first simple version.

QuickBASIC from Microsoft takes a giant leap beyond yesterday's BASIC, which was designed for beginners, to a truly structured and powerful, professional language. Since it has its roots in Microsoft BASIC, it is still easy to learn and use. Most of your own BASIC programs can be run from QuickBASIC. However, you will soon be rewriting old BASIC programs to take advantage of QuickBASIC's advanced features.

Using QuickBASIC version 4, you can edit, compile, run, and debug programs within a single environment. All of QuickBASIC's programming tools are contained in one integrated package, ready for use at any time.

About This Book

This book assumes that you have previously programmed in some version of BASIC. If you have used some form of Microsoft BASIC, that will be even more helpful. A knowledge of the Microsoft Disk Operating System (referred to in this book as MS-DOS) will also be helpful, but is not absolutely necessary.

The QuickBASIC manuals *Learning and Using QuickBASIC, Programming in BASIC: Selected Topics,* and *Language Reference* cover three aspects of the language. These manuals plus the multi-disks containing the language and supporting files provide a powerful programming package.

This book offers a different point of view and a different approach to learning how to use the massive amount of information available from the Microsoft manuals and disks. A background is laid in the early chapters to provide readers with a common base from which to start. From this point a smooth transition to the rich language elements of QuickBASIC can be made.

The book contains many demonstration examples and programs to simplify the explanation of QuickBASIC procedures, statements, and functions in a meaningful context. Screen displays are used to show what is happening at critical stages in the development of the demonstrations.

As you work through *Using QuickBASIC,* you'll find it easier to learn and understand the discussions if you actually sit down at your computer and run the examples and demonstration programs. At times we describe specific steps in a given computer operation, but it is not practical to describe the steps for every conceivable computer configuration. Therefore, we describe steps for a minimal system with two floppy disk drives. It is much easier to transfer such information from a small to a large system than vice versa.

A consistent style of programming has been used in this book. Programs are easy to read and understand. Programming "tricks" and shortcuts that would detract from learning have been avoided.

After explaining how to configure a QuickBASIC work disk, we describe fundamental tools of QuickBASIC. Their use is demonstrated with practical examples. You learn how to move around in

QuickBASIC's menu system and to use the menus for loading, saving, and running programs.

After learning the basics, you are ready to move on to some of QuickBASIC's more powerful control structures. Editing tools are used to delete, insert, and copy characters, words, and blocks of text. Some editing tools are immediately available from the QuickBASIC editor. The more powerful ones are accessed from the Edit menu.

The features of QuickBASIC procedures, subprograms (SUB... END SUB), and function definitions (FUNCTION...END FUNCTION) are discussed and fully demonstrated. They are powerful structures that will enhance your programs. The View menu, used to access procedures after they have been created, is explained and demonstrated in many examples.

Data files, both sequential and random access, are discussed and used to demonstrate how many QuickBASIC features can be used in applications. Methods of scanning, copying, inserting, adding, and editing records within data files are described and many examples are shown.

The Debug menu is explained and used to show QuickBASIC tools for debugging programs. Single stepping through programs is demonstrated, along with the use of watch points, breakpoints, and program tracing and history.

The book concludes with a demonstration of making and running executable program files that will run directly from your disk operating system (MS-DOS, PC-DOS, and so on).

Microsoft QuickBASIC is an extremely powerful language that contains rich and elegant features. This book "walks" you through the fundamental features so that you will have the background necessary to further explore QuickBASIC in an intelligent way. Programming skills are developed by studying programs and experimenting with the elements of a language. You are encouraged to use this book as a beginning for such exploration and development.

—Don Inman
Bob Albrecht

Using QuickBASIC *Convenience Disk*

You may order a disk containing all programs, defined functions, and procedures discussed in *Using QuickBASIC*. This disk includes

■ All GW-BASIC and QuickBASIC programs shown in this book

■ All single-line and multi-line functions stored as separate files so you can easily merge them with your programs

■ All SUB and FUNCTION procedures stored as separate files so you can easily merge them with your programs

■ A bonus. The disk includes several files not described in the book: functions, procedures, and complete programs

All files are in ASCII format.

Using QuickBASIC disk: $14.95 (check or money order)

Name: _____

Address: _____

City, State, ZIP: _____

Send to: Don & Bob
Adventures in Learning
P.O. Box 7627
Menlo Park, CA 94026

California residents, please add applicable sales tax.

Osborne/McGraw-Hill assumes NO responsibility for this offer. This is solely an offer of the authors and not of Osborne/McGraw-Hill.

Using QuickBASIC *Teacher's Guide*

QuickBASIC is the ideal language for students in secondary schools. This teacher's guide includes exercises, solutions, COPY ME instructional material, and other things to help teachers teach QuickBASIC. Available February 1, 1988.

Using QuickBASIC Teacher's Guide: $9.95 (check or money order)

Name: _____

Address: _____

City, State, ZIP: _____

Send to: Don & Bob
Adventures in Learning
P.O. Box 7627
Menlo Park, CA 94026

California residents, please add applicable sales tax.

Osborne/McGraw-Hill assumes NO responsibility for this offer. This is solely an offer of the authors and not of Osborne/McGraw-Hill.

1 A Review of BASIC

BASIC was available as a programming language for large computers long before the first microcomputer appeared. BASIC arose from a quest whose purpose was to make computing power available to all people, not just those professional programmers who normally had access to large, expensive computers. Dartmouth professors John G. Kemeny and Thomas E. Kurtz developed the original BASIC language in 1963 and 1964 as an instructional tool for training novice programmers. Their purpose was to design a language that would be easy to learn, but still useful for any programming task. The success of BASIC (Beginners' All-purpose Symbolic Instructional Code) and its widespread use are due to its simplicity, ease of use, and general-purpose power.

In 1965, BASIC became available outside of Dartmouth, initially by means of time-sharing systems. Its use later spread to the "low-cost" (at that time) dedicated minicomputers. When microcomputers were introduced to the public as personal computers, the computer moved from the exclusive realm of the professional programmer into the domain of the creative amateur. The only higher-level language available for these early machines was BASIC. A short history of BASIC is shown in Table 1-1.

1956	Darsimco (Dartmouth Simplified Code), a simplified version of assembly language programming, was designed but did not catch on.
1956-57	Kemeny and Kurtz became increasingly aware of the shortcomings of batch-processing computer programs.
1957	Appearance of FORTRAN for experts.
Early 1960s	Kemeny and Kurtz began to seriously consider time sharing for computer use by many users.
	The National Science Foundation approved funding for a project staffed by Kemeny, Kurtz, and a dozen undergraduates to develop a time-sharing system at Dartmouth College. This marked the beginning of personalized, interactive computing.
	Kemeny, Kurtz, and students worked with compilers, FORTRAN, ALGOL, and experimental languages, all of which influenced later development of BASIC.
1963	A decision was made at Dartmouth to enable all students to become computer literate. Kemeny and Kurtz, with help from students, began the development of a general-purpose, time-sharing computer system and a new language (BASIC) to introduce beginners to programming and to serve all applications for large and small systems.
	The original features of BASIC were designed to
	■ Be general-purpose in nature for writing any type of program
	■ Allow for advanced features if needed later
	■ Provide for user/computer interaction
	■ Provide clear and friendly error messages
	■ Give a fast response for small programs
	■ Require no hardware knowledge
	■ Shield the user from the computer's operating system
1964	Equipment on which the time-sharing system and BASIC were to be developed arrived in February 1964. The equipment was fully functional by March 1, 1964.
	On May 1, 1964, at 4 A.M., John Kemeny and a student programmer entered and ran separate BASIC programs on the new system with success. Timesharing and BASIC were born.
1964-1971	The growth of BASIC in this period predated personal computers.
	BASIC at Dartmouth made the transition from a language suitable only for small programs to a language suitable for building large application programs.

Table 1-1.   *Early BASIC History**

Kemeny and Kurtz had sole responsibility for Dartmouth's first BASIC; then others became involved.

Two main genealogical lines grew out of the original Dartmouth BASIC. Large-machine BASIC versions were probably direct descendants of GE BASIC, which in turn descended from Dartmouth BASIC. Most small-machine BASIC versions descended from versions that first appeared on the Hewlett-Packard HP-2000 or the Digital Equipment PDP-8. GE BASIC and Dartmouth BASIC were almost the same until around 1970; Dartmouth had built its time-sharing systems around GE hardware.

Expanded PRINT statements and the introduction of the INPUT statement (almost two years after BASIC first appeared) greatly enhanced the interaction between user and computer.

The use of strings of characters (highly restricted in early BASIC) was expanded with the introduction of string variables.

The use of files for other purposes than saving programs was introduced.

Provision for "calling" external subroutines added flexibility to large programs.

By the end of 1971, Dartmouth BASIC had reached its sixth version and was a huge success.

*The material for this history was based on *Back to BASIC*, by J. G. Kemeny and T. E. Kurtz (Addison-Wesley, 1985), which is recommended reading.

Table 1-1. *Early BASIC History (continued)*

Because early microcomputers had limited memory, early versions of BASIC were crunched adaptations of Dartmouth BASIC. Today there is at least one version of BASIC available for each brand of microcomputer. Today's versions are more complete and powerful, but they are still easy to learn and use. BASIC is now built into, or bundled with, almost every computer that goes into businesses, homes, and schools.

BASIC provides immediate interaction with the user by means of commands that cause some action on the video screen. Therefore, a beginner receives immediate positive reinforcement through the person/computer relationship. After learning a small number of BASIC statements, a user can create programs in short, simple steps. The desire to solve interesting problems or create interesting video displays stimulates the desire, as well as the necessity, to learn more of BASIC's capabilities. This immediate and constant interaction between person and computer puts BASIC at the forefront of people-oriented computer languages.

Many languages are now available for microcomputers — COBOL, FORTRAN, LOGO, Pascal, Modula-2, and C, to name a few. The list of candidates in the battle for computer language supremacy goes on and on. Each language has its own group of proponents who expound the virtues of their choice.

BASIC is not a standardized language. Different versions have been created to fit the unique hardware characteristics of individual computers. The programming styles of users also vary widely — people often write programs that work but are impossible for anyone other than the programmer to read. Even the programmer may have trouble reading the program after some time has passed.

Proponents of other computer languages attack BASIC with the claim that it does not lend itself to well-structured programs. With a little planning and effort on the part of a programmer, however, BASIC programs can be structured into functional blocks of program lines. In addition, new BASIC interpreters and compilers, such as QuickBASIC, qualify as fully structured languages with multiline functions, procedures with both local and global variables, and structures such as IF...THEN...ELSE...END IF and WHILE... WEND. And now some versions of BASIC, including QuickBASIC, have all the "goodies" that proponents of other languages have bragged about in the past.

BASIC has also been criticized because of its lack of speed. This was true in the past, since most versions of BASIC were written as interpreters. The microprocessor of a computer cannot directly execute BASIC statements; it can only execute its own binary machine-language instructions. Therefore, before BASIC statements can be executed, they must be translated into the machine language of the processor.

There are two ways to provide this translation, by interpreter and by compiler. Nearly all versions of BASIC developed in the past, and most versions of the present, are interpreted. Each BASIC statement is translated (interpreted) as it is executed. This line-by-line interpretation takes place every time the BASIC program is run, slowing the execution of the program.

The original version of BASIC and its further development at Dartmouth used a compiler to convert BASIC programs into machine language directly. A compiler translates (compiles) the BASIC statements before the program is run. The program is first compiled to produce an executable machine-language file. When this file is run, it runs very quickly, since it is in the machine's native language. The translation has already taken place, so no time is lost during the program's execution. Most commercial software operates in this way.

There are advantages and disadvantages to both methods of translation. Much time is spent in writing an error-free, compiled program. Each time an error is discovered in the executable machine-language file, the original BASIC program (called the source code) must be corrected. The program must then be recompiled before its executable file (called the object code) can be run again. If more errors are discovered, the original program must be corrected and recompiled. Although the compiled code runs very swiftly, writing an error-free source program can be time-consuming. Interpreted BASIC, on the other hand, is translated line by line, and errors are discovered and corrected quickly. The execution time is much slower than that of a compiled program, however.

QuickBASIC: The Best of Two Worlds

QuickBASIC is a new version of BASIC from Microsoft Corporation that can run much more quickly than interpreted versions, and it also retains the interactive qualities of the language. Designed for IBM PC and PC-compatible computers, QuickBASIC offers functions and speed previously unavailable from other versions of BASIC. It combines the interactive strength of interpreted BASIC with the structured, modular approach of languages such as Pascal.

QuickBASIC employs the same powerful yet easy-to-use language environment that is characteristic of other versions of Microsoft BASIC. It is compatible with IBM's Advanced BASIC (BASICA) and

Microsoft's GW-BASIC, which runs on the Tandy 1000 and other computers. The QuickBASIC compiler is intended for users familiar with those interpreted versions of Microsoft BASIC.

Major features of QuickBASIC are as follows:

■ It is compatible with Microsoft GW-BASIC and IBM BASICA.

■ It offers a built-in, full-screen editor, compiler, and debugger with pull-down menus, dialog boxes, and on-line help.

■ Commands may be selected from menus by using the keyboard or a mouse.

■ It can compile entirely in memory to save time.

■ Its editor locates errors and highlights them with the cursor.

■ Programs can be compiled to optimize speed or to optimize memory.

■ It supports structured programming with alphanumeric labels, structured logic statements, subprograms, and multiline functions, which makes programs easier to read and understand.

■ It supports graphics (including EGA modes), BLOAD/BSAVE, sound, music, and event trapping.

A Common BASIC Starting Point

Since readers of this book have a wide variety of computer experience, a brief review of a common set of BASIC statements, functions, and commands is in order. This book assumes that you have been using, and have some knowledge of, one or more versions of BASIC. Whether you have been using an Atari, Commodore, IBM PC, Tandy 1000, Apple II, or some other computer is of little consequence—all versions of BASIC used with those computers are similar.

This review is limited to GW-BASIC (or IBM BASICA, which is almost identical) and Applesoft BASIC for several reasons. To simplify the discussion, these versions of BASIC will be referred to as

GW-BASIC and Applesoft. Microsoft's GW-BASIC was chosen because it is one of the latest and most powerful versions of BASIC, is widely used, and is available for many brands of computers. Applesoft BASIC (which is licensed from Microsoft) was chosen because it is the language of the entire series of Apple II computers, which are widely used in schools. Applesoft is an older BASIC that is built into the Apple II, II+, IIc, IIe, and even the new IIGS. These new and older versions of BASIC provide a good contrast because of their differences and similarities. The contrast also illustrates the growth of BASIC from Applesoft's old and primitive version to the newer and more powerful GW-BASIC.

The series of short sample programs presented here will emphasize the similarities and differences of GW-BASIC and Applesoft. Table 1-2 lists the BASIC statements, functions, and operators reviewed in this chapter. If the statement, function, or operator is available in GW-BASIC or Applesoft, a plus mark (+) appears in the appropriate column. If not available, a zero (0) appears in the appropriate column.

The Applesoft programs included in this chapter will help Applesoft users make the transition from Applesoft to GW-BASIC and QuickBASIC. By comparing the two versions of each program, you will see how you can quickly and easily edit your Applesoft programs so they can be compiled and executed in QuickBASIC. In order to ease your task, the Applesoft and GW-BASIC versions have been made as similar as possible, so you can more easily see the differences and similarities. Of course, as you wend your way through this book, you will learn to use powerful QuickBASIC features that are not available in either Applesoft or GW-BASIC.

Many of you may want to just browse through the sample programs of this review, studying only those of interest. If you are a beginner, you should study each program and try it on your computer. REMARK (REM) statements are not executed when you run a program. Therefore, they may be omitted when testing these demonstration programs, which will save you a considerable amount of typing. REM statements are used to help you read and understand the program.

If you are an advanced BASIC user, you can skip through this chapter and move on to more advanced material.

Statements	GW-BASIC	Applesoft
ASC	+	+
CLS	+	0
DATA	+	+
DIM	+	+
ELSE	+	0
END	+	+
FOR...TO...STEP...NEXT	+	+
GET	0	+
GOSUB/RETURN	+	+
GOTO	+	+
HOME	0	+
HTAB	0	+
IF...THEN	+	+
INPUT	+	+
KEY OFF	+	0
LOCATE	+	0
PRINT	+	+
PRINT USING	+	0
READ	+	+
REM	+	+
SWAP	+	0
VTAB	0	+
WHILE...WEND	+	0
Functions		
CHR$	+	+
INKEY$	+	0
INT	+	+
LEN	+	+
MID$	+	+
SPACE$	+	0

Table 1-2.   *BASIC Statements, Functions, and Operators in Chapter 1*

Statements	GW-BASIC	Applesoft
SPC	+	+
TAB	+	+
Operators		
+	+	+
−	+	+
*	+	+
/	+	+
AND	+	+
OR	+	+
=	+	+
<	+	+
>	+	+

Table 1-2.   *BASIC Statements, Functions, and Operators in Chapter 1*
(continued)

Personal Applications

BASIC is known as a language for personal rather than commercial use. Therefore, the first programs here are applications that are common to many people. They are written in a style that is easy to read and understand. All variables are defined, and program functions are written as separate blocks.

Checking Up on Your Utility Company   Almost everyone has to deal with a monthly bill from a utility company. We usually pay the specified amount with little regard to its validity. Figure 1-1 shows a typical utility bill, which contains all the information needed to check its validity. You can also check the meter readings if you know what day of the month the meter person reads your meter.

   The UTIL BILL program is shown in two versions, one written in GW-BASIC and the other written in Applesoft. Program 1-1a, UTIL

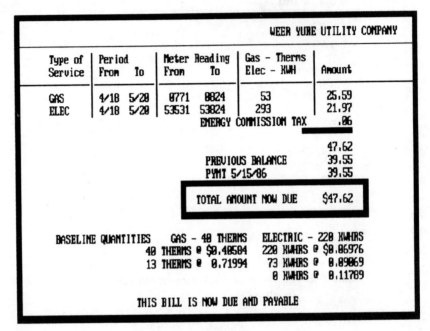

Figure 1-1.   *Utility bill*

BILL, is written in GW-BASIC. It is already in a form that is compatible with QuickBASIC, so you can use QuickBASIC to compile and run it. Remember, BASICA programs are also compatible with QuickBASIC. Program 1-1*b*, UTIL BILL, is written in Applesoft. This program is not compatible with QuickBASIC, so you cannot use QuickBASIC to compile and execute it.

Programs 1-1*a* and 1-1*b* demonstrate the style and many of the conventions used throughout this book. The programs use a common set of conventions and a structured style, which Chapter 2 discusses in detail. They are structured in functional blocks, or modules. This can be done even when you are using early versions of BASIC. Each functional block begins with a REMARK (REM) statement to identify the function performed. No GOTO, GOSUB, or other statement is made to a line that begins with a REMARK. Therefore, you may omit lines that begin with REM when entering the program; the program will run in the same way whether these lines are there or not.

The REM statements that identify the functional blocks in a

```
1 REM ** UTIL BILL **
2 REM ** GW-BASIC VERSION **
3 REM ** PROGRAM 1-1a **
4 REM ** 1/20/87 **
5 REM ** A COLD, RAINY DAY **
6 REM ** UTILITY BILL RISES **
9 '
100 REM ** VARIABLES USED **
110 ' EBA      - ELECTRIC BASE LINE LIMIT
120 ' KBP      - KWH BASE LINE PRICE
130 ' KPO      - KWH OVER BASE PRICE
140 ' KWH      - KWH USE - ENTRY
150 ' K1       - KWH OVER BASE LINE USE
160 ' GBA      - GAS BASE LINE LIMIT
170 ' TBP      - THERMS BASE LINE PRICE
180 ' THM      - THERMS USE - ENTRY
190 ' TPO      - THERMS OVER BASE PRICE
200 ' T1       - THERMS OVER BASE LINE USE
210 ' ELECT    - ELECTRIC CHARGE BEFORE ROUNDING
220 ' ELECTOT  - ELECTRIC CHARGE ROUNDED
230 ' GAS      - GAS CHARGE BEFORE ROUNDING
240 ' GASTOT   - GAS CHARGE ROUNDED
250 ' SUBTOT   - TOTAL CHARGES BEFORE TAX
260 ' TAX      - ENERGY COMMISSION TAX
270 ' TOTAL    - TOTAL INCLUDING TAX
280 ' TXR      - ENERGY COMMISSION TAX RATE
290 ' ST$      - STRING OUTPUT FORMAT
299 '
300 REM ** ASSIGN CONSTANTS **
310 EBA = 220               ' ELECTRIC BASE LINE AMOUNT
320 GBA = 40                ' GAS BASE LINE AMOUNT
330 KBP = .06976            ' KWH BASE LINE PRICE
340 KPO = .09069            ' KWH OVER BASE PRICE
350 TBP = .40584            ' THERMS BASE LINE PRICE
360 TPO = .71994            ' THERMS OVER BASE PRICE
370 TXR = .00125            ' ENERGY TAX RATE
380 ST$ = "$###.##"         ' STRING OUTPUT FORMAT
399 '
400 REM ** ENTER AMOUNTS **
410 CLS
420 INPUT "TOTAL    KWH"; KWH
430 INPUT "TOTAL THERMS"; THM
499 '
500 REM ** CALCULATE BILL **
510 K1 = 0: T1 = 0
520 IF KWH > EBA THEN K1 = KWH - EBA: KWH = EBA
530 IF THM > GBA THEN T1 = THM - GBA: THM = GBA
540 ELECT = KWH * KBP + K1 * KPO
550 GAS = THM * TBP + T1 * TPO
599 '
600 REM ** ROUND OFF & PRINT RESULTS **
610 ELECTOT = INT(ELECT * 100 + .5) / 100
620 GASTOT = INT(GAS * 100 + .5) / 100
630 PRINT: PRINT "TOTAL ELECTRIC = ";: PRINT USING ST$; ELECTOT
640 PRINT "TOTAL GAS      = ";: PRINT USING ST$; GASTOT

650 SUBTOTAL = ELECTOT + GASTOT
660 TAX = INT(TXR * SUBTOTAL * 100 + .5) / 100
670 PRINT "ENERGY TAX     = ";: PRINT USING ST$; TAX
680 TOTAL = SUBTOTAL + TAX
690 PRINT: PRINT "TOTAL BILL     = ";: PRINT USING ST$; TOTAL
700 END
```

Program 1-1a.   *UTIL BILL (GW-BASIC version)*

```
1 REM ** UTIL BILL **
2 REM ** APPLESOFT VERSION **
3 REM ** PROGRAM 1-1b **
4 REM ** 1/26/87 **
9 :
100 REM ** VARIABLES USED **
110 REM  EBL      - ELECTRIC BASE LINE LIMIT
120 REM  KBP      - KWH BASE LINE PRICE
130 REM  KPO      - KWH OVER BASE PRICE
140 REM  KWH      - KWH USE - ENTRY
150 REM  K1       - KWH OVER BASE LINE USE
160 REM  GBL      - GAS BASE LINE LIMIT
170 REM  TBP      - THERMS BASE LINE PRICE
180 REM  THM      - THERMS USE - ENTRY
190 REM  TPO      - THERMS OVER BASE PRICE
200 REM  T1       - THERMS OVER BASE LINE USE
210 REM  ELECT    - ELECTRIC CHARGE BEFORE ROUNDING
220 REM  TELEC    - ELECTRIC CHARGE ROUNDED
230 REM  GAS      - GAS CHARGE BEFORE ROUNDING
240 REM  TGAS     - GAS CHARGE ROUNDED
250 REM  SUBTTL   - TOTAL CHARGES BEFORE TAX
260 REM  TAX      - ENERGY COMMISSION TAX
270 REM  TT       - TOTAL INCLUDING TAX
280 REM  TXR      - ENERGY COMMISSION TAX RATE
299 :
300 REM ** ASSIGN CONSTANTS **
310 EBL = 220          :REM ELECTRIC BASE LINE AMOUNT
320 GBL = 40           :REM GAS BASE LINE AMOUNT
330 KBP = .06976       :REM KWH BASE LINE PRICE
340 KPO = .09069       :REM KWH OVER BASE PRICE
350 TBP = .40584       :REM THERMS BASE LINE PRICE
360 TPO = .71994       :REM THERMS OVER BASE PRICE
370 TXR = .00125       :REM ENERGY TAX RATE
399 :
400 REM ** ENTER AMOUNTS **
410 HOME
420 INPUT "TOTAL   KWH ? "; KWH
430 INPUT "TOTAL THERMS ? "; THM
499 :
500 REM ** CALCULATE BILL **
510 K1 = 0: T1 = 0
520 IF KWH > EBL THEN K1 = KWH - EBL: KWH = EBL
530 IF THM > GBL THEN T1 = THM - GBL: THM = GBL
540 ELECT = KWH * KBP + K1 * KPO
550 GAS = THM * TBP + T1 * TPO
599 :
600 REM ** ROUND OFF & PRINT RESULTS **
610 TELEC = INT(ELECT * 100 + .5) / 100
620 TGAS = INT(GAS * 100 + .5) / 100
630 PRINT: PRINT "TOTAL ELECTRIC = $ "; TELEC
640 PRINT "TOTAL GAS       = ? "; TGAS
650 SUBTTL = TELEC + TGAS
660 TAX = INT(TXR * SUBTTL * 100 + .5) / 100
670 PRINT "ENERGY TAX      = $ 0"; TAX
680 TT = SUBTTL + TAX
690 PRINT: PRINT "TOTAL BILL      = $ "; TT
700 END
```

Program 1-1b.   *UTIL BILL (Applesoft version)*

program can be used as an outline of the program. For example, here is an outline, in REM statements, of programs 1-1*a* and 1-1*b*:

```
1 REM ** UTIL BILL **              Block 1

100 REM ** VARIABLES USED **        Block 100

300 REM ** ASSIGN CONSTANTS **      Block 300

400 REM ** ENTER AMOUNTS **         Block 400

500 REM ** CALCULATE BILL **        Block 500

600 REM ** ROUND OFF & PRINT RESULTS **   Block 600
```

Notice that the opening block (Block 1) consists only of REMARK statements used to identify this particular program — name, number, computer version, and date. From time to time, other information in this block of program lines may be included. This information can be comments about the program, advice, or any subject. When you are writing programs, use comments in any way you want, but be sure to use them. In this way, your program becomes self-explanatory, which is especially important for long, complicated programs. Others can read and understand your programs, and you can read and understand a program you wrote a long time ago.

The second block (Block 100) names and briefly describes the variables used in the program. Applesoft users should compare Block 100 in the two programs. One of the most notable differences between GW-BASIC and Applesoft is the use of variable names. GW-BASIC and QuickBASIC accept long variable names of as many as 40 characters, but Applesoft only accepts variable names of 8 or fewer characters. Moreover, Applesoft recognizes only the two leftmost characters of a variable name. You must use great care when using Applesoft variable names that are longer than two letters. For example, *NUMBER, NUMBER1,* and *NUMBER2* are all recognized by their first two letters (*NU*) when Applesoft is used, so an Apple II considers them all to be the same. However, these three names would be recognized as three distinct variables by GW-BASIC or QuickBASIC. Therefore, GW-BASIC and QuickBASIC allow you to use names that are descriptive of the values that they represent.

The third block (Block 300) assigns values to some of the variables. The utility rates are constants but are given variable names so that you may easily change them to fit the rates charged by your utility company. The first program uses short variable names — they have the advantage of being typed quickly, but they might not be as descriptive as longer names. Even with short names, some will not work in the Applesoft version of the program.

Blocks 400, 500, and 600 compute and print the amount of the utility bill for the number of kilowatt hours (KWH) and therms of gas (THM) supplied by the user. Applesoft users should note the slight differences in the INPUT and PRINT statements. Also note the use of PRINT USING in lines 630, 640, 670, and 690 of the GW-BASIC program, which provides format control not available in Applesoft.

The indentations and spacing used in the GW-BASIC version are preserved when the program is listed. Applesoft removes the indentations and uses its own spacing conventions when listing a program. A listed Applesoft program will look quite different from the Applesoft version shown in the demonstration programs presented here. In fact, the spacing used by Applesoft may cause the use of reserved words that are completely unexpected. Consider the program line entered as

```
520 IF KWH > EBA THEN K1 = KWH - EBA: KWH = EBA
```

The variables in this line seem to contain no reserved words. However, when the line is listed, you will see

```
520 IF KWH > EB AT HENK1 = KWH - EBA: KWH = EBA
```

Applesoft finds the reserved word AT, separates it by spaces, and makes nonsense of the line. Changing the variable *EBA* to *EBL* for the Applesoft version will make everything work fine.

A similar problem was encountered in this line:

```
650 SUBTOTAL = TELEC + TGAS
```

When listed, the line became

```
650 SUB TO TAL = TELEC + TGAS
```

By changing *SUBTOTAL* to *SUBTTL,* you can make Applesoft accept the line. Applesoft users will be pleasantly surprised to discover the power and control over the computer that QuickBASIC gives you.

A screen print of a run made for the utility bill shown in Figure 1-1 is shown in Figure 1-2. Both GW-BASIC and Applesoft versions of the program produce the same result. The GW-BASIC version can be directly compiled by QuickBASIC. The Applesoft version cannot be compiled by QuickBASIC, but is shown as an aid to those of you with Applesoft experience. There are some differences in PRINT statements to make the outputs of the two versions conform in appearance. If you have moved up to an IBM PC or a PC-compatible computer, the Applesoft version will help you learn to convert Applesoft to GW-BASIC or BASICA, which are accepted by the QuickBASIC compiler.

Checking Up on Your Stocks   Those of you who follow the stock market may find the next demonstration program helpful. You can use it to calculate the average price per share of the stocks you own and

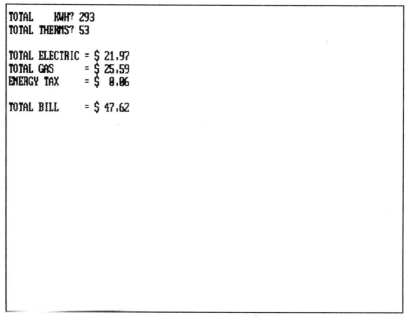

```
TOTAL    KWH? 293
TOTAL THERMS? 53

TOTAL ELECTRIC = $ 21.97
TOTAL GAS      = $ 25.59
ENERGY TAX     = $  0.06

TOTAL BILL     = $ 47.62
```

Figure 1-2.   *Output from Program 1-1a, UTIL BILL*

their total value. The short program consists of only four blocks—program identifier, variable definitions, data entry, and calculation. Here is an outline in REM statements:

```
1 REM ** AVERAGE PRICE OF STOCKS **

100 REM ** VARIABLES USED **

200 REM ** ENTER DATA **

300 REM ** CALCULATE & PRINT **
```

Program 1-2*a* is the GW-BASIC version and Program 1-2*b* is the Applesoft version of AVERAGE PRICE OF STOCKS. In each version, the data entry section asks for the number of shares and the price per share for each stock you own. If you have entered these values for all of your stocks, then enter a zero for the number of shares. The program will then leave the data entry section and move to the calculation module, which computes and prints the average price per

```
1 REM ** AVERAGE PRICE OF STOCKS **
2 REM ** GW-BASIC VERSION **
3 REM ** PROGRAM 1-2a **
4 REM ** 1/21/87 **
9 '
100 REM ** VARIABLES USED **
110 ' NUMS    - Number of shares, each stock
120 ' PPS     - Price per share, each stock
130 ' TSS     - Total stock shares owned
140 ' WORTH   - Total worth of stocks
150 ' AVE     - Average value per share
199 '
200 REM ** ENTER DATA **
210 CLS: TSS = 0: WORTH = 0
220 INPUT "NUMBER OF SHARES "; NUMS
230 IF NUMS = 0 THEN 310
240 INPUT "PRICE PER SHARE   "; PPS
250 WORTH = WORTH + NUMS * PPS
260 TSS = TSS + NUMS
270 PRINT: GOTO 220
299 '
300 REM ** CALCULATE **
310 AVE = INT(WORTH / TSS * 100 + .5) / 100
320 WORTH = INT(WORTH * 100 + .5) /100
330 PRINT: PRINT "AVERAGE PRICE FOR"; TSS; "SHARES IS $"; AVE
340 PRINT "TOTAL VALUE OF STOCKS = $"; WORTH
350 END
```

Program 1-2a. *AVERAGE PRICE OF STOCKS (GW-BASIC version)*

share and the total value of your portfolio.

Both versions of the program produce the same results. The variable in the GW-BASIC version, *WORTH*, was shortened to *WO* for Applesoft. Applesoft does not allow reserved words in variables, even when they are embedded within a variable. It looks at *WORTH* as if it is *W OR TH*. Since OR is a reserved Applesoft word, that combination of letters cannot be used as part of a variable name. You saw earlier that Applesoft will even pick out reserved words from two adjacent words: *EBA THEN* is interpreted as *EB AT HEN*. Applesoft uses HOME in place of the CLS of GW-BASIC. The only other differences in the two versions are in the spacing of PRINT statements and the spacing and use of the question mark in INPUT statements.

A typical run for this program is shown in Figure 1-3. The average price per share is rounded to the nearest cent. When this value is multiplied by the total number of shares owned, the result may differ from the total value shown. However, the result will be correct to within a few cents unless you have a very large number of stock shares.

```
1 REM ** AVERAGE PRICE OF STOCKS **
2 REM ** APPLESOFT VERSION **
3 REM ** PROGRAM 1-2b **
4 REM ** 1/21/87 **
9 :
100 REM ** VARIABLES USED **
110 REM   NUMS   - Number of shares, each stock
120 REM   PPS    - Price per share, each stock
130 REM   TSS    - Total stock shares owned
140 REM   TWR    - Total worth of stocks
150 REM   AVE    - Average value per share
199 :
200 REM ** ENTER DATA **
210 HOME: TSS = 0: TWR = 0
220 INPUT "NUMBER OF SHARES ? "; NUMS
230 IF NUMS = 0 THEN 310
240 INPUT "PRICE PER SHARE   ? "; PPS
250 TWR = TWR + NUMS * PPS
260 TSS = TSS + NUMS
270 PRINT: GOTO 220
299 :
300 REM ** CALCULATE **
310 AVE = INT(TWR / TSS * 100 + .5) / 100
320 PRINT: PRINT "AVERAGE PRICE FOR "; TSS; " SHARES IS $ "; AVE
330 PRINT "TOTAL VALUE OF STOCKS = $ "; TWR
340 END
```

Program 1-2b. *AVERAGE PRICE OF STOCKS (Applesoft version)*

```
NUMBER OF SHARES ? 50
PRICE PER SHARE  ? 62.125

NUMBER OF SHARES ? 23
PRICE PER SHARE  ? 10.5

NUMBER OF SHARES ? 44
PRICE PER SHARE  ? 16

NUMBER OF SHARES ? 0


AVERAGE PRICE FOR 117 SHARES IS $ 34.63
TOTAL VALUE OF STOCKS = $ 4051.75
```

Figure 1-3.   *Output from Program 1-2a, AVERAGE PRICE OF STOCKS*

Uppercase and Lowercase Utilities

It is often necessary for the computer to distinguish between upper- and lowercase letters. The next three programs include subroutines to convert lowercase letters to uppercase, and uppercase letters to lowercase.

If you have written many BASIC programs, you have probably faced the problem of recognizing whether characters are uppercase (capital letters) or lowercase (small letters). Look at the table of ASCII (American Standard Code for Information Interchange) codes for the letters of the alphabet in Appendix A. You will see a difference of 32 characters between the codes for the upper- and lowercase letters.

Here are some examples:

A = 65   a = 97

B = 66   b = 98

.   .

.   .

.   .

Z = 90   z = 122

You can use the BASIC ASC function to discover the ASCII code of a character. If it is a number from 97 to 122, inclusive, the letter is lowercase. You can change a lowercase character's code to an equivalent uppercase code by subtracting 32 and then using the CHR$ function to assign the new code to the character. The reverse procedure (adding 32) will change an uppercase letter to lowercase.

The next program, UPSHIFT/DOWNSHIFT, contains subroutines that perform the upper- and lowercase changes. The GW-BASIC version is shown in Program 1-3*a* and the Applesoft version is shown in Program 1-3*b*. Browse through the program by looking at the REM statements in lines 1, 100, 200, 1000, and 2000. You will find the QuickBASIC programs presented later in this book even easier to read and understand.

The main program block (Block 200) asks you to enter a long string. Type part of this string in capital letters and part of it as lowercase letters. Also use punctuation marks and other characters. When you have entered the string, the program goes to the UPSHIFT subroutine, where lowercase letters are changed to uppercase. When this is done, a return is made to the main program, and the uppercase string is printed. Characters that are not letters remain unchanged.

Although the subroutines begin with line numbers that are multiples of 1000, GOSUB statements are not made to REMARK statements. Instead, GOSUB 1010 and GOSUB 2010 are used. This is done so that you can omit REM statements when you enter a program simply to try it. However, it is recommended that you include all REM statements when you save a program for later use.

After you type a string and press ENTER (RETURN on the Apple II), the DOWNSHIFT subroutine (beginning at line 2000) is executed to

```
1 REM ** UPSHIFT/DOWNSHIFT **
2 REM ** GW-BASIC VERSION **
3 REM ** PROGRAM 1-3a **
4 REM ** 1/22/87 **
9 '
100 REM ** VARIABLES USED **
110 ' KY$     - Entry from keyboard
120 ' UP$     - All upper case string
130 ' LOW$    - All lower case string
140 ' TEMP$   - Temporary string being shifted
150 ' LETTER  - Individual character of string
160 ' CODE    - ASCII code for individual character
199 '
200 REM ** MAIN PROGRAM **
210 CLS
220 INPUT "ENTER A LONG STRING "; KY$
230 GOSUB 1010
240 PRINT: PRINT UP$
250 GOSUB 2010
260 PRINT LOW$
270 LOCATE 7,1: PRINT "PRESS Q TO QUIT  -";
280 PRINT SPC(2)"OR SPACE BAR FOR ANOTHER"
290 KY$ = INKEY$: IF KY$ = "" THEN 290
300 IF KY$ = CHR$(32) THEN 210
310 GOSUB 1010
320 IF UP$ = "Q" THEN END ELSE 290
399 '
1000 REM ** SUBROUTINE: UPSHIFT **
1010 TEMP$ = ""
1020 FOR LETTER = 1 TO LEN(KY$)
1030   CODE = ASC(MID$(KY$,LETTER,1))
1040   IF CODE > 96 AND CODE < 123 THEN CODE = CODE - 32
1050   TEMP$ = TEMP$ + CHR$(CODE)
1060 NEXT LETTER
1070 UP$ = TEMP$
1080 RETURN
1999 '
2000 REM ** SUBROUTINE: DOWNSHIFT **
2010 TEMP$ = ""
2020 FOR LETTER = 1 TO LEN(KY$)
2030   CODE = ASC(MID$(KY$,LETTER,1))
2040   IF CODE > 64 AND CODE < 91 THEN CODE = CODE + 32
2050   TEMP$ = TEMP$ + CHR$(CODE)
2060 NEXT LETTER
2070 LOW$ = TEMP$
2080 RETURN
```

Program 1-3a.   *UPSHIFT/DOWNSHIFT (GW-BASIC version)*

change the original string to all lowercase letters. The resulting string
is then printed on returning to the main program. All characters
except alphabetic characters remain the same as they were originally.
The program then provides a choice between typing another string or
stopping.

```
1 REM ** UPSHIFT/DOWNSHIFT **
2 REM ** APPLESOFT VERSION **
3 REM ** PROGRAM 1-3b **
4 REM ** 1/22/87 **
9 :
100 REM ** VARIABLES USED **
110 REM   KY$      - Entry from keyboard
120 REM   UP$      - All upper case string
130 REM   LOW$     - All lower case string
140 REM   TEMP$    - Temporary string being shifted
150 REM   LTTR     - Individual character of string
160 REM   CODE     - ASCII code for individual character
199 :
200 REM ** MAIN PROGRAM **
210 HOME
220 INPUT "ENTER A LONG STRING ? "; KY$
230 GOSUB 1010
240 PRINT: PRINT UP$
250 GOSUB 2010
260 PRINT LOW$
270 VTAB 7: HTAB 1: PRINT "PRESS Q TO QUIT   - ";
280 PRINT " OR SPACE BAR FOR ANOTHER"
290 GET KY$
300 IF KY$ = CHR$(32) THEN 210
310 GOSUB 1010
320 IF UP$ = "Q" THEN END
330 GOTO 290
399 :
1000 REM ** SUBROUTINE: UPSHIFT **
1010 TEMP$ = ""
1020 FOR LTTR = 1 TO LEN(KY$)
1030    CODE = ASC(MID$(KY$,LTTR,1))
1040    IF CODE > 96 AND CODE < 123 THEN CODE = CODE - 32
1050    TEMP$ = TEMP$ + CHR$(CODE)
1060 NEXT LTTR
1070 UP$ = TEMP$
1080 RETURN
1999 :
2000 REM ** SUBROUTINE: DOWNSHIFT **
2010 TEMP$ = ""
2020 FOR LTTR = 1 TO LEN(KY$)
2030    CODE = ASC(MID$(KY$,LTTR,1))
2040    IF CODE > 64 AND CODE < 91 THEN CODE = CODE + 32
2050    TEMP$ = TEMP$ + CHR$(CODE)
2060 NEXT LTTR
2070 LOW$ = TEMP$
2080 RETURN
```

Program 1-3b.   *UPSHIFT/DOWNSHIFT (Applesoft version)*

The GW-BASIC and Applesoft versions of this program are similar. GW-BASIC's CLS corresponds to Applesoft's HOME. GW-BASIC's INKEY$ function corresponds to Applesoft's GET function. GW-BASIC's LOCATE corresponds to Applesoft's combined VTAB and HTAB.

The AND Operator

For those of you who are not familiar with the logical operator AND, a brief explanation of its use in Program 1-3*a* is presented here. The UPSHIFT and DOWNSHIFT subroutines find the ASCII code of each character that you entered. The program must determine if the code of each entered character is in the range of 65 through 90 to determine if the character is an uppercase letter (A=65, B=66,..., Z=90). The AND operator performs this function by looking at the two conditions: CODE > 64 and CODE < 91. If both conditions are true, the character is an uppercase letter. If either condition is false, the letter is not uppercase. Line 2040 of the DOWNSHIFT subroutine uses AND in its IF...THEN statement to ensure that all uppercase letters are changed to lowercase.

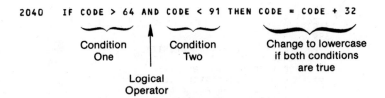

Line 1040 of the UPSHIFT subroutine performs a similar function to change lowercase letters to uppercase:

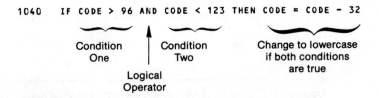

Table 1-3 contains a truth table identifying all possible combinations of the two conditions when combined with the AND operator. Line 2050 of the DOWNSHIFT subroutine builds up a new string (TEMP$) composed of all lowercase letters plus all non-alphabetic characters from your entry. Table 1-4 shows how key values change as the program progresses through the FOR...NEXT loop of the subroutine.

Condition One	Condition Two	Condition One AND Condition Two
TRUE	TRUE	TRUE
TRUE	FALSE	FALSE
FALSE	TRUE	FALSE
FALSE	FALSE	FALSE

Table 1-3. *AND Truth Table*

If the entered string was *UP and doWN*

Value of CHAR	Letter and Code Before Line 2040	Letter and Code After Line 2040	TEMP$ After Line 2050
1	U = 85	u = 117	u
2	P = 80	p = 112	up
3	space = 32	space = 32	up
4	a = 97	a = 97	up a
5	n = 110	n = 110	up an
6	d = 100	d = 100	up and
7	space = 32	space = 32	up and
8	d = 100	d = 100	up and d
9	o = 111	o = 111	up and do
10	W = 87	w = 119	up and dow
11	N = 78	n = 110	up and down

Table 1-4. *DOWNSHIFT Subroutine Results for the String "UP and doWN"*

All variables in the two versions of the program are the same except for *LETTER*, which contains the reserved word LET and cannot be used in the Applesoft version; for this example, *LTTR* was used instead of *LETTER*. A typical run is shown in Figure 1-4.

```
ENTER A LONG STRING ? Now is the time for CAP's.

NOW IS THE TIME FOR CAP'S.
now is the time for cap's.


PRESS Q TO QUIT - OR SPACE BAR FOR ANOTHER
```

Figure 1-4. *Output from Program 1-3a, UPSHIFT/DOWNSHIFT*

The Bubble Sort

A computer can handle lots of data, but human beings are often overwhelmed by it. We can use every bit of help that a computer can provide to arrange data in a way that is useful. For instance, suppose you use a mailing list of names and addresses. One time you might want to print it in alphabetical order by name. Another time you might want to print it by ZIP code. The next program is an example of computer assistance in sorting data.

There are many ways to sort information, and many algorithms exist to sort in different ways. Some ways are easy to understand, but slow. Simple sorting programs are adequate for sorting small files of information. For large files, more sophisticated methods are appropriate.

The bubble sort is a simple and widely used sorting method, suitable for small files of information. A bubble sort starts at the bottom of a list and then proceeds upward, comparing each item in the list with the item above it. If the two items being compared are not in the proper order, their positions in the list are interchanged. In this way, the item that comes first alphabetically is "bubbled" to the top of the list. A bubble sort is not an efficient way to sort data, but it is one of the easiest to understand and is useful for small amounts of information. Later in this book, you will learn about more efficient sorting methods.

As an example, suppose you have a list of four names:

KIT
DON
BOB
MARIKO

The computer starts at the bottom of the list. It first compares items 3 and 4, MARIKO and BOB. Since they are in the proper order, the list remains the same. The computer then compares items 2 and 3, BOB and DON. They are out of order, so their positions are interchanged. The list becomes

KIT
BOB
DON
MARIKO

The computer next compares items 1 and 2, KIT and BOB. They are out of order, so their positions are interchanged:

BOB
KIT
DON
MARIKO

The computer has now completed the first pass through the list of names. It has bubbled the name BOB to the top of the list. However, other items may still be out of order. The computer returns to the bottom of the list to begin its second pass through the list. It compares items 3 and 4, DON and MARIKO. Since they are ordered properly, the computer then compares items 2 and 3, KIT and DON. They are out of order and are interchanged:

BOB
DON
KIT
MARIKO

Since **BOB** was already bubbled to the top of the list during the first pass, there is no need to compare items 1 and 2, BOB and DON. The second pass through the list has bubbled the second name, DON, into its proper place.

The computer once again returns to the bottom of the list for a third pass. It compares KIT and MARIKO. They are in the proper place, so no change is made. Since there were only four names in the list and the top three have been bubbled to their proper places, all necessary changes have been made, and the list is now in alphabetical order. The first pass made three comparisons and any necessary changes; the name was bubbled to the top. The second pass made two comparisons and any necessary changes; the name was bubbled to the second position on the list. The third pass made one comparison and any necessary change; the name was bubbled to the third position on the list. The total number of passes through the list is one less than the number of names. Each pass makes one less comparison than the pass that preceded it.

Program 1-4*a*, BUBBLE SORT, is written in GW-BASIC. It contains six modules, two of which are subroutines. The subroutine beginning at line 2000 reads 19 unordered names from a data list. You can change the number of names in the list, provided you also change the value of the variable *NUMNAMES* (line 2010) and the DIM statement in line 220. (Later on you will find that QuickBASIC is much more flexible for working with arrays.) The subroutine beginning at line 3000 prints the list of names after they have been sorted into alphabetical order.

The first module contains the program identification information, and the second module lists the program variables and their uses.

```
1 REM ** BUBBLE SORT **
2 REM ** GW-BASIC VERSION **
3 REM ** Program 1-4a **
4 REM ** 1/26/87 **
5 REM ** BUBBLE SORT IS NOT EFFICIENT **
99 '
100 REM ** VARIABLES USED **
110 ' NAYM$    - Array of names
120 ' TOP      - First position in list of names being sorted
130 ' BOTTOM   - Last position in list of names
140 ' HERE     - FOR-NEXT loop counter; position of compared names
150 ' NUMNAMES - Number of names in list
160 ' NAYM     - Counter used to subscript array items
199 '
200 REM ** INITIALIZE **
210 KEY OFF: CLS
220 DIM NAYM$(20)
230 GOSUB 2010
299 '
300 REM ** SORT NAMES **
310 LOCATE 10,30: PRINT "DATA BEING SORTED"
320 TOP = 2: BOTTOM = NUMNAMES
330 WHILE TOP <= BOTTOM
340    FOR HERE = BOTTOM TO TOP STEP -1
350      IF NAYM$(HERE) > NAYM$(HERE - 1) THEN 370
360      SWAP NAYM$(HERE), NAYM$(HERE - 1)
370    NEXT HERE
380    TOP = TOP + 1
390 WEND
400 LOCATE 10,30: PRINT SPACES(17)
410 GOSUB 3010
420 END
499 '
2000 REM ** SUBROUTINE: READ LIST INTO ARRAY **
2010 NUMNAMES = 19
2020 DATA SMITH, JONES, BIDWELL, PRESLEY, DECKLE, PORTER, CRANE
2030 DATA TIBBETTS, ROBBINS, GRAHAM, BOCZKOWSKI, HAVENS, STETLER
2040 DATA CHAMBERS, COLE, JAMES, TOLAND, HARRIS, MCCLELLAN
2050 FOR NAYM = 1 TO NUMNAMES
2060    READ NAYM$(NAYM)
2070 NEXT NAYM
2080 RETURN
2999 '
3000 REM ** SUBROUTINE: PRINT SORTED LIST **
3010 LOCATE 1,1: PRINT "SORTED LIST": PRINT
3020 FOR NAYM = 1 TO NUMNAMES
3030    PRINT "NUMBER"; NAYM; TAB(12); NAYM$(NAYM)
3040 NEXT NAYM
3050 RETURN
```

Program 1-4a.   *BUBBLE SORT (GW-BASIC version)*

Since the function-key information at the bottom of the screen can be distracting, the third module uses KEY OFF to erase it. The screen is cleared, the *NAYM$* array is dimensioned, and the READ DATA subroutine is called. Notice that the use of *NAME$* was avoided as the name for the array, since NAME is a reserved word in GW-BASIC.

The fourth module, which sorts the names, is the main body of the program. It contains a WHILE...WEND loop to control the number of times the nested FOR...NEXT loop is executed. The Applesoft version uses a FOR...NEXT loop to control the number of passes through the inner FOR...NEXT loop, since it does not have the WHILE...WEND statement.

GW-BASIC has a SWAP statement that is used in line 360 to interchange out-of-order names. This statement is convenient when sorting data. It is not available in Applesoft, but the result can be duplicated by using an intermediate variable to hold the first value while the second value is moved into the first value's position. The intermediate variable's value is then moved into the second value's position to complete the swap. Figure 1-5 compares the two swapping methods.

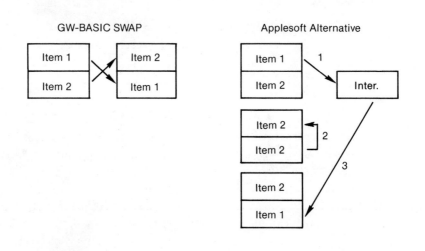

Figure 1-5. *SWAP items*

The following listing shows that the upper limit of the nested FOR...NEXT loop gets smaller, since *TOP* increases (moves down the list) as names bubble to the top.

```
FOR HERE = 19 TO 2  STEP - 1
          .
          .
          .
FOR HERE = 19 TO 3  STEP - 1
          .
          .
          .
       ETC.
          .
          .
          .
FOR HERE = 19 TO 19  STEP - 1
```

A WHILE...WEND loop controls how many times the nested FOR...NEXT loop is executed:

```
WHILE TOP <= BOTTOM
```

In this example, *BOTTOM* is the number of names in the list, and *TOP* is equal to 2 as the FOR...NEXT loop is entered the first time. The FOR...NEXT loop runs from HERE = 19 TO 2. It compares two adjacent names in line 350. If the compared names are in the correct alphabetical order, the THEN clause of line 350 causes line 360 to be omitted (THEN 370), and no SWAP occurs. If the two names are out of order, line 360 SWAPs the order of the two names.

Each time an exit is made from the FOR...NEXT loop, *TOP* is incremented by 1 at line 380. After the last pass through the loop, *TOP* is incremented to 20 and the WHILE limit is exceeded. The sort has been completed. The subroutine beginning at line 3000 is called to print the sorted list of names, and the program ends.

The Applesoft version of BUBBLE SORT is shown in Program 1-4*b*, BUBBLE SORT. In addition to the usual changes of HOME for CLS, VTAB/HTAB for LOCATE, and spacing changes, a major change was made to replace GW-BASIC's WHILE...WEND loop with a FOR...NEXT loop. Within this loop, the Applesoft version

```
1 REM ** BUBBLE SORT **
2 REM ** APPLESOFT VERSION **
3 REM ** Program 1-4b **
4 REM ** 1/26/87 **
99 :
100 REM ** VARIABLES USED **
110 REM   NAYM$   - Array for holding names
120 REM   PASS    - Counter for FOR-NEXT loop
130 REM   TP      - First position in list of names being sorted
140 REM   BOTM    - Last position in list of names
150 REM   HERE    - Counter used to subscript array items when compared
160 REM   NUM     - Number of array entries
170 REM   NAYM    - Counter used to subscript array items when READ
199 :
200 REM ** INITIALIZE **
210 HOME
220 DIM NAYM$(20)
230 GOSUB 2010
299 :
300 REM ** SORT NAMES **
310 VTAB 10: HTAB 30: PRINT "DATA BEING SORTED"
320 TP = 2: BOTM = NUM
330 FOR PASS = 1 TO NUM-1
340   FOR HERE = BOTM TO TP STEP -1
350     IF NAYM$(HERE) < NAYM$(HERE-1) THEN GOSUB 1010
360   NEXT HERE
370   TP = TP + 1
380 NEXT PASS
390 VTAB 10: HTAB 30: PRINT TAB(47)
400 GOSUB 3010
410 END
420 :
1000 REM ** SUBROUTINE: SWAP NAMES **
1010 TEMP$ = NAYM$(HERE)
1020 NAYM$(HERE) = NAYM$(HERE-1)
1030 NAYM$(HERE-1) = TEMP$
1040 RETURN
1999 :
2000 REM ** SUBROUTINE: READ LIST INTO ARRAY **
2010 NUM = 19
2020 DATA SMITH, JONES, BIDWELL, PRESLEY, DECKLE, PORTER, CRANE
2030 DATA TIBBETTS, ROBBINS, GRAHAM, BOCZKOWSKI, HAVENS, STETLER
2040 DATA CHAMBERS, COLE, JAMES, TOLAND, HARRIS, MCCLELLAN
2050 FOR NAYM = 1 TO NUM
2060   READ NAYM$(NAYM)
2070 NEXT NAYM
2080 RETURN
2999 :
3000 REM ** SUBROUTINE: PRINT SORTED LIST **
3010 VTAB 1: HTAB 1: PRINT "SORTED LIST": PRINT
3020 FOR NAYM = 1 TO NUM
3030   PRINT "NUMBER "; NAYM; TAB(12); NAYM$(NAYM)
3040 NEXT NAYM
3050 RETURN
```

Program 1-4b. *BUBBLE SORT (Applesoft version)*

```
SORTED LIST

NUMBER 1    BIDWELL
NUMBER 2    BOCZKOWSKI
NUMBER 3    CHAMBERS
NUMBER 4    COLE
NUMBER 5    CRANE
NUMBER 6    DECKLE
NUMBER 7    GRAHAM
NUMBER 8    HARRIS
NUMBER 9    HAVENS
NUMBER 10   JAMES
NUMBER 11   JONES
NUMBER 12   MCCLELLAN
NUMBER 13   PORTER
NUMBER 14   PRESLEY
NUMBER 15   ROBBINS
NUMBER 16   SMITH
NUMBER 17   STETLER
NUMBER 18   TIBBETTS
NUMBER 19   TOLAND
```

Figure 1-6. *Output from Program 1-4a, BUBBLE SORT*

uses a subroutine to replace the SWAP statement of GW-BASIC, as shown in Figure 1-5. TAB is used in the Applesoft version (instead of SPACE$) to erase a line of text from the screen. Variable names were also changed to avoid Applesoft reserved words. Both versions of the BUBBLE SORT program produce the sorted list shown in Figure 1-6.

Review

In this chapter you were given a brief history of BASIC. You reviewed the advantages and disadvantages of the two methods of translating BASIC to the computer's native machine language— by compiler and by interpreter. A glimpse of QuickBASIC was presented.

The chapter also gave you a tour of BASIC through demonstration programs. These programs used the statements and functions shown in Table 1-2. Some actions performed by GW-BASIC or QuickBASIC statements require different statements or functions for Applesoft. Some GW-BASIC or QuickBASIC statements can only be duplicated by a more complex series of statements in Applesoft.

You have learned that GW-BASIC and QuickBASIC are more flexible than Applesoft in the accepted length and use of variables.

Applesoft recognizes only the first two characters of a variable name as unique—it will not allow reserved words embedded in a variable name. GW-BASIC and QuickBASIC recognize long variable names. A variable name may not be identical to a reserved word, but reserved words may be embedded in a variable name that is longer than the reserved word.

This chapter has provided readers with a common starting point for the BASIC statements and functions that will be used throughout the book.

2 Conventions and Style

Learning to program offers an opportunity to increase problem-solving abilities—not just mathematical problem-solving, but any problem-solving task that you may wish to do. The computer is a valuable tool for learning to think logically. The problem-solving process becomes: defining the problem, breaking the problem down into a series of smaller subproblems, and then writing a computer program in small, functional blocks to fit the subproblems. The solution is reached more logically, more quickly, and more reliably when this process is followed. During the process, one becomes acutely aware of the capabilities and the limitations of the computer. The human element is more important in problem-solving than the tools that are used.

This chapter discusses certain conventions that are used in this book to promote good programming style and structure. These conventions will lead you gently into the style of programming that is supported by QuickBASIC. Structure and good style are practices that you should use for all programs in any BASIC. The computer is a machine that is used by people. Therefore, people should write programs that are easy for other people to read and understand.

The conventions used in this book will provide standardization and a learning environment that will make a smooth and easy transition from the version of BASIC with which you are familiar to Microsoft's QuickBASIC compiler language.

Notational Conventions

This book generally follows the conventions used in the Microsoft QuickBASIC manual. These conventions conform to descriptions in most BASIC reference books, with some noted exceptions. Some of the examples shown use QuickBASIC statements that will not be accepted by other versions of BASIC. Most versions of BASIC cannot use line labels in the way QuickBASIC does.

Ellipses

Ellipses consist of three horizontal dots (...) and indicate that an entry may be repeated as many times as needed or desired. In the example below, ellipses indicate that additional line numbers may be used:

```
ON expression GOSUB linenumber1, linenumber2, ...
```

As many line numbers (linenumber1, linenumber2, linenumber3, and so on) may be supplied as needed.

Vertical Ellipses

Vertical ellipses (three vertical dots) indicate that a portion of the program has been omitted. The following example shows the first and last lines of a subroutine with vertical ellipses indicating the missing lines:

```
1100 REM ** SUBROUTINE: SWAP NAMES **
.
.
.
1040 RETURN
```

Brackets ([ ])

Square brackets indicate that the information enclosed is optional: [optional information]. A default value is used when you do not provide explicit information.

```
FOR counter = first TO last [STEP increment]
```

The square brackets around "STEP increment" indicate that you are not required to supply the STEP information. When it is not supplied, the increment for the loop is +1 by default, as in the following example:

```
FOR A = 1 TO 5
.
.
.
NEXT A
```

If you desire a STEP different from +1, a STEP value must be provided. In the example below, a STEP value of 2 is given:

```
FOR A = 1 TO 5 STEP 2
.
.
.
NEXT A
```

Braces ({ })

Braces indicate that you have the choice of two or more entries following the BASIC keyword. A slash separates choices within braces. At least one of the entries must be chosen unless the entries are also enclosed in square brackets. In the following example, you must state either a line number or a line label following the keyword GOSUB:

```
GOSUB {linenumber/linelabel}
```

Here are specific examples illustrating the two possible choices:

```
GOSUB 330            (a line number follows GOSUB)

GOSUB upcount        (a line label follows GOSUB)
```

Both braces and square brackets are used in the following description of the RETURN statement:

```
RETURN [{linenumber/linelabel}]
```

In this case no entry is necessary following the RETURN statement because of the square brackets. However, either a line number or a line label may be used, if desired. All three possibilities are shown here:

```
RETURN

RETURN 370

RETURN backyonder
```

Programming Conventions and Style

A computer accepts information, processes the information according to specific instructions, and provides the results of the process as new information. The primary reason for learning to program is to be able to use your computer as flexibly as possible. Commercial programs are available for many purposes, but they are seldom written for an individual's specific needs. They are written to be used by as many different people as possible so as to increase sales. By learning to write your own programs, you can make the computer do what you want it to do in the way that you want it done.

While programming, you will develop skills useful in solving problems. You will learn to define a problem and break it down into smaller, more manageable parts. Then you can write a series of instructions that solve the parts. These blocks of instructions, called modules, each solve a particular portion of your original problem. The solution to your problem is finalized by linking the modules together into a complete program.

It is important that your instructions to the computer (in other words, your program) are written in such a way that they can be understood by your computer. The instructions should also be easy to read, understand, and use — for you or anyone else who might read them or use them.

It is tempting to write programs for yourself with little thought to their logic or structure. You may think that you will only use the program once and that no one else will ever use it. However, you never know when you may end up with a real gem that you may want to use again or share with friends. You may even submit it to a magazine. Good programming style is a good habit that leads to good programs.

This book provides carefully designed examples that use a consistent set of programming conventions and structured style. Programs can be structured into functional blocks, or modules, even when you are using versions of BASIC other than QuickBASIC. Several elements of style are shown in this chapter. Additional elements of style are explained as needed in later chapters. The following sections contain the conventions and style used in this book's programs.

Statements

In the programs in this book, each functional block begins with at least one REM (REMARK) statement to indicate clearly the function of that part of the program. Statements that change the flow of the program (such as GOTO or GOSUB) never direct execution to a line that begins with a REM statement.

Each program begins with a series of REM statements numbered 1, 2, 3, and so on. The first REM states the name of the program.

Another gives the program number. Other descriptive information may be given in other REMs of the first program block. Put in whatever information you want. Remember, REM statements are not executed, but they supply descriptive information. In fact, in Quick-BASIC, REM statements are not included in the compiled program. Here is an example from Program 1-1a:

```
1 REM ** UTIL BILL **
2 REM ** GW-BASIC VERSION **
3 REM ** PROGRAM 1-1a **
4 REM ** 1/20/87 **
5 REM ** A COLD, RAINY DAY **
6 REM ** UTILITY BILL RISES **
```

GW-BASIC and QuickBASIC will also accept the apostrophe (') as an alternate way to indicate REM statements. This shortened form can be used to provide comments at the end of some executable lines. Notice the apostrophe used as a break between blocks in line 299 in the following example. This additional separation between blocks makes the programs easier to read.

```
.
.
.
280 ' TXR        - ENERGY COMMISSION TAX RATE
290 ' ST$        - STRING OUTPUT FORMAT
299 '
300 REM ** ASSIGN CONSTANTS **
310 EBA = 200     ' ELECTRIC BASE LINE AMOUNT
.
.
.
```

You may have noticed a difference in the Applesoft programs shown in Chapter 1. Applesoft does not recognize the apostrophe as a replacement for REM. A colon (:) was used to separate blocks in the Applesoft programs, as in line 299 of the following example. REMs used at the end of executable lines were implemented by using multi-line statements, as shown here:

```
.
.
.
270 REM  TT       - TOTAL INCLUDING TAX
280 REM  TXR      - ENERGY COMMISSION TAX
299 :
300 REM ** ASSIGN CONSTANTS **
310 EBL = 200     : REM ELECTRIC BASE LINE AMOUNT
.
.
.
```

You use asterisks (**) to set off the REMARKs that describe the program in the first block and that are used as the first line of all other blocks. This makes it easier to browse through a program and find the REMs. The REMs provide an outline of a program as shown below.

```
1 REM ** UTIL BILL **                              Block 1
100 REM ** VARIABLES USED **                       Block 100
300 REM ** ASSIGN CONSTANTS **                     Block 300
400 REM ** ENTER AMOUNTS **                        Block 400
500 REM ** CALCULATE BILL **                       Block 500
600 REM ** ROUND OFF AND PRINT RESULTS **          Block 600
```

When you outline your programs with REM statements before you write the program, you have made the first step to structuring it. The REM statements provide you with a plan. The plan may change as you write the program, but the REMs give you a place to start.

BASIC Keywords

In Applesoft, BASIC keywords (PRINT, INPUT, and so on) must be typed in uppercase. In GW-BASIC or BASICA, keywords may be typed in uppercase or lowercase. However, when a program is listed, keywords will appear in uppercase regardless of how they were entered.

In QuickBASIC, keywords may be typed in either uppercase or lowercase. The QuickBASIC editor will change keywords to all uppercase letters. This book will consistently use uppercase for keywords.

Variables

GW-BASIC, BASICA, and QuickBASIC allow and recognize long, unique variables (up to 40 characters). Applesoft BASIC allows only eight characters for a variable and recognizes only the first two characters. If you are an Applesoft BASIC user, keep in mind that the first two characters of each Applesoft variable must be different if the variables are to be recognized as distinct from one another.

In Applesoft, letters that appear in variables must be typed in uppercase. GW-BASIC or BASICA variables may be typed using either uppercase or lowercase letters. However, when listed, they appear in uppercase. QuickBASIC variables may be typed in upper case or lowercase and will appear exactly as typed when listed.

The Applesoft and GW-BASIC programs presented in this book use only uppercase letters as variables. This is required in Applesoft. Although not required in GW-BASIC, programs that are listed show variables in uppercase only, regardless of how they were originally typed. QuickBASIC variables will be shown in lowercase and keywords in uppercase as shown below.

```
QuickBASIC :  IF code > 96 AND code < 123 THEN code = code - 32
```

This convention makes programs easier to read.

Line Numbering

Line numbers are required in Applesoft or GW-BASIC. Lines in the opening module are always assigned line numbers less than 100. Other modules always begin with a line number that is a multiple of 100. Subroutines begin with a line number that is a multiple of 1000.

```
1 REM ** UPSHIFT/DOWNSHIFT **              Block 1
2 REM ** GW-BASIC VERSION **
3 REM ** PROGRAM 1-3a **
4 REM ** 1/22/87 **
.
.
.
100 REM ** VARIABLES USED **              Block 100
.
.
.
200 REM ** MAIN PROGRAM **                Block 200
.
.
1000 REM ** SUBROUTINE: UPSHIFT **        Block 1000
.
.
2000 REM ** SUBROUTINE: DOWNSHIFT **      Block 2000
.
.
.
```

In QuickBASIC, line numbers are not required, as you will see later in this chapter and in the rest of this book.

Punctuation Conventions (, ; :)

When a comma, semicolon, or colon is used, it will always be followed by a space, as shown in the following examples:

```
CLS: INPUT "Enter state desired"; NM$
MID$(NM$, LETTER, 1)
PRINT: PRINT "TOTAL ELECTRIC $ "; TELEC
LOCATE 10, 30: PRINT "DATA BEING SORTED"
```


Operation and Relational Symbols

The format in this book places one space before and after an operation symbol ($+ - * /$) or relational symbol ($= < > <= >= <>$). Here are some examples:

```
AVE = INT(WORTH / TSS * 100 + .5) / 100
IF CODE > 64 AND CODE < 91 THEN CODE = CODE + 32
SWAP NAYM$(HERE), NAYM$(HERE - 1)
IF FLAG <> 0 THEN AFTER$ = AFTER$ + CHAR$
```

There is one exception: when the dash ($-$) is used to denote a negative number, it is not followed by a space.

```
FOR HERE = BOTTOM TO TOP STEP -1
```

Liberal spacing in programs makes them much easier to read. You will see programs that are "crunched" in magazines and even in some books. At one time, when memory was expensive, it was necessary to eliminate as many characters as possible so that programs would fit into the memory-starved computers. It is seldom necessary today. This is how Applesoft Program 1-2*b* could be entered in crunched form:

```
210HOME:TSS=0:WWR=0
220INPUT"NUMBER OF SHARES ? ";NUMS
230IFNUMS=0THEN310
240INPUT"PRICE PER SHARE  ? ";PPS
250TWR=TWR+NUMS+PPS
260TSS=TSS+NUMS
270PRINT:GOTO220
310AVE=INT(TWR/TSS*100+.5)/100
320PRINT:PRINT"AVERAGE PRICE FOR ";TSS;" SHARES IS $ ";AVE
330PRINT"TOTAL VALUE OF STOCK  - $ ";TWR
340END
```

The program would run as shown. Of course, if you list the program, Applesoft will put in some spaces.

FOR...NEXT Loops

A FOR...NEXT loop begins with a FOR statement and ends with a NEXT statement. The lines between these two are called the body of the loop. The FOR format places one space between items. The NEXT statement is always followed by the variable name used to open the loop. Indentations are used to delineate the body of each loop. Both GW-BASIC and QuickBASIC allow the omission of the variable following NEXT. However, this variable is included throughout this book to show clearly where each loop ends. In the following example, lines 2050 through 2070 illustrate a single FOR...NEXT loop, and lines 330 through 380 illustrate a FOR...NEXT loop nested within a FOR...NEXT loop:

```
330 FOR PASS = 1 TO NUM - 1
340    FOR HERE = BOTM TO TP STEP -1
350       IF NAYMS(HERE) < NAYMS(HERE - 1) THEN GOSUB 1010
360    NEXT HERE
370    TP = TP + 1
380 NEXT PASS
   .
   .
   .
2050 FOR NAYM = 1 TO NUM
2060    READ NAYMS(NAYM)
2070 NEXT NAYM
```

Multiple Statements

Multiple statements are only used when the statements form a compound function—statements that together perform some action.

Examples are when a REM follows an executable statement in an Applesoft program or when a print statement is being formatted. Here is an example from Program 1-1*b:*

```
310 EBL = 220                :REM ELECTRIC BASE LINE LIMIT
   .
   .
   .
630 PRINT: PRINT "TOTAL ELECTRIC = $ "; TELEC
```

When multiple statements are used on the same line, one space follows the colon separator, except in the case of REMs as used in the previous example. Multiple statements on one line are sometimes used to set an initial value for variables before the beginning of a loop, as is done in line 320 in the following example:

```
300 REM ** SORT NAMES **
310 LOCATE 10,30: PRINT "DATA BEING SORTED"
320 TOP = 2: BOTTOM = NUMNAMES
330 WHILE TOP <= BOTTOM
   .
   .                              multiple statement lines
   .
390 WEND
400 LOCATE 10, 30: PRINT SPACES(17)
```

Other conventions are introduced throughout this book as needed.

Demonstrating the Conventions

Program 2-1, STATES AND ABBREVIATIONS, demonstrates the conventions and style that have been discussed so far in this chapter. It is a practical application that provides a search for the two-letter postal abbreviation for any state or territory of the United States. It is written in GW-BASIC and can be compiled by QuickBASIC.

To use Program 2-1, enter the name of the state or territory for which you require an abbreviation, and the computer will find the state and its abbreviation. If you enter only the first letter of the state, the program will print all the states and territories that begin with that letter. You can enter the first two letters or the first three letters of the name of the state. Try it. The program examines your entry from left to right and searches for all states and territories that match your entry.

```
1 REM ** STATES & ABBREVIATIONS **
2 REM ** PROGRAM 2-1 **
3 REM ** 1/30/87 **
9 '
100 REM ** VARIABLES USED **
110 ' STATES(ST)            - Array variable, state name
120 ' ABBREVS(ST)           - Array variable, state abbreviation
130 ' ST                    - Subscript in STATES and ABBREVS arrays
140 ' FINDS                 - Name of state to look for
150 ' UNSQZDS               - Unsqueezed string in UPSQUEEZE
160 ' SQZDS                 - String squeezed by UPSQUEEZE
170 ' L                     - FOR-NEXT loop counter in UPSQUEEZE
180 ' CODE                  - ASCII code in UPSQUEEZE
190 ' FLAG                  - Match or No Match in MATCH NAMES
200 ' STATES                - Squeezed State Name in MATCH NAMES
299 '
300 REM ** THE ACTION DIRECTOR **
310 DIM STATES(60), ABBREVS(60)
320 GOSUB 3010
330 CLS: INPUT "Enter state desired"; FINDS
340 UNSQZDS = FINDS: GOSUB 1010
350 FINDS = SQZDS: GOSUB 2010
400 REM ** SEARCH AGAIN ? **
410 LOCATE 15, 5: PRINT "PRESS Q TO QUIT, SPACE BAR FOR ANOTHER"
420 KYS = INKEYS: IF KYS = "" THEN 420
430 IF KYS = "Q" OR KYS = "q" THEN CLS: END
440 IF ASC(KYS) = 32 THEN 330 ELSE 420
499 '
1000 REM ** SUBROUTINE: UPSQUEEZE **
1010 SQZDS = ""
1020 FOR L = 1 TO LEN(UNSQZDS)
1030    CODE = ASC(MIDS(UNSQZDS, L, 1))
1040    IF CODE > 96 AND CODE < 123 THEN CODE = CODE - 32
1050    IF CODE <> 32 THEN SQZDS = SQZDS + CHRS(CODE)
1060 NEXT L
1070 RETURN
1999 '
2000 REM ** SUBROUTINE: MATCH NAMES **
2010 FLAG = 0
2020 FOR ST = 1 TO 59
2030    UNSQZDS = STATES(ST): GOSUB 1010
2040    STATES = SQZDS
2050    IF FINDS <> LEFTS(STATES, LEN(FINDS)) THEN 2070
2060    PRINT STATES(ST); TAB(20); ABBREVS(ST): FLAG = 1
2070 NEXT ST
2080 IF FLAG = 0 THEN PRINT "State not found"
2090 RETURN
2999 '
3000 REM ** SUBROUTINE: READ DATA FOR STATES **
3010 FOR ST = 1 TO 59
3020    READ STATES(ST), ABBREVS(ST)
3030 NEXT ST
3040 DATA ALABAMA,AL, ALASKA,AK, AMERICAN SAMOA,AS, ARIZONA,AZ
3060 DATA ARKANSAS,AR. CALIFORNIA,CA, COLORADO,CO, CONNECTICUT,CT
3070 DATA DELAWARE,DE, DISTRICT OF COLUMBIA,DC, FLORIDA,FL
3080 DATA GEORGIA,GA, GUAM,GU, HAWAII,HI, IDAHO,ID, ILLINOIS,IL
3090 DATA INDIANA,IN, IOWA,IA, KANSAS,KS, KENTUCKY, KY
4000 DATA LOUISIANA,LA, MAINE,ME, MARSHALL ISLANDS,TT, MARYLAND,MD
4010 DATA MASSACHUSETTS,MA, MICHIGAN,MI, MICRONESIA,TT
4020 DATA MINNESOTA,MN, MISSISSIPPI,MS, MISSOURI,MO, MONTANA,MT
4030 DATA NEBRASKA,NE, NEVADA,NV, NEW HAMPSHIRE, NH, NEW JERSEY,NJ
4040 DATA NEW MEXICO,NM, NEW YORK,NY, NORTH CAROLINA,NC
4050 DATA NORTH DAKOTA,ND, NORTHERN MARIANA ISLANDS,CM, OHIO,OH
4060 DATA OKLAHOMA,OK, OREGON,OR, PALAU,TT, PENNSYLVANIA,PA
4070 DATA PUERTO RICO, PR, RHODE ISLAND,RI, SOUTH CAROLINA,SC
4080 DATA SOUTH DAKOTA,SD, TENNESSEE,TN, TEXAS,TX, UTAH,UT
4090 DATA VERMONT,VT, VIRGIN ISLANDS,VI, VIRGINIA,VA
4100 DATA WASHINGTON,WA, WEST VIRGINIA,WV, WISCONSIN,WI, WYOMING,WY
4130 RETURN
```

Program 2-1. *STATES AND ABBREVIATIONS*

You enter	Computer prints
C	CALIFORNIA CA
	COLORADO CO
	CONNECTICUT CT
nor	NORTH CAROLINA NC
	NORTH DAKOTA ND
	NORTHERN MARIANA ISLANDS CM
VIRGIN	VIRGIN ISLANDS VI
	VIRGINIA VA
NUBRASKA	No State Found
Nebraska	NEBRASKA NE

Table 2-1. *Samples from Program 2-1*

Names of states and territories may be entered in any mix of upper- and lowercase letters. Examples of entries and the printed results are shown in Table 2-1.

A REM Outline of Program 2-1

Program 2-1 is divided into four main sections—the main program and three subroutines. The main program consists of four blocks. A program outline is formed by the first lines of each block, as shown below:

```
1 REM ** STATES AND ABBREVIATIONS **              Block 1

100 REM ** VARIABLES USED **                      Block 100

300 REM ** THE ACTION DIRECTOR **                 Block 300

400 REM ** SEARCH AGAIN ? **                      Block 400

1000 REM ** SUBROUTINE: UPSQUEEZE **              Block 1000

2000 REM ** SUBROUTINE: MATCH NAMES **            Block 2000

3000 REM ** SUBROUTINE: READ DATA FOR STATES **   Block 3000
```

The subroutine beginning at line 3000 is called first from the main program to read the names and abbreviations into appropriate arrays. After the program returns to the main program, the desired state name is entered. The UPSQUEEZE subroutine (beginning at line 1000) is then called to change any lowercase characters in the entry to uppercase characters. In addition, the subroutine removes any blank spaces (blanks) from the entry.

The program then returns again to the main program. The MATCH NAMES subroutine (beginning at line 2000) is called. It makes a search for all states that match the letters entered. The UPSQUEEZE subroutine is also called from this subroutine to squeeze out any blanks in the names of the states from the stored data list. The matching subroutine prints the complete name and abbreviation of the matching states or territories. Control then passes back to the main program, where you are given the choice of entering another state or ending the program.

A Detailed Description of Program 2-1

The program consists of a main program and three subroutines. The main program is broken into four blocks. The first block of the main program provides the name and other descriptive information about the program.

```
1 REM ** STATES & ABBREVIATIONS **
2 REM ** PROGRAM 2-1 **
3 REM ** 1/30/87 **
```

The second block (beginning at line 100) consists of REMARK statements that describe the variables used in the program.

```
100 REM ** VARIABLES USED **
110 ' STATE$(ST)          - Array variable, state name
120 ' ABBREV$(ST)         - Array variable, state abbreviation
130 ' ST                  - Subscript in STATE$ and ABBREV$ arrays
140 ' FIND$               - Name of state to look for
150 ' UNSQZD$             - Unsqueezed string in UPSQUEEZE
160 ' SQZD$               - String squeezed by UPSQUEEZE
170 ' L                   - FOR-NEXT loop counter in UPSQUEEZE
180 ' CODE                - ASCII code in UPSQUEEZE
190 ' FLAG                - Match or No Match in MATCH NAMES
200 ' STATE$              - Squeezed State Name in MATCH NAMES
```

The third block controls and directs most of the work done by the program.

```
300 REM ** THE ACTION DIRECTOR **
310 DIM STATES(60), ABBREV$(60)
320 GOSUB 3010
330 CLS: INPUT "Enter state desired"; FIND$
340 UNSQZD$ = FIND$: GOSUB 1010
350 FIND$ = SQZD$: GOSUB 2010
```

Lines 310 and 320 dimension the *STATE\$* and *ABBREV\$* arrays and call the READ DATA FOR STATES subroutine. Line 330 requests the name of the state whose abbreviation is wanted. Lines 340 and 350 call the UPSQUEEZE program to convert lowercase letters and squeeze out any blanks, or spaces, and then calls the MATCH NAMES subroutine, which searches for states that match the requested name.

After the completion of a search, the SEARCH AGAIN? block is executed. It allows you to select whether to search for another state or to end the program.

```
400 REM ** SEARCH AGAIN ? **
410 LOCATE 15, 5: PRINT "PRESS Q TO QUIT, SPACE BAR FOR ANOTHER"
420 KY$ = INKEY$: IF KY$ = "" THEN 420
430 IF KY$ = "Q" OR KY$ = "q" THEN CLS: END
440 IF ASC(KY$) = 32 THEN 330 ELSE 420
```

Most of the work is done by subroutines called from the main program. The READ DATA FOR STATES subroutine is called first. It uses a FOR...NEXT loop to fill the two arrays. Items in the data list are listed in pairs—complete name first, then abbreviation. The loop reads the first of each pair of items into the *STATE\$* array. The second item of each pair is read into the *ABBREV\$* array.

```
3000 REM ** SUBROUTINE: READ DATA FOR STATES **
3010 FOR ST = 1 TO 59
3020   READ STATES(ST), ABBREV$(ST)
3030 NEXT ST
3040 DATA ALABAMA,AL, ALASKA,AK, AMERICAN SAMOA,AS, ARIZONA,AZ
3060 DATA ARKANSAS,AR, CALIFORNIA,CA, COLORADO,CO, CONNECTICUT,CT
3070 DATA DELAWARE,DE, DISTRICT OF COLUMBIA,DC, FLORIDA,FL
3080 DATA GEORGIA,GA, GUAM,GU, HAWAII,HI, IDAHO,ID, ILLINOIS,IL
3090 DATA INDIANA,IN, IOWA,IA, KANSAS,KS, KENTUCKY,KY
4000 DATA LOUISIANA,LA, MAINE,ME, MARSHALL ISLANDS,TT, MARYLAND,MD
4010 DATA MASSACHUSETTS,MA, MICHIGAN,MI, MICRONESIA,TT
4020 DATA MINNESOTA,MN, MISSISSIPPI,MS, MISSOURI,MO, MONTANA,MT
4030 DATA NEBRASKA,NE, NEVADA,NV, NEW HAMPSHIRE,NH, NEW JERSEY,NJ
4040 DATA NEW MEXICO,NM, NEW YORK,NY, NORTH CAROLINA,NC
4050 DATA NORTH DAKOTA,ND, NORTHERN MARIANA ISLANDS,CM, OHIO,OH
4060 DATA OKLAHOMA,OK, OREGON,OR, PALAU,TT, PENNSYLVANIA,PA
4070 DATA PUERTO RICO,PR, RHODE ISLAND,RI, SOUTH CAROLINA,SC
4080 DATA SOUTH DAKOTA,SD, TENNESSEE,TN, TEXAS,TX, UTAH,UT
4090 DATA VERMONT,VT, VIRGIN ISLANDS,VI, VIRGINIA,VA
4100 DATA WASHINGTON,WA, WEST VIRGINIA,WV, WISCONSIN,WI, WYOMING,WY
```

The UPSQUEEZE subroutine begins with an "unsqueezed" string called *UNSQZD$* and produces a string called *SQZD$*, in which all lowercase letters have been changed to uppercase and all blanks removed.

```
1000 REM ** SUBROUTINE: UPSQUEEZE **
1010 SQZD$ = ""
1020 FOR L = 1 TO LEN(UNSQZD$)
1030    CODE = ASC(MID$(UNSQZD$, L, 1)
1040    IF CODE > 96 AND CODE < 123 THEN CODE = CODE - 32
1050    IF CODE <> 32 THEN SQZD$ = SQZD$ + CHR$(CODE)
1060 NEXT L
1070 RETURN
```

UPSQUEEZE changes lowercase letters to uppercase, removes blanks, and copies any other characters into the *SQZD$* string. It begins by setting *SQZD$* equal to the empty string (""), a string containing no characters. It then scans the string contained in *UNSQZD$* from left to right. In line 1040, lowercase ASCII codes are detected and changed to the corresponding uppercase codes. In line 1050, characters other than spaces are appended to the value of SQZD$. Table 2-2 shows the value of *SQZD$* produced for various values of *UNSQZD$*.

The MATCH NAMES subroutine searches the entire list of 59 states and territories, and prints each match found. If no match is found, it prints the message "State not found".

```
2000 REM ** SUBROUTINE: MATCH NAMES **
2010 FLAG = 0
2020 FOR ST = 1 TO 59
2030    UNSQZD$ = STATE$(ST): GOSUB 1010
2040    STATE$ = SQZD$
2050    IF FIND$ <> LEFT$(STATE$, LEN(FIND$)) THEN 2070
2060    PRINT STATE$(ST); TAB(20); ABBREV$(ST): FLAG = 1
2070 NEXT ST
2080 IF FLAG = 0 THEN PRINT "State not found"
2090 RETURN
```

A flag is set to zero by line 2010, before the loop is entered. The variable, *FLAG*, will remain zero unless at least one match is found. If no match is found, *FLAG* will still be equal to zero when the FOR... NEXT loop is completed. Line 2080 will then print the message "State not found", and control will return to the main program. If a match is found, the matching state and its abbreviation will be printed and *FLAG* will be set to one. When the FOR...NEXT loop is

UNSQZD$	SQZD$
South Dakota	SOUTHDAKOTA
nOr	NOR
VIRGIN Islands	VIRGINISLANDS
Washington D. C.	WASHINGTOND.C.

Table 2-2. *Unsqueezed and Squeezed Words*

completed, the THEN clause of line 2080 will be ignored. The list of matching states and their abbreviations will be on the screen as control passes back to the main program.

The FOR...NEXT loop (lines 2020-2070) compares the state requested (*FIND$*) with every state in the *STATE$* array. Remember, *FIND$* has been squeezed by the UPSQUEEZE subroutine. In lines 2030 and 2040, the name of the current state from the array is also squeezed.

Line 2050 compares the search key (*FIND$*) with the left portion of *STATE$*. If there is no match, line 2060 is skipped. If a match occurs, line 2060 is executed. This use of the LEFT$ function allows you to enter only the first few letters of the state you want to find. The computer will find and print all states for which the left part of the state name matches the string of letters you entered. Refer back to Table 2-1 to see what the computer prints in response to state names or portions of state names that you enter.

Keeping Characters in a String

Program 2-2, KEEP CHARACTERS, demonstrates a useful subroutine that scans a string and keeps only those characters that are contained in another string named *KEEP$*. This program uses decimal digits in *KEEP$*, but you can substitute other characters in the string. Using the *KEEP$* string "0123456789", a number in the

```
1 REM ** KEEP CHARACTERS **
2 REM ** PROGRAM 2-2 **
3 REM ** 3/17/87 **
4 REM ** ST. PATRICK'S DAY **
99 '
100 REM ** VARIABLES USED **
110 ' KEEP$            - STRING OF CHARACTERS TO KEEP
120 ' BEFORE$          - ORIGINAL STRING
130 ' AFTER$           - FINAL STRING
140 ' CPOS             - COUNTER FOR CHARACTER POSITION
150 ' CHAR$            - SINGLE CHARACTER FROM BEFORE$
160 ' FLAG             - NOT ZERO IF CHAR$ IS IN KEEP$
199 '
200 REM ** MAIN PROGRAM **
210 KEEP$ = "0123456789"
220 CLS
230 PRINT "Enter a Telephone number including area code"
240 LINE INPUT BEFORE$
250 GOSUB 1010
260 PRINT AFTER$
270 PRINT: GOTO 230
999 '
1000 REM ** SUBROUTINE: KEEP ONLY CHARACTERS IN KEEP$ **
1010 AFTER$ = ""
1020 FOR CPOS = 1 TO LEN(BEFORE$)
1030    CHAR$ = MID$(BEFORE$, CPOS, 1)
1040    FLAG = INSTR(KEEP$, CHAR$)
1050    IF FLAG <> 0 THEN AFTER$ = AFTER$ + CHAR$
1060 NEXT CPOS
1070 RETURN
```

Program 2-2.   *KEEP CHARACTERS*

form of a social security number, such as 000-98-7654, would be printed as: 000987654. The hyphens (-) would be removed.

The subroutine scans the string *BEFORE$* from left to right as the value of *CPOS* goes from 1 to the length of *BEFORE$*. Each character of *BEFORE$* is temporarily assigned as the value of *CHAR$*. Therefore, *CHAR$* is a single character from *BEFORE$*.

A single character from *BEFORE$* is assigned to the variable *CHAR$* in line 1030. INSTR then compares *CHAR$* with each of the characters in *KEEP$* in line 1040. If the character (*CHAR$*) is in *KEEP$*, INSTR assigns its position in *KEEP$* to the variable *FLAG*. If the character (*CHAR$*) is not in *KEEP$*, a value of zero is assigned to *FLAG*. When *FLAG* is a nonzero number, line 1050 adds the character to the new string *AFTER$*.

When all characters of *BEFORE$* have been examined, a RETURN from the subroutine occurs. Line 260 prints the string of characters that were kept (*AFTER$*), and it then prints a line space and goes back for another value of *BEFORE$*.

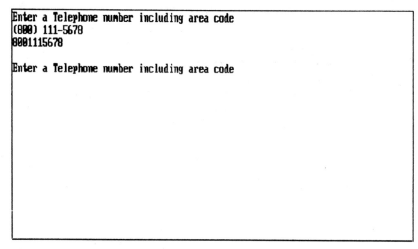
```
Enter a Telephone number including area code
(800) 111-5678
8001115678

Enter a Telephone number including area code
```

Figure 2-1. *Output of Program 2-2*

Program 2-2 has been run with the fictitious phone number (800) 111-5678. The result was 8001115678, as shown in Figure 2-1. These are the digits that would actually be dialed to reach the fictitious phone destination. You don't enter parentheses and blank spaces when dialing a phone number.

Enter Program 2-2 and try various combinations of digits and other characters. Then set *KEEP$* to the set of characters you want to keep. Run the program with your set of characters.

Purging Characters from a String

Program 2-3, PURGE CHARACTERS, demonstrates the converse application — purging, or removing, characters from a given string. You enter two strings. The first is the string of characters you want to purge (*PURGE$*). The second is the string that you want purged (*BEFORE$*).

The subroutine in this program is almost a duplicate of that used in Program 2-2. Slight, but important, differences occur in lines 1040 and 1050. The string variable *PURGE$* is used in line 1040 in place of *KEEP$* (used in Program 2-2). If a character (*CHAR$*) of *BEFORE$*

```
1 REM ** PURGE CHARACTERS **
2 REM ** PROGRAM 2-3 **
3 REM ** 3/17/87 **
4 REM ** ST. PATRICK'S DAY **
99 '
100 REM ** VARIABLES USED **
110 ' PURGE$          - CHARACTERS TO BE PURGED
120 ' BEFORE$         - ORIGINAL STRING
130 ' AFTER$          - FINAL STRING
140 ' CPOS            - COUNTER FOR CHARACTER POSITION
150 ' CHAR$           - SINGLE CHARACTER FROM BEFORE$
160 ' FLAG            - ZERO IF CHARACTER IS NOT IN PURGE$
199 '
200 REM ** MAIN PROGRAM **
210 CLS
220 PRINT "Enter characters to be purged"
230 LINE INPUT PURGE$
240 PRINT "Enter a string you want purged"
250 LINE INPUT BEFORE$
260 GOSUB 1010
270 PRINT AFTER$
280 PRINT: GOTO 220
999 '
1000 REM ** SUBROUTINE: PURGE CHARACTERS IN PURGE$ **
1010 AFTER$ = ""
1020 FOR CPOS = 1 TO LEN(BEFORE$)
1030    CHAR$ = MID$(BEFORE$, CPOS, 1)
1040    FLAG = INSTR(PURGE$, CHAR$)
1050    IF FLAG = 0 THEN AFTER$ = AFTER$ + CHAR$
1060 NEXT CPOS
1070 RETURN
```

Program 2-3.   *PURGE CHARACTERS*

matches a character of *PURGE$*, INSTR will assign its position, a nonzero number, to *FLAG*. In this case, the character will not be concatenated to *AFTER$* in line 1050.

Suppose the character (*CHAR$*) does not match a character in *PURGE$*. In this case, INSTR assigns the value zero to *FLAG* and, in line 1050, the character will be concatenated to *AFTER$*. Once again, the resulting string is printed after the subroutine has been completed.

Figure 2-2 shows a test run of Program 2-3. All parentheses and dollar signs were removed from the string: "Purge all (parentheses) and $dollar signs." Try entering a variety of purge strings and strings to be purged. Since LINE INPUT is used (line 250) to enter strings, you may enter up to 255 characters, including punctuation marks such as commas, and even quotation marks. You can use LINE INPUT to enter the strings. LINE INPUT accepts a maximum of 255 characters from the keyboard, including such punctuation marks as commas and quotation marks.

```
Enter characters to be purged
()$
Enter a string you want purged
Purge all (parentheses) and $dollar signs.
Purge all parentheses and dollar signs.

Enter characters to be purged
```

Figure 2-2. *Output of Program 2-3*

Executive Recreations

After working through these first two chapters, you might enjoy the following application.

Words are the basis for communication among people. Some words are more valuable than others. However, a word's value may be determined in many different ways. Two different ways to determine the value of a word are presented in Program 2-4, WORDSWORTH.

Each letter of the alphabet is assigned a value, called a letter score, according to its relative position in the list that follows:

A=1	J=10	S=19
B=2	K=11	T=20
C=3	L=12	U=21
D=4	M=13	V=22
E=5	N=14	W=23
F=6	O=15	X=24
G=7	P=16	Y=25
H=8	Q=17	Z=26
I=9	R=18	

```
1 REM ** WORDSWORTH **
2 REM ** PROGRAM 2-4 **
3 REM ** 2/7/87 **
99 '
100 REM ** VARIABLES USED **
110 ' W                    - Used to define all W variables double precision
120 ' WORD$                - Word entered by user
130 ' WW1                  - WORDSWORTH #1
140 ' WW2                  - WORDSWORTH #2
150 ' L                    - Counter in FOR-NEXT loop
160 ' LTTR$                - Single letter from WORD$
170 ' LSCORE               - Letter score
180 ' CPOS                 - Counter in FOR-NEXT loop
190 ' CODE                 - ASCII code of a character in WORD$
199 '
200 REM ** INITIALIZE **
210 DEFDBL W
220 CLS
299 '
300 REM ** GET WORD AND UPCASE IT **
310 INPUT "Your word"; WORD$
320 GOSUB 1010
399 '
400 REM ** INITIALIZE WW1 & WW2 **
410 WW1 = 0
420 WW2 = 1
499 '
500 REM ** COMPUTE WW1 & ;WW2 **
510 FOR L = 1 TO LEN(WORD$)
520    LTTR$ = MID$(WORD$, L, 1)
530    IF LTTR$ < "A" OR LTTR$ > "Z" THEN 570
540    LSCORE = ASC(LTTR$) - 64
550    WW1 = WW1 + LSCORE
560    WW2 = WW2 * LSCORE
570 NEXT L
599 '
600 REM ** PRINT WW1 & WW2, GO FOR MORE
610 PRINT "WORDSWORTH #1 IS "; WW1
620 PRINT "WORDSWORTH #2 IS "; WW2
630 PRINT: GOTO 310
699 '
1000 REM ** SUBROUTINE: UPCASE **
1010 FOR CPOS = 1 TO LEN(WORD$)
1020    CODE = ASC(MID$(WORD$, CPOS, 1))
1030    IF CODE > 96 AND CODE < 123 THEN MID$(WORD$, CPOS) = CHR$(CODE - 32)
1040 NEXT CPOS
1050 RETURN
```

Program 2-4.   *WORDSWORTH*

The first way to determine the value of a word, WORDSWORTH #1, is
the numerical score of a word obtained by adding the letter scores of
all the letters in the word. Here are some examples:

FAST:	6 + 1 + 19 + 20 = 46
Quick:	17 + 21 + 9 + 3 + 11 = 61
BASIC:	2 + 1 + 19 + 9 + 3 = 34

A second way to determine the value of a word, WORDSWORTH #2, is the numerical score of a word obtained by multiplying the letter scores of all the letters in a word. Some examples are shown here:

Use:	21 * 19 * 5 = 1995
Quick:	17 * 21 * 9 * 3 * 11 = 106029
BASIC:	2 * 1 * 19 * 9 * 3 = 1026

Program 2-4 allows you to enter words in uppercase (A, B, C, and so on), lowercase (a, b, c, and so on), or any mixture of upper- and lowercase. You can include blanks, hyphens, apostrophes, and other nonalphabetic characters in your word; the program will ignore them in calculating the WORDSWORTH values. However, do not use a comma unless you enclose your entry in quotation marks. GW-BASIC uses a comma to separate multiple variable entries. When it sees a comma, it normally treats it as a separation symbol between multiple entries. If commas are used within quotation marks, they are not treated as entry separators.

Figure 2-3 shows the results obtained in a test run of the program. Program 2-4 uses conventions and programming techniques that are very similar to those used in earlier programs. However, you might be unfamiliar with the use of MID$ as a statement in line 1030. This cannot be done in Applesoft but is allowed in GW-BASIC, BASICA,

```
Your word? QuickBASIC
WORDSWORTH #1 IS  95
WORDSWORTH #2 IS  108785754

Your word?
```

Figure 2-3. *WORDSWORTH Results*

and QuickBASIC. Line 1030 is shown here:

```
1030   IF CODE > 96 AND CODE < 123 THEN MID$(WORD$, CPOS) = CHR$(CODE-32)
```

If the value of *CODE* is in the range 97-122, the MID$ statement following THEN is executed. It causes the computer to replace the lowercase letter at character position *CPOS* in *WORD$* with the corresponding uppercase letter, CHR$(*CODE*−32).

The UPCASE subroutine replaces all lowercase letters in *WORD$* with uppercase letters, but leaves all other characters unchanged. Try your hand at writing a *LOCASE* subroutine to change uppercase letters to lowercase. Here are some questions you might explore. Try them with both WORDSWORTH #1 and WORDSWORTH #2.

1. What three-letter word has the smallest WORDSWORTH?

2. What three-letter word has the largest WORDSWORTH?

3. What four-letter word has the smallest WORDSWORTH?

4. What four-letter word has the largest WORDSWORTH?

5. What is the first word (alphabetically) to have a WORDSWORTH of exactly 100? Exactly 1000? Exactly equal to a number you choose?

6. What is the last word (alphabetically) to have a WORDSWORTH of exactly 100?

7. In the dictionary you use, what word has the largest WORDS-WORTH?

8. What is the longest word (most letters) that has a WORDS-WORTH equal to the number of weeks in a year?

9. For WORDSWORTH #2, find the longest word (with the most letters) that has a WORDSWORTH #2 of less than or equal to 1,000,000.

10. What word has a WORDSWORTH #2 closest to 1,000,000? The value can be less than or greater than 1,000,000.

11. The word Ratio has a WORDSWORTH #1 (WW1) of 63. The number of letters (NL) in Ratio is 5. WW1 / NL = 63 / 5 = 12.6. What word with 4 or more letters has the largest ratio of WW1 / NL?

12. What word with four or more letters has the smallest ratio of WW1/NL?

QuickBASIC Preview

You may have used some GW-BASIC statements and functions in your previous programs that cannot be used in QuickBASIC. Some statements and functions also require additional information in Quick-BASIC that is unnecessary in GW-BASIC. Table 2-3 contains a list of GW-BASIC statements and functions that cannot be used in a compiled QuickBASIC program. Examine this list carefully. These items perform editing operations on the source file, interfere with program execution, or require cassette support. Their functions are performed in some other way or are unnecessary in QuickBASIC.

Statement	Description
AUTO	Automatically generates a line number when you press ENTER. QuickBASIC does not need line numbers.
CONT	Resumes execution of a program. The QuickBASIC debugger performs this function.
DEF USR	Defines the user number and segment offset of a subroutine to be called by a USR function. User functions are created and used differently in QuickBASIC.
DELETE	Deletes specified lines or ranges of lines in a program. This function is performed in the QuickBASIC editor in a different way.
EDIT	Enters the GW-BASIC edit mode. QuickBASIC's editor is chosen from the Edit Menu.
LIST	Lists a program in memory to the display. QuickBASIC displays a program in a list window from the File Menu.
LLIST	Lists a program in memory to the printer. QuickBASIC uses a PRINT command selected from items in the File Menu.

Table 2-3. *Prohibited Statements and Functions*

Statement	Description
LOAD	Loads a GW-BASIC program from disk to memory. QuickBASIC uses an OPEN command selected from items in the File Menu.
MERGE	Loads a GW-BASIC program and merges it with a program currently in memory. QuickBASIC uses a different technique to link modules.
MOTOR	Turns the cassette motor on or off. The cassette motor is not supported by QuickBASIC.
NEW	Deletes the GW-BASIC program currently in memory. QuickBASIC performs this function through its File Menu.
RENUM	Renumbers the lines of the GW-BASIC program currently in memory. Line numbers are unnecessary in QuickBASIC.
SAVE	Saves a program to disk. This is performed by the SAVE command in the File Menu.
USR	Calls a user assembly language subroutine. The CALL statement is used in QuickBASIC.

Table 2-3.   *Prohibited Statements and Functions (continued)*

Table 2-4 contains statements and functions that must be modified to run in QuickBASIC. If you want to compile any of your GW-BASIC programs, check the items in Table 2-3. Consult your Quick-BASIC manual for detailed information on how to modify these statements and functions.

Program 2-5, **KEEP CHARACTERS** (QuickBASIC version), gives you a preview of QuickBASIC programs. Notice that there are no line numbers in this program. Lines can be inserted between other QuickBASIC lines as needed using the built-in editor. Forget about the RENUM statement of GW-BASIC when you are writing programs in QuickBASIC. Of course, RENUM can be used to organize a GW-BASIC program. However, do not include a RENUM statement in the program if it is to be compiled by QuickBASIC. RENUM cannot be used in a QuickBASIC program, as shown in Table 2-3.

Program 2-5 works the same way as the GW-BASIC version (Program 2-2). You will only notice differences in the appearance of the two versions. The QuickBASIC version uses lowercase letters for variables and for line labels.

Statement	Modification
BLOAD/BSAVE	Memory locations available may be different for Quick-BASIC.
CALL name	The name argument is the name of the subroutine or subprogram being called.
CHAIN	The compiler does not support the ALL, MERGE, DELETE, or linenumber options.
DEF type	DEF type statements should be moved to the beginning of compiled programs
DEF SEG	Memory use of the interpreter and compiler are different.
DIM	All DIM statements declaring static arrays must appear at the beginning of compiled programs.
DRAW	The compiler requires that the VARPRTR$ function be used with embedded variables.
PEEK	Memory use of the interpreter and compiler are different.
PLAY	The compiler requires that the VARPRTR$ function be used with embedded variables.
POKE	Memory use of the interpreter and compiler are different.
RESUME	If an error occurs in a single-line function, the compiler attempts to resume program execution at the line containing the function.
RUN	The object of a RUN statement cannot be a .BAS file. It must be an .EXE file. The interpreter R option is not supported. RUN {linenumber/linelabel} is supported. This starts the program at the specified line.

Table 2-4. *Statements Requiring Modification*

Program 2-5 uses the line labels *start* and *keep* as shown below.

```
REM ** MAIN PROGRAM **
  .
  .
  .
start:
  .
  .
  .
```

```
REM ** KEEP CHARACTERS **
REM ** PROGRAM 2-5 **
REM ** QUICKBASIC VERSION OF KEEP CHARACTERS **
REM ** 3/30/87

REM ** VARIABLES USED **
' keep$          - String of characters to keep
' before$        - Original string
' after$         - Final string
' cpos           - Counter for character position
' char$          - Single character from before$
' flag           - Not zero if char$ is in keep$

REM ** MAIN PROGRAM **
keep$ = "0123456789"
CLS
start:
PRINT "Enter a Telephone number including area code"
LINE INPUT before$
GOSUB keep
PRINT after$
PRINT : GOTO start

REM ** SUBROUTINE: Keep Only Characters in keep$ **
keep:
after$ = ""
FOR cpos = 1 TO LEN(before$)
  char$ = MID$(before$, cpos, 1)
  flag = INSTR(keep$, char$)
  IF flag <> 0 THEN after$ = after$ + char$
NEXT cpos
RETURN
```

Program 2-5.   *KEEP CHARACTERS (QuickBASIC Version)*

```
GOSUB keep
.
.
.
REM ** SUBROUTINE: keep **
keep:
.
.
.
```

Notice that line labels are followed by a colon. The colon is not used in the statements that refer to the label. It is only used following the label in the labeled line.

Program 2-5 produces the same output as Program 2-2, which was shown in Figure 2-1. Using Program 2-5 as a guide, see if you can write a QuickBASIC version of Program 2-3.

Review

This chapter has shown you what programming conventions and style to expect in the rest of this book. If conventions and style are consistent, programs and text are much easier to read and understand.

Programs are separated into functional blocks, or modules. REM statements are used to document program modules. Multiple statements on a line are used only if the statements are clearly related. Descriptive variable names are used, and spacing is consistent and designed for clarity.

Five programs demonstrate the conventions and style used throughout the book. Program 2-5 was written in QuickBASIC to give you a preview of things to come. Table 2-3 listed the GW-BASIC statements and functions that cannot be used in QuickBASIC, and Table 2-4 listed GW-BASIC statements and functions that must be modified when used in QuickBASIC.

3 An Overview of QuickBASIC

This chapter describes how to prepare and use a QuickBASIC work disk. You are taken through the steps of compiling three different types of programs:

1. A new QuickBASIC program
2. A previously saved QuickBASIC program
3. A GW-BASIC program previously saved in ASCII format

You will learn how to use the File menu and the Run menu to write, save, print, compile, and run a program. Dialog boxes, which appear when selected menu items need additional information, are explained. Simple editing techniques are introduced.

The Microsoft QuickBASIC compiler requires at least one floppy disk drive and 256K of RAM, but Microsoft recommends two disk drives. More memory is necessary if you are going to write long programs.

The discussions in this chapter assume that you have two floppy disk drives but no hard disk. If you are using a hard disk system, merely copy all the files on the Microsoft QuickBASIC disks to a directory on your hard disk. In this case, some of the screens will be different from those shown in this book.

It is also assumed that you have some knowledge of MS-DOS. Otherwise, stop now and browse through your MS-DOS reference manual. The following MS-DOS commands are used in this chapter:

DIR	Lists the files on a disk
DISKCOPY	Copies all files from one disk to another
COPY	Copies one file
FORMAT	Formats a disk

Making Backup Copies of QuickBASIC

QuickBASIC version 4 is discussed in this book. It has easy-to-use menus so that you don't have to memorize all of the command symbols associated with most other compilers. You can edit, compile, run, debug, and recompile programs without leaving QuickBASIC. If you have used earlier versions of QuickBASIC, you will find version 4 easier to use and more powerful.

QuickBASIC uses an 8087 or 80287 math coprocessor when one is present in your computer system. These coprocessors provide fast, accurate floating-point calculations. If a coprocessor is not present in your system, QuickBASIC uses software routines to emulate a coprocessor. Emulation is slower but provides a similar degree of precision.

The first thing you should do is to make backup copies of all original QuickBASIC disks. Put the original disks in a safe place (a locked vault?) so that they will remain in near virgin condition. Use the MS-DOS DISKCOPY command to copy the original Microsoft QuickBASIC disks to your backup disks.

There are many files on the backup disks you have just made. For the first few chapters that follow, you will need only two files from the backup disks plus one file from your MS-DOS disk. The work disk should contain the following files:

COMMAND	COM	From MS-DOS
QB	EXE	From one of the QuickBASIC backup disks
QB	HLP	From one of the QuickBASIC backup disks

Preparing a QuickBASIC Work Disk (QB Work Disk)

Many of the files on the QuickBASIC backup disks are sample QuickBASIC programs. Other files on the backup disks enable you to do things at an advanced level and are discussed in later chapters. You do not need everything on the disks to begin using QuickBASIC. The steps that follow tell you how to prepare a QuickBASIC work disk with which you can begin exploring QuickBASIC. You can add other files from the backup disks when you need them.

Use the backup copies of QuickBASIC to prepare the work disk. You will need some blank, formatted disks for this task. You may want to make more than one work disk. Other blank disks will be needed to hold your QuickBASIC programs and other data files.

Check the directory of each backup disk by using the MS-DOS DIR command. Find where the QB.EXE and QB.HLP files are located. They may be on different disks.

With the backup copies, you are ready to produce a QuickBASIC work disk. You will use the work disk to prepare, save, compile, and run your QuickBASIC programs.

You need a blank, formatted disk for making the work disk. Format the disk with the /S option, if you wish. This option formats the disk and copies the COMMAND.COM file from the MS-DOS disk. This file should be on your work disk so that you can boot the work disk without needing to load MS-DOS first from the system disk. This option is not needed on the disks used for your program files, the QuickBASIC programs that you write.

When you have formatted your working disk, it will have only the COMMAND.COM file on it. The next step is to copy two files from the QuickBASIC backup disks.

First, find the QB.EXE file. It is the "work horse" of QuickBASIC. Copy the QB.EXE file to the work disk.

After you have copied QB.EXE to your work disk, find the disk containing the QB.HLP file. The QB.HLP file contains helpful information that you can access while creating your source files. Copy the QB.HLP file to your work disk.

Copying these two files completes the preparation of your work disk. Label it "QB Work Disk." You may also want to add "Drive A" to the label to remind you where it should be loaded.

Put your QuickBASIC backup disks away in a safe place. You will need only the QB work disk that you just prepared and a few blank, formatted disks on which to write your programs.

Place your new QB work disk in Drive A and use a directory command to make sure you have the necessary files on the disk. It should show these files:

COMMAND   COM

QB   EXE

QB   HLP

If these files are on your QB work disk, you are ready to explore QuickBASIC. If all three files are not on the disk, try copying the missing files again.

Using the QuickBASIC Compiler

Once you have prepared your QB work disk, remove it from Drive B. From now on, the QB work disk will be used in Drive A. Disks in Drive B will be used to store programs and data files that you enter.

There are essentially three procedures for using QuickBASIC, as follows:

1. As a new QuickBASIC program:
   a. Put the QB work disk in Drive A.
   b. Put a blank, formatted disk in Drive B.
   c. Enter the QuickBASIC editor.
   d. Type in the new program.
   e. Save the program to the disk in Drive B.
   f. Compile and run the program.

2. As a QuickBASIC program that has been previously saved:
   a. Put the QB work disk in Drive A.
   b. Put the disk containing the QuickBASIC program in Drive B.
   c. Load the program from the MS-DOS command line (A>) or from the QuickBASIC File menu.
   d. Compile and run the program.

3. As a GW-BASIC program that has been previously saved in ASCII format:
   a. Put the QB work disk in Drive A.
   b. Put the disk containing the GW-BASIC program in Drive B. (The GW-BASIC program must be in ASCII format.)
   c. Load the program from the MS-DOS command line (A>) or from the QuickBASIC File menu.
   d. Remove the disk with the GW-BASIC program from Drive B.
   e. Put the disk on which you want to save the QuickBASIC version of the program in Drive B.
   f. Save the program to the QuickBASIC program disk in Drive B.
   g. Compile and run the program.

Each of these procedures is discussed in more detail in the sections that follow.

A New QuickBASIC Program

The QB work disk will be used to enter, save, compile, and run a program that simulates coin flipping. Simulations are powerful tools used to solve many types of tasks. Some are simple and some are

```
REM ** COIN FLIPPER **
' Program 3-1  7/18/87

REM ** GET NUMBER OF FLIPS & FLIP COINS **

start:
' Get number of coins to flip
CLS
INPUT "I flip coins. How many should I flip"; nflips
PRINT

' Flip Coins
FOR counter = 1 TO nflips
  flip = INT(2 * RND(1))
  IF flip = 0 THEN PRINT "HEADS",  ELSE PRINT "TAILS",
NEXT counter

END
```

Program 3-1. *COIN FLIPPER*

complex. This one is simple so that you don't get tangled up in the task being performed. Most of the REM (REMARK) statements you have seen in past programs have been omitted so that you can concentrate on the process of entering Program 3-1, COIN FLIPPER.

First, make sure you have the QB work disk in Drive A. Then place a blank, formatted disk in Drive B. At the MS-DOS prompt (A>), type the letters **QB** in either upper- or lowercase.

```
A>QB
```

The command QB tells the computer to load QuickBASIC (the QB.EXE file). After typing **QB**, press the ENTER key.

Entering the COIN FLIPPER Program

When you start QuickBASIC without a file name, the screen is cleared, ready for entering the program shown in Figure 3-1.

The cursor (the blinking underscore character) shows where the text that you type will appear. If you have had a mouse installed, the mouse pointer (a small, rectangular block) appears near the center of the screen.

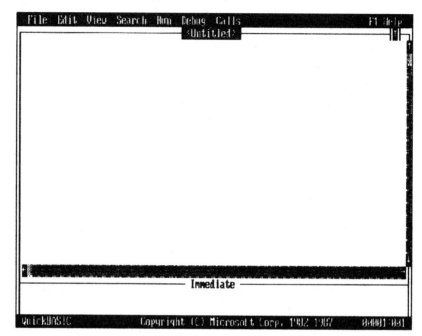

Figure 3-1. *Opening editing screen*

You enter text in the View window. It can be split into two separate windows and the size of each can be adjusted. If one window contains the text of your source file (main module of your program), the second window can be opened and used for working on any other part of your program. You can edit the text in either window. This procedure is discussed in Chapter 6.

Each View window has a title bar that displays the name of the file in the window below. If the window contains a subprogram or function (described in Chapter 6), the title bar shows both the module name and the procedure name. If no file is loaded or if you are working on a new program, "Untitled" appears in the title area. The title area of the active window (the window currently affected by editing and file commands) is highlighted (appears in reverse video).

The long, rectangular window near the bottom of the screen is the Immediate window. You can enter and execute BASIC statements directly in this window.

The menu bar, at the top of the screen, contains the names of the QuickBASIC command menus: File, Edit, View, Search, Run, Debug, and Calls.

Scroll bars at the right side and bottom of the active window show your relative position in the file and appear only in the active window. They can be toggled on and off through the View menu's Options... dialog box, discussed later in this chapter.

When you first load QuickBASIC, the status line at the bottom of the screen displays the QuickBASIC copyright notice. On the far right, the current cursor position is displayed as a combination of line and column numbers. Just to the left of this cursor position display, the letters *C* or *N* appear when the CAPS LOCK or NUM LOCK key is toggled on. When these keys are off these letters do not appear.

At the right end of the menu bar (top of the screen), notice **F1=Help**. Press the F1 key and a Help screen appears, as shown in Figure 3-2. Keyboard combinations used to perform specified functions are listed in separate boxes. You may want to make a screen print

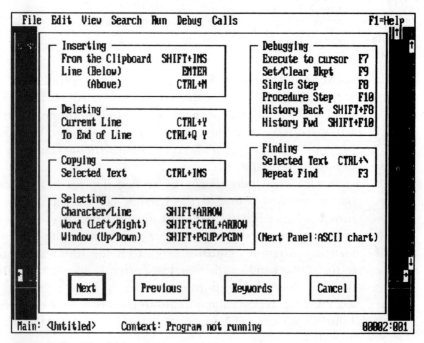

Figure 3-2.   *First Help screen*

of this window so that you will have a hard copy of the keys used for these functions. You can return to the editing screen any time by pressing the ESC key. Press ESC now, and then press F1 to get back to the Help screen.

Buttons labeled Next, Previous, Keywords, and Cancel are positioned at the bottom of the Help screen. In Figure 3-2, the Next button is highlighted and therefore active. You can move the highlight from button to button by pressing the TAB key. If ENTER is pressed while a button is highlighted (active), that action is carried out. Use the Next and Previous buttons to explore the Help pages, then return to the first Help page.

Use the TAB key to move the cursor to the Keywords button and press ENTER. A list of BASIC keywords is displayed, as shown in Figure 3-3. To see information on a given keyword, use the arrow keys to move the highlight to the desired keyword and press ENTER. To move to another entire page of keywords, use the PGUP and PGDN keys. To return to the editing screen, press the ESC key.

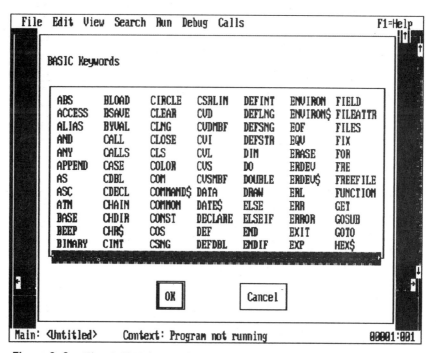

Figure 3-3. *First BASIC keywords screen*

Changing the Active Window When you start QuickBASIC without a file name, two windows appear: a View window above and an Immediate window below. Later, when you load a program, the main module of the program appears in the upper window. To move from the upper window to the Immediate window, press F6. Press F6 a second time to move back to the upper window. F6 acts as a toggle to switch back and forth between the two windows.

Now use F6 to move to the Immediate window. Type **BEEP** and press ENTER. You will hear a beep because the BEEP instruction occurs immediately. Press F6 to return to the View window.

Using the Editor Here are some basic editing aids. A more complete discussion of the editor and its uses appears in a later chapter. For the present, type carefully to keep errors to a minimum. If you make a mistake in typing, there are two easy ways to erase it:

1. Press the BACKSPACE key to erase the character to the left of the cursor.

2. Press the DEL key to erase the character at the cursor position.

The four arrow keys — up (↑), down (↓), left (←), and right (→) — move the cursor over characters without erasing them.

Enter Program 3-1, COIN FLIPPER. Read it once more for any errors you might have overlooked. If you find an error, move the cursor to the appropriate position and correct the error.

Rather than compiling and running the program immediately after you have entered it, first save it. If you run the program before saving it, some logical error may cause the program to malfunction. You may not be able to recover the program without resetting the computer and losing it from memory. To avoid any chance of having to reenter the program from the keyboard, save it first. It may then be reloaded at any time from the File menu, as described later on in the chapter.

Saving the COIN FLIPPER Program

When you are satisfied that the program has been entered correctly, press the ALT+F key combination to access the File menu. The File

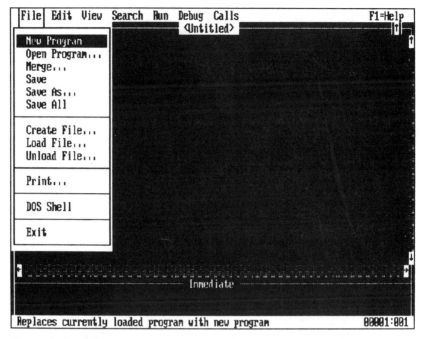

Figure 3-4. *File menu (New Program highlighted)*

menu, shown in Figure 3-4, appears in a window near the top-left hand corner of the screen. Press the down arrow key. Each time you press the down arrow key, the highlight moves down one item, unless it is already on the last item. In that case, it moves to the top of the list. The up arrow moves the highlight up one item until it reaches the top. Pressing the up arrow at this point moves the highlight to the bottom of the list.

Notice that some of the commands are followed by an ellipsis (...), which indicates that more information is needed when the command is selected. If an ellipsis does not appear after a command, the command is executed immediately without any further information.

There are three ways to save a program from the File menu. Since you have not provided a name for the program, move the highlight to the Save As... command in order to give it a name before saving. Then press ENTER. A Save dialog box prompts you for the name to be used

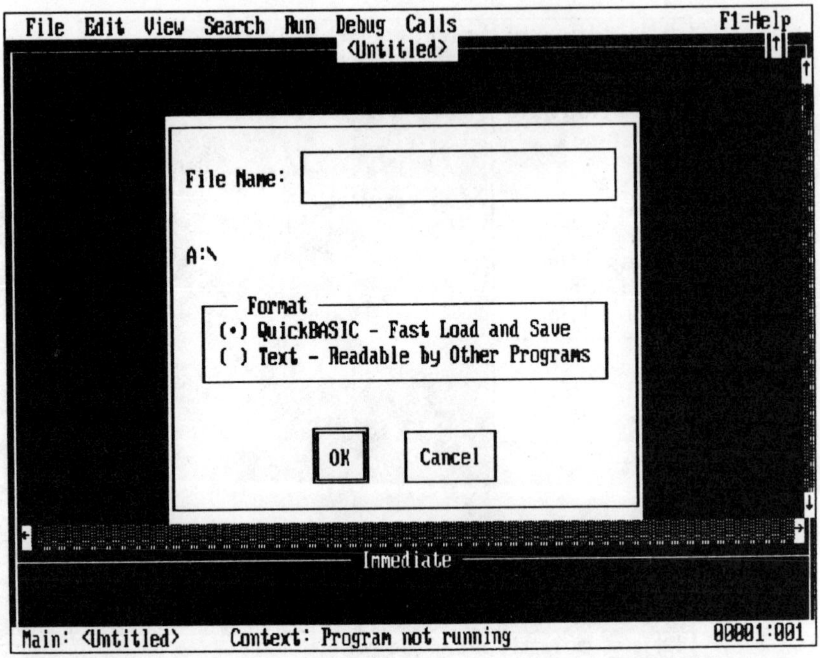

```
 File  Edit  View  Search  Run  Debug  Calls                    F1=Help
                            <Untitled>


            File Name:


            A:\


               ┌─ Format ──────────────────────────────┐
               │ (•) QuickBASIC - Fast Load and Save    │
               │ ( ) Text - Readable by Other Programs  │
               └────────────────────────────────────────┘



                         ┌────┐   ┌────────┐
                         │ OK │   │ Cancel │
                         └────┘   └────────┘


                             Immediate


 Main: <Untitled>       Context: Program not running        00001:001
```

Figure 3-5. *Save As... dialog box*

for the file, as shown in Figure 3-5. You can use the TAB key to move the cursor from box to box and the arrow keys to move the cursor within a box.

Use the TAB key to move the cursor into the Format box. Use the arrow keys to select the line that reads **Text - Readable by Other Programs**.

Use the TAB key to move to the File Name box. Make sure that you have a blank, formatted disk in Drive B. Then enter

```
File Name:   B:PRO3-1
```

File names must conform to the MS-DOS format. There can be no more than eight characters plus a three-letter extension. If no extension is provided, QuickBASIC automatically supplies .BAS (for BASIC).

If you choose the Save or Save All command when no file name has been given and press ENTER, the dialog box shown in Figure 3-5 will appear. If you have already given the file a name, Save or Save All will immediately save the program.

After saving the program, you may wish to print out a hard copy. Access the File menu (ALT F), move the highlight in the File menu to the Print . . . command and press ENTER. A dialog box will appear, as shown in Figure 3-6.

You can select one of the four print options, which are as follows:

Selected Text   Prints only the text selected (highlighted) in the active window.

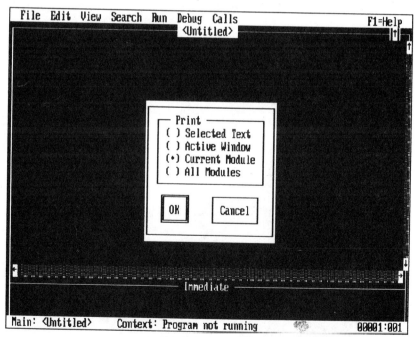

Figure 3-6.   *Print . . . dialog box*

Active Window   Prints the contents of the active window, usually a complete main module, function, or subprogram.

Current Module   Prints the contents of the file associated with the active window.

All Modules   Prints the contents of all modules, include files, and document files in memory. Use the All Modules option when you are working with multiple modules and want to print all of them.

When you first access the Print ... dialog box, note that the Current Module option is active (solid dot in parentheses). Since you have a simple source program for this program, any of the last three options will work.

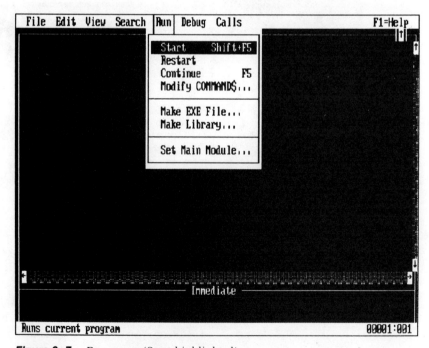

Figure 3-7. *Run menu (Start highlighted)*

Compiling and Running
the COIN FLIPPER Program

Press the ALT+R key combination and the Run menu appears in a
window near the top of the screen. The Start command is highlighted,
as shown in Figure 3-7. To run the program press the ENTER key.

Your program is scanned for errors. Suppose you have no errors in
the program: The program is immediately compiled and run. The
screen clears and the coin flipper input prompt appears at the top of
the output screen.

```
I flip coins.   How many should I flip? _
```

A run is shown in Figure 3-8. Results will vary as heads or tails is
randomly selected. When the run is completed, at the bottom of the

```
I flip coins.  How many should I flip? 58

TAILS       TAILS       TAILS       HEADS       HEADS
HEADS       TAILS       TAILS       TAILS       HEADS
HEADS       TAILS       HEADS       TAILS       HEADS
TAILS       TAILS       TAILS       HEADS       HEADS
HEADS       HEADS       HEADS       HEADS       TAILS
HEADS       HEADS       HEADS       TAILS       TAILS
HEADS       HEADS       HEADS       TAILS       HEADS
HEADS       TAILS       TAILS       HEADS       TAILS
HEADS       HEADS       HEADS       HEADS       HEADS
TAILS       HEADS       TAILS       HEADS       TAILS


















Press any key to continue
```

Figure 3-8.   *Output of Program 3-1*

screen you will see the line **Press any key to continue**. Press any key and you are returned to the View window with the program displayed.

Now consider the case in which an error occurs in the program. To create an error, move the cursor to the *N* of the NEXT statement in the FLIP COINS block, as shown below.

```
        .
        .
        .
' Flip Coins
FOR counter = 1 to nftips
    flip = INT(2 * RND(1))
    IF flip = 0 THEN PRINT "HEADS",  ELSE PRINT "TAILS",
NEXT counter

END
```

Press the DEL key until the NEXT statement has been deleted.

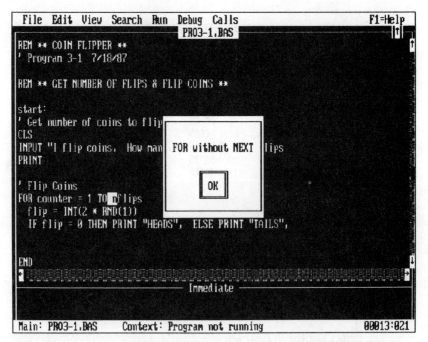

Figure 3-9.   *Error dialog box*

```
   .
   .
   .
' Flip Coins
FOR counter = 1 to nflips
   flip = INT(2 * RND(1))
   IF flip = 0 THEN PRINT "HEADS",  ELSE PRINT "TAILS",
   _

END
```

You have introduced an error and QuickBASIC should find it for you. Access the Start command from the Run menu and press ENTER. When the program is scanned for errors this time, an error is detected. An error dialog box appears near the center of the screen, showing the type of error and highlighting the OK button (see Figure 3-9).

Press the ENTER key. The dialog box disappears. The blinking cursor appears at a place related to the error in your program, as shown in Figure 3-10. Move the cursor to the end of the FOR...

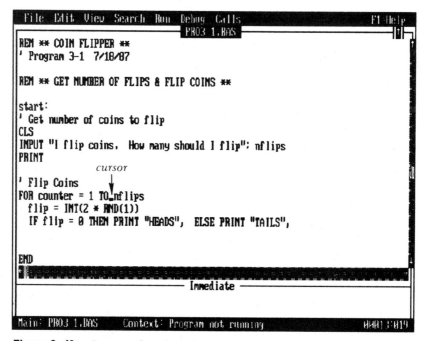

Figure 3-10. *Cursor at location of error*

NEXT loop and type in the missing line:

```
NEXT counter
```

Then go back to the Run menu and run the corrected program. Also make sure Program 3-1 is saved to disk; you will use it in the next section.

A Previously Saved QuickBASIC Program

This method is the simplest of all, since you already have a working QuickBASIC program to use.

Make sure the QB work disk is in Drive A and the disk with the previously saved QuickBASIC program is in Drive B. Since you have already created and saved Program 3-1, use it for this demonstration.

Loading a Previously Saved QuickBASIC Program

You can load Program 3-1 in two ways:

1. Use the MS-DOS command line to load the program. Include the name of the program:

```
A>QB B:PRO3-1
```

This method loads QuickBASIC from Drive A and loads PRO3-1 from Drive B. You bypass the File menu and go directly to the editor. You then proceed to the Run menu to compile and run the program.

2. Load QuickBASIC only with the command

```
A>QB
```

Use ALT+F to access the File menu. Move the highlight to the Open Program ... item as shown in Figure 3-11, and press ENTER. The Open Program ... dialog box appears, as shown in Figure 3-12. Type the file name in the File Name window near the top of the screen.

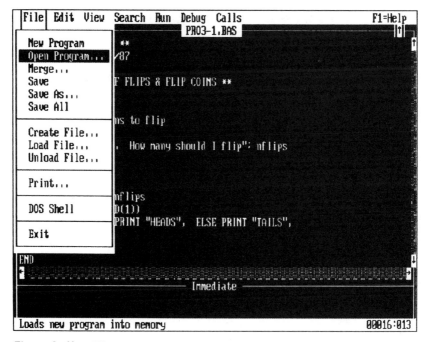

Figure 3-11. *File menu (Open Program ... highlighted)*

File Name: B:PRO3-1

Notice the OK and Cancel buttons near the bottom of the screen. The Cancel button is used to abort the Open Program ... command. Use the TAB key to move from box to box. If the OK button is highlighted (a double border), press ENTER to load the program. However, if you change your mind, there are two ways to leave this window: (1) move the cursor to the Cancel button and press ENTER or (2) press the ESC key.

Compiling and Running the QuickBASIC Program

Use the ALT+R key combination to access the Run menu. It appears in a window with the Start ... command highlighted, as shown in Figure 3-13. Press the ENTER key to compile and run the program.

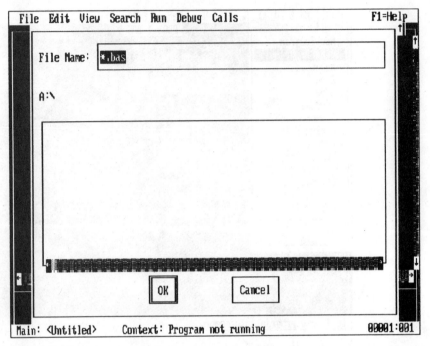

Figure 3-12.   *Open Program...dialog box*

A Previously Saved GW-BASIC Program

A GW-BASIC program must be in ASCII format before QuickBASIC can compile it. It is assumed that you have previously saved Program 1-2*a*, AVERAGE PRICE OF STOCKS, in ASCII format. If you have not saved the program in ASCII format, stop now, return to GW-BASIC, load or enter Program 1-2*a*, and save it in ASCII format with the file name PRO1-2A.

Place the disk containing Program 1-2*a* (in ASCII format) in Drive B. Place your QB work disk in Drive A if it is not already there. At the MS-DOS prompt, type **QB** and press ENTER. When the blank editing screen appears as shown previously in Figure 3-1, press ALT+F to access the File menu.

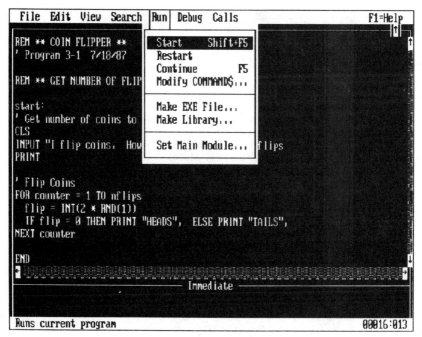

Figure 3-13. *Run menu (Start highlighted)*

Loading the GW-BASIC Program

Press the down arrow key until the Open Program . . . command of the File menu is highlighted (refer to Figure 3-11). Then press ENTER.

A dialog box prompts you for the name of the file that you want to load, as shown previously in Figure 3-12. Note that the default disk drive is Drive A, as shown below **File Name:**. Be sure to type in the disk drive of your program disk (Drive B) and a colon before the name used to save Program 1-2a in ASCII format:

```
File Name:  B:PRO1-2A
```

Press ENTER to load the program. Figure 3-14 shows the beginning of Program 1-2a after it was loaded.

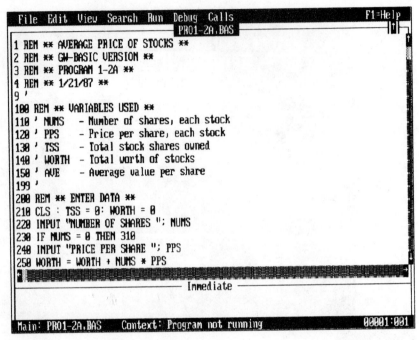

Figure 3-14. *Beginning of Program 1-2a*

Press the down arrow key to scroll the screen if you want to see the rest of the program. When the cursor reaches the bottom of the screen, the program will scroll up one line each time you press the down arrow key. You can return the cursor to the first line of the program by holding down CTRL and pressing HOME. If a program contains any long lines that go off the screen to the right, you can scroll the screen to the right by pressing the right arrow key as many times as necessary to see the end of the line.

QuickBASIC places up to 255 characters on a single line. To scroll the screen back to its original position, press the left arrow key until the line numbers appear at the left side of the screen. You should now save the program to the QuickBASIC data disk that was used to save Program 3-1.

Saving the GW-BASIC Program

In Drive B, replace the disk containing the original GW-BASIC program with the disk containing QuickBASIC Program 3-1. Save Program 1-2*a* to this disk so that both programs are on the same disk. To do this, select the Save command from the File menu since the program has already been named. Then press the ENTER key. When saving is completed, you are ready to compile and run the program.

Compiling and Running the GW-BASIC Program

Press the ALT+R key combination to access the Run menu. The Start command is highlighted. Press ENTER to compile and run the program. Since you have already successfully run Program 1-2*a* using GW-BASIC and it contained no prohibited statements, you can expect it to run successfully.

The program will work the same way it did in Chapter 1. Entries are necessary for the number of shares and price per share of each stock. The average price per share and total value of your portfolio is displayed.

The File Menu

The File menu, shown previously in Figure 3-4, is shown here again as Figure 3-15.

All File menu commands are described below.

New Program	Used to create a new file. It can also be used to erase any file currently in memory.
Open Program ...	Loads a file from disk into memory. You can also use this command to list the files and directories in your system.

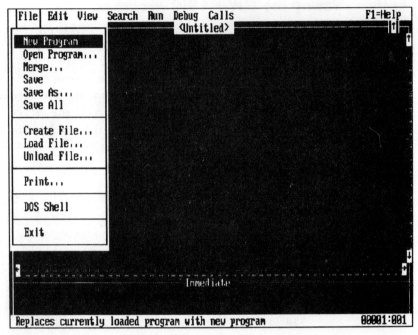

Figure 3-15.   *File menu (New Program highlighted)*

Merge ...	Used to merge files.
Save	Saves a previously named file to disk.
Save As ...	Prompts you for a file name. Writes the current module (the one in the active window) to a disk file. You can also use this command to change file names.
Save All	Saves to disk all modules that have changed since the last save.
Create File ...	Creates a file in memory.
Load File ...	Loads a file from a disk.
Unload File ...	Erases a file from a program.
Print ...	Prints selected text from the active window, the complete active window, the current module, or the current program.

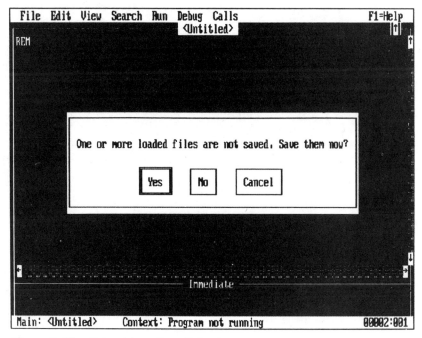

Figure 3-16. *Exit without Save dialog box*

DOS Shell

Lets you temporarily return to the DOS command level, from which you can execute other programs and DOS commands. Quick-BASIC remains in memory. Access to COM-MAND.COM, which you copied to your QB work disk, is necessary. To return to Quick-BASIC from DOS, type **Exit** and press ENTER. The QuickBASIC screen reappears just as you left it.

Exit

Removes QuickBASIC from memory and returns you to the DOS prompt. When you have a new or modified program that has not been saved, QuickBASIC will ask if you want to save the program (see Figure 3-16). To save the program, press ENTER when the Yes button is highlighted. If the program has no

name, the Save As . . . dialog box (shown in
Figure 3-5) is displayed. If you do not want to
save the program, press TAB to highlight the
No button. Then press ENTER.

To select a command from the File menu, use the cursor control
keys or mouse to highlight the desired command, and then press
ENTER. Commands that are followed by an ellipsis, such as Open
Program . . ., require more information and will display a dialog box
with prompts for the information you need to enter.

New Program Command

Select the New Program command. A blank editing screen is displayed, ready for you to enter a new file.

Open Program . . . Command

Select the Open Program. . . command. The dialog box shown previously as Figure 3-12 and shown here again as Figure 3-17 appears.
 The window has two dialog boxes, one labeled File Name and a
larger untitled box. At the bottom of the screen are two buttons, OK
and Cancel. Use the TAB key to move from box to box.

File Name: Enter the name of a file you wish to load.

A: \.   This is the current pathspec. The value shown here
               (A: \) indicates Drive A.

OK and Cancel are the "buttons" that activate the selections made.

OK   If OK is highlighted, the chosen action is taken when
               the ENTER key is pressed.

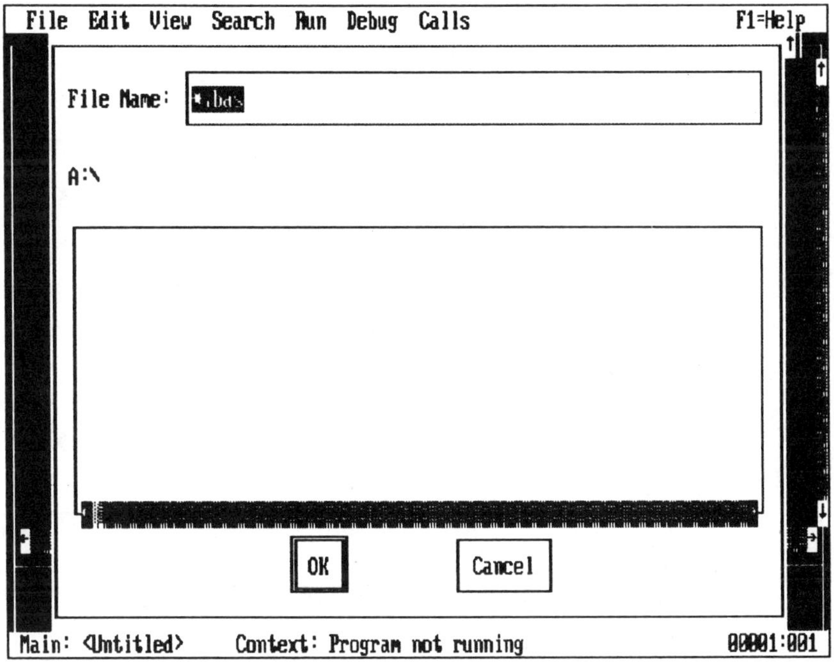

```
 File  Edit  View  Search  Run  Debug  Calls                    F1=Help
```

File Name: `*.bas`

A:\

OK   Cancel

```
 Main: <Untitled>     Context: Program not running        00001:001
```

Figure 3-17. *Open Program... dialog box*

Cancel   If Cancel is highlighted, pressing ENTER cancels the
                selection.

You can use the Open Program ... dialog box to list the files in
any directory. File names are displayed in lowercase in the File Name
box.

You can list all the files on the disk in Drive B in one of two ways
depending on the filespec displayed.

1. If the filespec displayed is **A:**, type **B:*.*** and the File Name box
will appear as shown below. Press ENTER.

`File Name:   B:*.*`

2. If the filespec displayed is **B:**, type ***.*** and press ENTER.

Figure 3-18 displays an example of the resulting file directory.

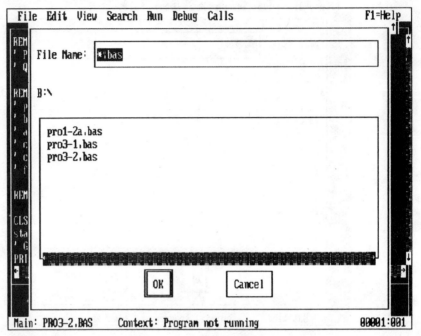

Figure 3-18.   *Open Program... dialog box (files displayed)*

Merge ... Command

The Merge ... command inserts a file from a disk at the point just ahead of the position at which you place the cursor. When this command is selected, the dialog box shown in Figure 3-19 is displayed.

File Name: Enter the name of the file you wish to merge with the current file in memory.

B: \.   The current filespec. The value shown here (**B:** \) indicates Drive B.

OK   If the OK button is highlighted, press ENTER to merge the file.

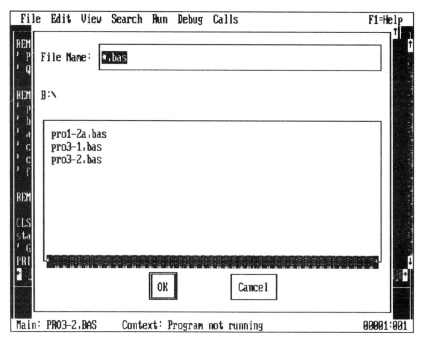

Figure 3-19.   *Merge... dialog box*

Cancel   If the Cancel button is highlighted, press ENTER to
                 cancel the Merge ... selection. You are returned to the
                 editor.

The large, empty box is used to list files from a disk so that you can
select the file you want to merge. It is used in the same way as the File
Name box in the Open Program ... command.

Save Command

Select the Save command when you wish to save a program that has a
file name. No dialog box appears when you press the ENTER key. The
file is immediately saved under its current name. If you make this

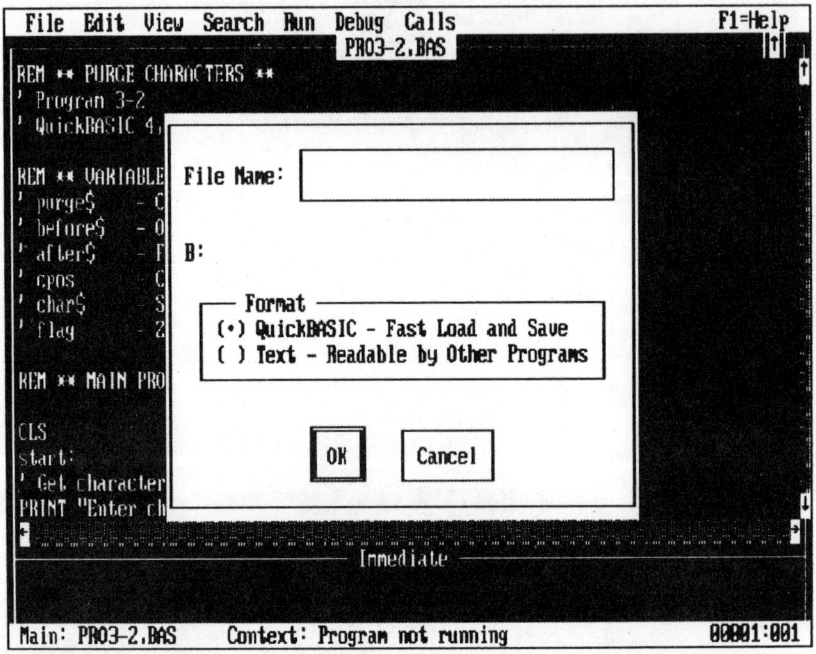

Figure 3-20. *Save As... and Save All dialog box*

selection before a file is named, the dialog box shown in Figure 3-20 appears so that you can name the file now.

Save As ... and Save All Commands

Select either the Save As ... or Save All command, and the dialog box shown in Figure 3-20 appears. (Exception: The dialog box will not appear for Save All if all modules have previously been named.)

File Name: If you are working with a new, unnamed file, enter the file name in this box. If the file has already been named, it appears in the box. If you want to change the name, type in the name that replaces the old name.

B: \.	The current filespec. The value shown here (**B:** \) indicates Drive **B**.
QuickBASIC	This option saves the file in compressed format. A compressed file loads faster than a text file, takes up less space on a disk, and can be edited by the QuickBASIC editor. Because it is a non-ASCII file, it cannot be processed by another text editor.
Text	Stores the file on disk in ASCII format. Text files can be read, modified, or printed by any editor or word processor that reads ASCII files.
OK	After choosing a format option, press ENTER to save if OK is highlighted.
Cancel	To cancel the save selection, press ENTER if Cancel is highlighted or press ESC if Cancel is not highlighted. You are returned to the editor.

Create File ... Command

Select the Create File ... command to create a new module to be used in your program. The dialog box shown in Figure 3-21 appears.

Load File ... Command

Select the Load File ... command to load a module to be used in your program. The dialog box shown in Figure 3-22 appears.

Unload File ... Command

Select the Unload File ... command to erase a module currently in your program. The dialog box shown in Figure 3-23 appears.

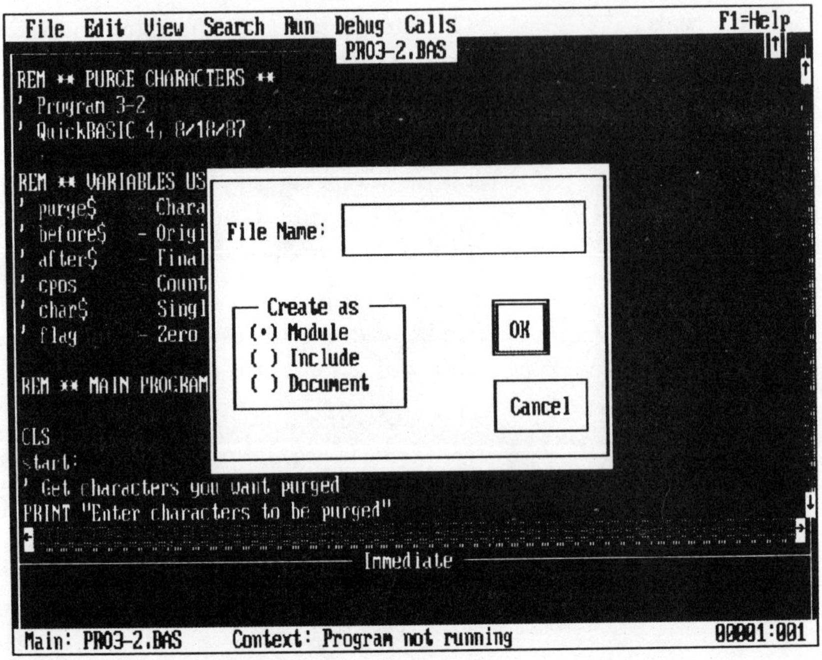

Figure 3-21.   *Create File... dialog box*

Print ... Command

Select the Print ... command. The dialog box shown previously as
Figure 3-6 and again here as Figure 3-24 appears.

Use the TAB key and arrow keys to move from place to place. Your
printer must be connected to LPT1 to operate properly.

Select Text	Prints only the text highlighted in the active window. Be sure to select some text before using this dialog box.
Active Window	Prints the contents of the active window, usually a main module, function, or subprogram.

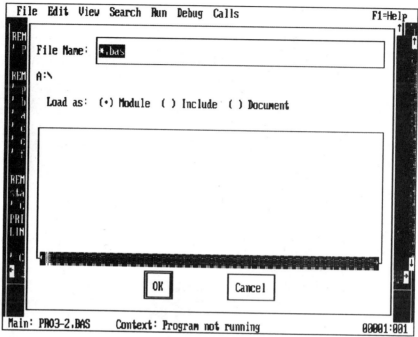

Figure 3-22.   *Load File . . . dialog box*

Current Module	Prints the contents of the file associated with, but not in, the active window.
All Modules	Prints the contents of all modules, include files, and document files in memory.
OK	Press ENTER when the OK button is highlighted to execute the selected print option.
Cancel	When highlighted, press ENTER to cancel the selected print option. You are returned to the editor.

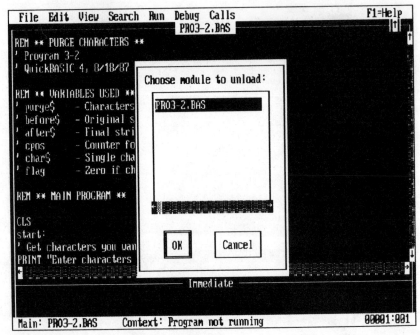

Figure 3-23.   *Unload File... dialog box*

DOS Shell Command

This command returns you to DOS, where you can execute other programs and DOS commands. QuickBASIC remains in memory. Access to COMMAND.COM, which you copied to your QB work disk, is necessary. To return to QuickBASIC, type **Exit** and press ENTER. The QuickBASIC screen reappears just as you left it.

Exit Command

Exit removes QuickBASIC from memory and returns you to the DOS prompt. When you have a new or modified program that has not been saved, QuickBASIC will ask if you want to save the program, as shown previously in Figure 3-16 and again here as Figure 3-25.

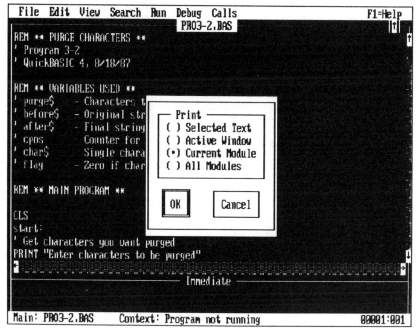

Figure 3-24. *Print... dialog box*

To save the program, press ENTER after highlighting the Yes button. If the program has no name, the Save ... dialog box, shown previously in Figures 3-5 and 3-20, is displayed. If you do not want to save the program, press TAB to highlight the No button and press ENTER.

The Run Menu

There are two ways to run a program from within QuickBASIC:

1. Move the cursor to the Immediate window by pressing the F6 key; type **Run** and press ENTER.

2. Use commands from the Run menu.

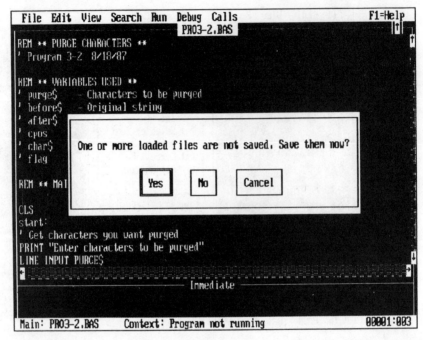

Figure 3-25.   *Exit without Save dialog box*

To select the Run menu, press the ALT+R key combination. The Run menu appears with the Start command highlighted, shown previously as Figure 3-7 and shown again here as Figure 3-26.

Start
Compiles and runs the program currently in memory, beginning with the main module. The shortcut keys for Start are SHIFT+F5.

Restart
Gets the program in memory ready to run again. After a Restart command, the next Continue or debugging Step command executes the first statement in the main program. A Restart command does not actually run the program.

Continue
Resumes running a stopped program. It is usually used in debugging. The shortcut key for Continue is F5.

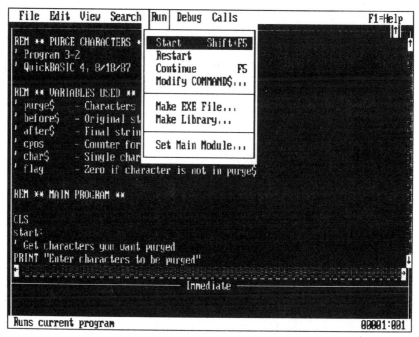

Figure 3-26. *Run menu (Start highlighted)*

Modify COM-MAND$ ...	Sets the string returned by the COMMAND$ function.
Make EXE File ...	Creates an executable file from the source program currently in memory and writes it to disk. The LINK.EXE file and any stand-alone library associated with the Quick library currently in memory must be available.
Make Library ...	Compiles all loaded modules into a Quick library and into a stand-alone library. The LINK.EXE file must be available.
Set Main Module ...	Sets which module of your program QuickBASIC treats as the main module.

Run menu selections other than Start are discussed in later chapters.

When errors are detected in a program when it is run, an Error dialog box is displayed. QuickBASIC opens a View window, if necessary, and places the cursor on the statement in which the error was detected, as was demonstrated in the earlier discussion of Program 3-1. You can then correct the error and rerun the program.

Using the File and Run Menus

New programs entered from the keyboard use the New Program command from the File menu. You used this command to enter Program 3-1.

With the QB work disk in Drive A and a program disk in Drive B, use the following steps to enter, compile, and run Program 3-2, **PURGE CHARACTERS**, in QuickBASIC.

1. From the MS-DOS prompt, type **QB** and press ENTER:

```
A>QB
```

2. To select the File menu from the menu bar, press ALT+F. A box around the title File on the menu bar indicates that the File menu has been chosen. The commands for this menu were displayed in Figure 3-15.

3. The New Program command is highlighted when the File menu has just been selected. If you should accidentally press the down arrow key, the highlight will move to the next item. You can press the up arrow key to move the highlight back to New Program or the down arrow key to move through the other commands until the highlight returns to New Program.

4. When you select New Program and press ENTER, a blank window appears with a blinking cursor in the upper-left-hand corner. You are in the editor. Enter Program 3-2. Use the editor as you would use a word processor. Incorporating indentations and blank lines will make the program easy to read.

```
REM ** PURGE CHARACTERS **
' Program 3-2  8/18/87

REM ** VARIABLES USED **
' purge$     - Characters to be purged
' before$    - Original string
' after$     - Final string
' cpos       - Counter for character position
' char$      - Single character from before$
' flag       - Zero if character is not in purge$

REM ** MAIN PROGRAM **

CLS
start:
' Get characters you want purged
PRINT "Enter characters to be purged"
LINE INPUT purge$

' Get string to be purged
PRINT "Enter a string you want purged"
LINE INPUT before$

' Purge the characters
GOSUB purge

' Print the purged string & go back
PRINT after$
PRINT : GOTO start

REM ** SUBROUTINE: PURGE **
purge:
after$ = ""
FOR cpos = 1 TO LEN(before$)
  char$ = MID$(before$, cpos, 1)
  flag = INSTR(purge$, char$)
  IF flag = 0 THEN after$ = after$ + char$
NEXT cpos
RETURN
```

Program 3-2. *PURGE CHARACTERS*

5. After you have entered the program, use the ALT+F key combination
to access the File menu. Use the down arrow key to highlight the Save
As . . . command and press ENTER. The Save As . . . dialog box shown
in Figure 3-20 appears. Since you have not given the program a name,
enter **B:PRO3-2** in the File Name box. Press ENTER to save the
program.

6. When the program has been saved, use the ALT+R keys to access the
Run menu. Press ENTER to compile and run the program.

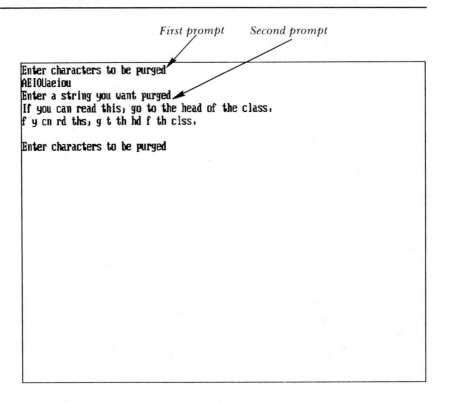

First prompt   *Second prompt*

```
Enter characters to be purged
AEIOUaeiou
Enter a string you want purged
If you can read this, go to the head of the class.
f y cn rd ths, g t th hd f th clss.

Enter characters to be purged
```

Figure 3-27.   *Output of Program 3-2*

At the first prompt enter the string of characters that you want to purge. At the second prompt enter the string that you want purged. A sample run is shown in Figure 3-27.

Review

In this chapter, you have learned how to prepare a QB work disk. You have used the work disk to write, save, print, compile, and run a new QuickBASIC program, COIN FLIPPER. You also used the QB work disk to load, compile, and run a previously saved QuickBASIC program and a GW-BASIC program, AVERAGE PRICE OF STOCKS, that had previously been saved in ASCII format. You then entered a QuickBASIC program, PURGE CHARACTERS, using the QuickBASIC editor. The File and Run menus were discussed and used to produce and test the QuickBASIC programs. You learned how to respond to dialog boxes that are displayed when a menu command needs more information.

4 *Building a Toolkit*

Every language has its own set of rules that must be followed for effective communication. This chapter discusses some of the most important rules to follow when using QuickBASIC, rules that allow you to take advantage of such QuickBASIC enhancements as long strings and variables, blocked program statements, structured formats, line labels, and subprograms. Tables illustrate new, enhanced, and prohibited statements and functions.

This chapter begins building programming tools that you can use in later programs. If a tool is saved to disk as a separate file, it can later be merged with your programs as needed. Much of this chapter is devoted to single-line and multiline functions. Local and global variables are discussed. A local variable has a value only within a particular unit of a program. A global variable has a value that is available throughout all parts of a program. Logical (Boolean) operations are explained and frequently used.

Three QuickBASIC control structures are introduced and discussed: Block IF...THEN...ELSE, SELECT CASE, and DO... LOOP. The Block IF...THEN...ELSE structure extends GW-BASIC's single-line IF...THEN statement to a multiline block, making the structure easier to read and providing more flexibility. The SELECT CASE structure allows for multiple-choice decisions depending on the value of an expression. The expression can be either numeric or string. The DO...LOOP structure allows you to test for a true or false condition at either the beginning or the end of a loop. The loop is executed either WHILE a condition is satisfied or UNTIL a condition is satisfied.

Making a Toolkit

The idea of building programming tools was introduced earlier in this book with GW-BASIC subroutines that performed such functions as squeezing spaces out of strings, changing lowercase letters to uppercase, purging certain characters from a string, and keeping only certain characters in a string. It is time to plan ways of collecting tools that you might want to use in the future, especially the single-line and multiline functions introduced in this chapter. You can save time and write programs more efficiently if you save often-used functions in one place, thereby creating a handy toolkit. Your programming toolkit can consist of many function definitions saved as individual files, all on the same disk. Using the Merge... command from the File menu, you can easily add the desired functions to any program.

When a function is needed in a program, place the disk containing your function definitions in Drive B. Move the cursor to the location in the program where you wish to place the definition. Select the Merge... command from the File menu. When the dialog box appears, type the file name of the function definition in the File box. This process will be explained in more detail later in the chapter.

You should give considerable thought to naming the files that contain the function definition. The name should describe what the function does, but it must be short since MS-DOS file names are restricted to eight characters. If the file name is the same as the name given to the function definition, it will be easy to identify the desired file. For example, you will later see a single-line function definition that rounds money to the nearest cent. The function is named FNroundcnt, so ROUNDCNT would be an appropriate name for the file. Since the name describes the function it defines (round to the nearest cent), it will be easy to locate from a list of files.

Variables and Data Types

QuickBASIC uses two types of variables: string and numeric. A variable must always match the type of expression assigned to it, string type with strings and numeric type with numbers:

city$* = *"CHICAGO"*   (both *city$ and *"CHICAGO"* are strings)

zip = *94026*   (both *zip* and *94026* are numeric)

QuickBASIC variable names may contain as many as 40 characters. Accepted characters are letters, numbers, the decimal point, and type declaration characters ($, %, &, !, and #). The first character of a variable must be a letter. A variable cannot be a reserved word (keyword), although reserved words may be embedded in a variable. For example, IF, which is a keyword, can be embedded in STIFF, which is a variable, not a reserve word.

Letters in a variable name may be uppercase or lowercase. *ZIP*, *Zip*, and *zip* are all the same variable. From now on, variables will appear in three possible ways:

1. Lowercase only: *zip city$ year%   money#*

2. First letter capitalized: *Agent007$ Zip*

3. Selected letters capitalized: *ZipCode$ BigNumber#*

Although technically possible, variables do not appear in this book in all uppercase letters. This makes variables in a program easy to distinguish from keywords, which appear in all uppercase. Variables are italicized in the text.

Five special characters ($, %, &, !, and #) are used to specify variables as string ($), short integer (%), long integer (&), single precision (!), or double precision (#).

1. The dollar sign ($) For example: *state$*. The dollar sign specifies that the variable *state$* represents a string of characters. Long strings—up to 32,767 characters—can be used.

2. The percent sign (%) For example: *calories%*. The percent sign specifies that the variable *calories%* represents an integer. Integers are numeric values stored internally as 16-bit integers in the range −32,768 through 32,767.

3. The ampersand (&) For example: *pennies&*. The ampersand specifies that the variable *pennies&* represents a long integer, stored as a 32-bit integer in the range −2,147,483,648 to 2,147,483,647 (-2^{31} to $2^{31}-1$).

4. The exclamation mark (!) For example: *AveragePrice!*. The exclamation mark specifies that the variable *AveragePrice!* represents a single-precision floating point number. Single-precision numbers are precise to about seven decimal digits. Their range can be from approximately −3.37E+38 to −8.43E−37 for negative numbers, zero, and from 8.43E−37 to 3.37E+38 for positive numbers.

5. The number sign (#) For example: *Lotsamoney#*. The number sign specifies that the variable *Lotsamoney#* represents a double-precision floating point number. Double-precision numbers are precise to about 15 decimal digits in the approximate range of −1.67D+308 to −4.19D−307 for negative numbers, zero, and of 4.19D−307 to 1.67D+308 for positive numbers. The letter *D* is used in place of *E* to designate the power of ten in double-precision numbers.

The default type for a variable when $, %, &, !, or # is not specified is a single-precision floating point.

You can use the above data specifications to conserve memory. There are some differences in execution speed for the different data types. Data is stored in the following way:

Short integer (%)	2 bytes	
Long integer (&)	4 bytes	
Single precision (!)	4 bytes	*floating point*
Double precision (#)	8 bytes	''
Strings ($)	6 bytes per string plus 1 byte per character	

Obviously, a substantial amount of memory can be saved by using short integers whenever possible.

Two useful operations are associated with integer data: the backslash (\ ) and the MOD operation. The backslash performs integer division, rounding both the divisor and the dividend to the nearest integer. When the division is completed the result is truncated (the decimal part dropped), producing an integer quotient. Here are some examples:

```
20 \ 3      = 6
20.49 \ 3.1 = 6  (the same as 20 \ 3 = 6)
20.51 \ 3.1 = 7  (the same as 21 \ 3 = 7)
19.49 \ 3.6 = 4  (the same as 19 \ 4 = 4)
19.51 \ 3.6 = 5  (the same as 20 \ 4 = 5)
```

The MOD operator computes the remainder with integer division. For example:

```
20 MOD 3 = 2
20 MOD 4 = C
20 MOD 5 = 0
1987 MOD 4 = 3
```

This operation is also called "modulo arithmetic" and MOD is sometimes called the "modulus operator."

Local and Global Variables

QuickBASIC uses variables in two ways. They are either *local* to a specific part of a program or *global*, that is, available throughout the entire program.

A local variable has a value only within a particular unit of a program, such as a user-defined function or a subprogram. A global variable has a value that is available throughout all parts of a program.

The STATIC statement designates variables as local to a function definition or subprogram and preserves their values when the function or subprogram is exited and later reentered. The STATIC statement can appear only within a multiline function definition or a named subprogram.

Program Lines

A program line can contain a maximum of 255 characters, including blank spaces. A line is terminated by pressing the ENTER key. If you enter a line that contains more than 80 characters, the screen will scroll to the right after the first 80 characters are typed. Think of the line moving to the left or the screen moving to the right. When you press the ENTER key at the end of the line, the screen will scroll back to its original position at the far left. Only the first 80 characters of the line will be visible. If you want to see the rest of the line, hold down the right arrow key; the screen will scroll to the right. To move back to the beginning of the line hold down the left arrow key.

A program is hard to read on the screen if it contains lines longer than the width of the screen. Also, if you list a program on an 80-column printer, lines longer than 80 characters will be broken into two or more printed lines, usually at some awkward place. The result is a hard-to-read listing that doesn't look exactly like the program shown on the screen. In the interests of good programming style, it is highly recommended that you keep line length to 80 characters or less. From now on, programs in this book will heed this recommendation.

As you have seen, you do not have to use line numbers in a QuickBASIC program. However, there are times when it helps to be able to identify a line. Two types of line identifiers may be used: line numbers and alphanumeric labels. Line-number identifiers are like those used in GW-BASIC. A line number may be any integer from 0 through 65,529. Since line numbers are not required, they are used only when previous GW-BASIC programs are discussed or when comparing QuickBASIC with GW-BASIC.

An alphanumeric line label can be any combination of 1 to 40 letters and digits; the label must end with a colon. QuickBASIC keywords are not permitted as line labels by themselves, but may be embedded in a line label. Upper- or lowercase has no significance. STARTHERE:, starthere:, Starthere:, and StartHere: are all the same label. From now on, line labels will conform to the same conventions as variable names.

In a statement that references a line label, the colon at the end of the label is omitted, as these two examples show.

```
GOTO start

ON direction GOTO north, east, south, west
```

When using line labels, an IF...THEN...ELSE statement must have this form:

```
IF condition THEN GOTO linelabel [ELSE GOTO linelabel]
```

For example:

```
IF amount > 0 THEN GOTO Aok ELSE GOTO NotSoGood
   .
   .
   .
Aok:
   .
   .
   .
NotSoGood:
   .
   .
   .
```

A line label can occur at the beginning of a line that contains other things. For example:

```
waitkey: kbd$ = INKEY$: IF kbd$ = "" THEN GOTO waitkey
```

A line label can occur alone on a line, as in the following two-line block:

```
waitkey:
IF INKEY$ = "" THEN GOTO waitkey ELSE GOTO start
```

Built-in Functions

QuickBASIC has a rich repertoire of built-in functions. A function operates on one or more arguments and produces, or returns, one value. Arguments can be numeric or string. A function can be a numeric function or a string function. A numeric function returns a numeric value and a string function returns a string value. Here are some examples of numeric and string functions:

Numeric functions: ASC INSTR INT LEN RND VAL

String functions: CHR$ MID$ SPACE$ STR$ STRING$

The name of a string function always ends with a dollar sign ($).

Many combinations of function and argument are possible, as listed below:

Numeric function of a numeric argument	INT(100 * *money* + .5)
Numeric function of a string argument	LEN(*word$*)
String function of a numeric argument	STR$(*zipcode*)
String function of a string argument	UCASE$(*state$*)
Numeric function, mixed arguments	INSTR(*start%*, *strng$*, *substrng$*)
String function, mixed arguments	MID$(*word$*, *position%*, 1)

QuickBASIC provides functions that are not available in Applesoft BASIC or GW-BASIC, including the useful LCASE$ and UCASE$. LCASE$(*stringexpression*) is a string function of a string argument. It returns the value of a string expression with all uppercase letters changed to lowercase. Characters that are not letters are unchanged. UCASE$(*stringexpression*) also is a string function of a string argument. It returns the value of *stringexpression* with lowercase letters changed to uppercase. Characters that are not letters are unchanged. Other QuickBASIC functions that are not available in GW-BASIC are introduced as they are needed.

User-defined Functions

You can use the DEF FN statement to name and define your own functions. QuickBASIC allows you to define single-line functions in the same way that functions are defined in GW-BASIC or Applesoft BASIC. QuickBASIC also has a powerful multiline function definition that is not available in GW-BASIC or Applesoft BASIC.

A single-line function is named and defined in the following way:

```
DEF FNname [(parameterlist)] = functiondefinition
```

where

name is any legal variable name. This name, preceded by FN, is the name of the function. If *name* is a numeric variable, the function is a numeric function. If *name* is a string variable, the function is a string function.

parameterlist is a list of variable names separated by commas. These are dummy variables and have no meaning outside the function definition. You may use the same names as variables elsewhere in the program.

functiondefinition is an expression that computes the string or numeric value assigned to the function. It must be the same type (string or numeric) as the variable that names the function.

A function must be defined before it is called or used. Therefore, you should place function definitions near the beginning of a program.

Program 4-1, **DOLLARS AND CENTS**, demonstrates a numeric function of a numeric variable to round a number to the nearest penny.

Figure 4-1 shows a test run of the program. Note that negative numbers are properly rounded to two decimal places.

The function FNroundcnt# is defined as a double-precision function so that it can work with up to 15 decimal digits. The single-precision version shown below is limited to numbers with up to about seven decimal digits:

```
DEF FNroundcnt (money)=SGN(money)*INT(100*ABS(money)+.5)/100
```

Both of these functions are useful for rounding numbers for internal use. Use the **PRINT USING** statement to format numbers for printing.

Caution: Internally, numbers are stored in binary. For nonintegers, the binary representation may not be exactly equal to the decimal value. Thus, occasionally a simple function such as FNroundcnt# may fail to properly round a number whose decimal value has exactly three decimal places in which the third place is a 5.

```
REM ** DOLLARS AND CENTS **
' Program 4-1  7/20/87

REM ** DEFINE FUNCTION FNroundcnt# **
DEF FNroundcnt# (money#) = SGN(money#) * INT(100 * ABS(money#) + .5) / 100
' Double precision function to round a
' double precision number to two places

REM ** MAIN PROGRAM TO TEST FUNCTION **

CLS

getdata:
INPUT "Number, please"; testdata#
PRINT "Rounded value is "; FNroundcnt#(testdata#)
PRINT : GOTO getdata
```

Program 4-1. *DOLLARS AND CENTS*

```
Number, please? 123.456
Rounded value is  123.46

Number, please? 123.455
Rounded value is  123.46

Number, please? 123.454
Rounded value is  123.45

Number, please? -123.456
Rounded value is -123.46

Number, please? -123.455
Rounded value is -123.46

Number, please? -123.454
Rounded value is -123.45

Number, please? 123456789.946
Rounded value is  123456789.95

Number, please?
```

Figure 4-1. *Output of Program 4-1*

Your Toolkit Disk

You can begin your toolkit disk by saving the FNroundcnt# function as a separate file. You don't need to save Program 4-1; save only the function definition. Delete everything from Program 4-1 except the function definition and descriptive remarks.

```
REM ** DEFINE FUNCTION FNroundcnt# **
' Double precision function to round a
' double precision number to two places
DEF FNroundcnt# (money#) = SGN(money#) * INT(100 * ABS(money#) + .5) / 100
```

To save the function, access the Save As... command from the File menu. At the File Name dialog box enter **ROUNDCNT.BAS** as the

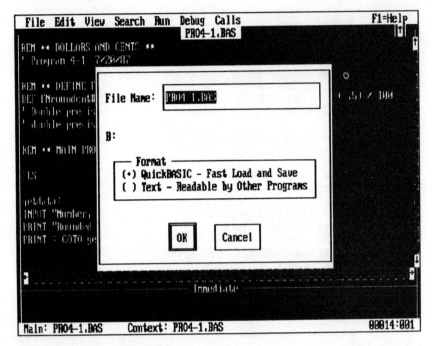

Figure 4-2. *Fast Load and Save*

file name. Look at the Format dialog box shown in Figure 4-2. If
QuickBASIC - Fast Load and Save is highlighted, change the format
selection to **Text - Readable by Other Programs**. Since you are merging the function definition with a main program, the function must
be saved in text format. Press the TAB key to move to the Format box.
Then press the down arrow key to move the highlight to the **Text -
Readable by Other Programs** selection. Press the TAB key once more to
highlight the OK box. See Figure 4-3. Press the ENTER key to save the
function definition.

　　If you want to verify that the function definition has been saved,
access the Open Program...dialog box from the File menu. You can
view the directory of the disk in Drive B by typing **b:*.*** into the File
Name box as follows:

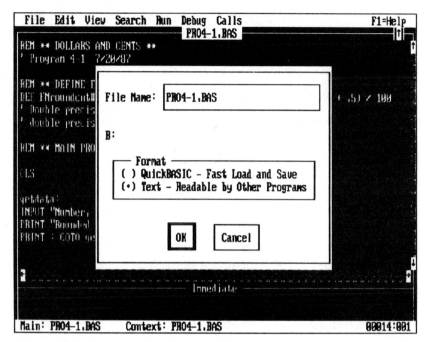

Figure 4-3. *Text Save*

Now that you have begun to assemble your toolkit of function definitions, try it out by merging it with Program 4-2*a*, TOOL MERGE DEMO.

```
REM ** TOOL MERGE DEMO **
' Program 4-2a  7/20/87

REM ** MAIN PROGRAM **

CLS

getmoolah:
INPUT "How much money"; moolah#
PRINT "Round value is  $"; FNroundcnt#(moolah#)
PRINT : GOTO getmoolah
```

Program 4-2a. *TOOL MERGE DEMO*

Merge the function definition from your toolkit in this way:

1. Make sure your toolkit disk is in Drive B if you are using a two-drive system.

2. Enter Program 4-2*a*, TOOL MERGE DEMO.

3. Move the cursor to the place at which you want to merge the function definition, as demonstrated below:

```
REM ** TOOL MERGE DEMO **
' Program 4-2  7/20/87

REM ** MAIN PROGRAM **
   .
   .
   .
```

4. Access the File menu, move the highlight down to the Merge... command, and press ENTER.

5. At the File Name box, enter the file name of the function definition,

```
File Name:  B:ROUNDCNT
```

6. Press ENTER.

```
REM ** TOOL MERGE DEMO **
' Program 4-2b  7/20/87

REM ** DEFINE FUNCTION FNroundcnt# **
DEF FNroundcnt# (money#) = SGN(money#) * INT(100 * ABS(money#) + .5) / 100
' Double precision function to round a
' double precision number to two places

REM ** MAIN PROGRAM **

CLS

getmoolah:
INPUT "How much money"; moolah#
PRINT "Rounded value is  $"; FNroundcnt#(moolah#)
PRINT : GOTO getmoolah
```

Program 4-2b. *TOOL MERGE DEMO; AFTER MERGE*

The final version of TOOL MERGE DEMO, Program 4-2*b*, shows the function definition merged at the selected location in the program. Any file from your toolkit disk can be merged with a program in memory in this way. This method of merging files is fine for small tools. In Chapter 6 you will learn a better way to assemble larger tools in your toolkit.

A Flock of Function Definitions

A numeric function can be a short-integer function, long-integer function, single-precision function, or double-precision function, as determined by the variable used to name the function. The following shows four ways of defining a function to return an integer random number in the range 1 to n, where n is a positive integer:

```
Short integer function: DEF FNrndint% (n%) = INT(n% * RND(1)) + 1

Long integer function: DEF FNrndint& (n&) = INT(n& * RND(1)) + 1

Single-precision function: DEF FNrndint (n) = INT(n * RND(1)) + 1

Double-precision function: DEF FNrndint# (n#) = INT n# * RND(1)) + 1
```

Select the one appropriate to your needs. Remember, the range of FNrndint%(n%) is 1 to 32767.

Minimum and Maximum Functions

A numeric function can be defined to return the minimum of two numbers as

```
DEF FNmin (num1, num2) = num1 * ABS(num1 <= num2) + num2 * ABS(num1 > num2)
```

How does it work? Suppose the value of *num1* is 4 and the value of *num2* is 7. In this case, the value of *num1* $<=$ *num2* is -1 (*true*) and the value of *num1* $>$ *num2* is 0 (*false*). Therefore, the value of the entire expression is *num1*:

$$num1 \; * \; \underbrace{ABS(num1 \; <= \; num2)}_{1} \; + \; num2 \; * \; \underbrace{ABS(num1 \; > \; num2)}_{0} \; = \; num1$$

So the value of FNmin is *num1 * 1 + num2 * 0 = num1*.

Now suppose *num1* is 6 and *num2* is 3. In this case,

$$num1 \; * \; \underbrace{ABS(num1 \; <= \; num2)}_{0} \; + \; num2 \; * \; \underbrace{ABS(num1 \; > \; num2)}_{1} \; = \; num2$$

The value of FNmin is *num1 * 0 + num2 * 1 = num2*. If *num1* and *num2* are equal, the value of *num1* is returned.

A similar function, FNmax, returns the maximum of two numbers:

```
DEF FNmax (num1, num2) = num1 * ABS(num1 >= num2) + num2 * ABS(num1 < num2)
```

Program 4-3, MINIMUM AND MAXIMUM, demonstrates both functions.

If you think these functions might be useful sometime, save each function as a separate file on your toolkit disk. You might also want to write and save short-integer, long-integer, and double-precision versions of both functions.

Choose function names and file names so that it is easy for you to recognize the function you want. For example:

```
FNMININT   for the short integer function FNmin%
FNMINLNG   for the long integer function FNmin&
FNMINSCL   for the single precision function FNmin
FNMINDBL   for the double precision function FNmin#
```

It is also a good idea to make a hard copy of the toolkit disk directory. Slip it into the disk envelope along with the disk.

```
REM ** MINIMUM AND MAXIMUM **
' Program 4-3  7/20/87

REM ** FUNCTION DEFINITIONS **

DEF FNmin (num1, num2) = num1 * ABS(num1 <= num2) + num2 * ABS(num1 > num2)
' FNmin returns the minimum of two numbers

DEF FNmax (num1, num2) = num1 * ABS(num1 >= num2) + num2 * ABS(num1 < num2)
' FNmax returns the maximum of two numbers

REM ** MAIN PROGRAM TO TEST FUNCTIONS **

CLS

getdata:
INPUT "First number"; first
INPUT "Second number"; second
PRINT "Minimum is"; FNmin(first, second)
PRINT "Maximum is"; FNmax(first, second)
PRINT : GOTO getdata
```

Program 4-3. *MINIMUM AND MAXIMUM*

Defining Functions Without Parameters

A function can be defined without specifying a list of parameters. Here are some examples.

The function FNroll3D6% simulates rolling three six-sided dice (3d6). It returns an integer in the range 3 to 18:

```
DEF FNroll3D6% = INT(6 * RND(1)) + INT(6 * RND(1)) + INT(6 * RND(1)) + 3
```

The function FNflip$ simulates flipping a coin. It returns a string value, "HEAD" or "TAIL", selected randomly:

```
DEF FNflip$ = MID$("HEADTAIL", 4 * INT(2 * RND(1)) + 1, 4)
```

The function FNrndvowel$ returns a random vowel:

```
DEF FNrndvowel$ = MID$("aeiou", INT(5 * RND(1)) + 1, 1)
```

Using Function Definitions

Two programs showing the use of function definitions follow. The first program determines whether a year is a leap year or a common year. The second program generates random five-letter words.

Types of Years   A year is either a common year (365 days) or a leap year (366 days) according to the Gregorian calendar introduced in 1582. A leap year is a year that is divisible by 4, except for centurial years. Centurial years are years that are multiples of 100 (1800, 1900, 2000, and so on). A centurial year qualifies as a leap year only if it is divisible by 400. The year 2000 will be a leap year, but 1900 was not. So a year is a leap year if it is (1) divisible by four and not a centurial year or (2) divisible by 400. This fact is used in the function FNleap%, shown in Program 4-4, LEAP YEAR OR COMMON YEAR.

The results of a test run are shown in Figure 4-4. The program seems to work properly, but further testing is always advisable.

The function FNleap% returns the value −1 if the argument is a leap year or the value 0 if the argument is not a leap year. Thus, FNleap% is essentially a logical, or Boolean, function returning values of true (−1) or false (0). Table 4-1 shows how the value of FNleap% is determined for several values of the argument.

```
REM ** LEAP YEAR OR COMMON YEAR **
' Program 4-4  7/21/87

REM ** DEFINE FUNCTION **
DEF FNleap% (yr%) = (yr% MOD 4 = 0 AND yr% MOD 100 <> 0) OR yr% MOD 400 = 0
' FNleap% returns values as follows:
'  -1 if the argument is a leap year
'   0 if the argument is not a leap year

REM ** MAIN PROGRAM **

CLS

getyear:
INPUT "Year"; year%
IF FNleap%(year%) THEN PRINT "Leap year" ELSE PRINT "Common year"
PRINT : GOTO getyear
```

Program 4-4.   *LEAP YEAR OR COMMON YEAR*

```
Year? 1582
Common year

Year? 1988
Leap year

Year? 1900
Common year

Year? 2000
Leap year

Year?
```

Figure 4-4. *Output of Program 4-4*

In the following table, the letters A, B, and C are used as follows:

A: yr% MOD 4 = 0
B: yr% MOD 100 < > 0
C: yr% MOD 400 = 0

yr%	A	B	A and B	C	(A and B) or C	FNleap%
1900	−1	0	0	0	0	0
1987	0	−1	0	0	0	0
1988	−1	−1	−1	0	−1	−1
2000	−1	0	0	−1	−1	−1

Table 4-1. *Determining the Value of FNleap%*

Inventing Words Computers are handy devices for inventing words. Program 4-5, WORDMAKER NUMBER 1, generates random five-letter combinations in the form of consonant, vowel, consonant, vowel, consonant. Much of the work is done by the string function FNrndchr$, which selects one character at random from a string of consonants or vowels.

The results of a test run are shown in Figure 4-5. Each word has the form CVCVC, where C is a consonant and V is a vowel. The letter Y can appear in any position, since it appears in both strings, *consonant$* and *vowel$*.

The next time you want to coin a name for a company, a product, or a character in a novel you are writing, try using FNrndchr$. You

```
REM ** WORDMAKER **
' Program 4-5  7/20/87
' Generates random 5-letter words of the form
' consonant, vowel, consonant, vowel, consonant

REM ** FUNCTION DEFINITION **
DEF FNrndchr$ (strng$) = MID$(strng$, INT(LEN(strng$) * RND(1)) + 1, 1)
' FNrndchr$ returns a random character from a string

REM ** MAIN PROGRAM **

' Define string variables
consonant$ = "BCDFGHJKLMNPQRSTVWXYZ"
vowel$ = "AEIOUY"

printwords:
CLS
word$ = ""
FOR k% = 1 TO 80
  word$ = FNrndchr$(consonant$)
  word$ = word$ + FNrndchr$(vowel$)
  word$ = word$ + FNrndchr$(consonant$)
  word$ = word$ + FNrndchr$(vowel$)
  word$ = word$ + FNrndchr$(consonant$)
  PRINT word$,
NEXT k%

END
```

Program 4-5. *WORDMAKER NUMBER 1*

SYWIB	COTYK	GOGUG	YYWIH	FALAS
KECUQ	GIKOJ	FYPAT	JEBAK	TIXAN
TEWUW	JODIZ	DOSEW	DETUC	WUVUU
DOSYQ	DASIW	PUKEC	JIJEG	HAMAG
HALON	CURED	GUXIQ	DUBYY	PACIW
ZODAN	XUXYQ	QIYEX	HIGEP	LUMYR
COQEY	DEJIK	DECIF	DEROH	QYWYT
JABEP	DUBEL	JEWAR	VUZIX	LOYYK
CYZAR	DOXOD	ROVOQ	HAFER	ZEGYU
DOZYW	VIXAT	LAKIP	YOBUL	XOMIW
JUJUR	PODOF	HEJIB	GABYD	BYJIV
BOWOL	WAQER	HUGEL	XENOL	ZOPIF
NUJUT	LAVUX	SYBYM	GOPIR	DYBEB
GUXIY	YYKOZ	TEPID	NILIF	JEZOT
JIYIG	KIPET	WEYID	FYKUS	WAKYR
REZAR	FIJEX	XUWEB	TASES	ZEXOL

Press any key to continue

Figure 4-5. *Output of Program 4-5*

can quickly write a program that generates random words having any desired consonant-vowel structure by changing only the assignment statements used to compute the value of *word$*.

To summarize, the single-line DEF FN function definition performs the operation that is defined by the expression on the right side of the equal sign. This statement is limited to a single logical line. Variable names that appear in the expression are local to the expression and serve to define the function. They do not affect program variables that have the same name. Hence, they are called dummy variables. If a variable name is in the parameter list, the parameter is supplied when the function is referenced (called by the program). If a variable name is not in the parameter list, it is treated as a global variable and the current value is used when the function is referenced.

Multiline Functions

QuickBASIC has two more ways to define functions. One is the
FUNCTION...END FUNCTION procedure, which is discussed in a
later chapter. The other is the multiline DEF FN...END DEF function definition described here.

DEF FN...END DEF evolved from the single-line DEF FN
statement. It provides a way to define more complex function definitions that cannot be squeezed into a single line. Therefore, it is much
more powerful than the single-line function definition. A multiline
function definition is simple and straightforward. It can often be used
in place of the more indirect subroutine structure. Programs with
multiline functions flow more smoothly than programs with subroutines. A multiline function is defined and named in this way:

```
DEF FNname [(parameterlist)]
    .
    .
    .
    FNname = expression
    .
    .
    .
    [EXIT DEF]
    .
    .
    .
END DEF
```

where

name is any legal variable name. This name, preceded by FN, becomes
the name of the function. If *name* is a numeric variable, the function is
a numeric function. If *name* is a string variable, the function is a
string function. For example:

```
DEF FNsqueeze$
```

parameterlist is a list of variable names separated by commas. These
are dummy variables. When the function is referenced, each variable
in the parameter list is assigned a value from the statement that
references the function. In the example that follows, the value of

teststring\$ is assigned to the dummy variable *strng\$* in the function
definition:

```
DEF FNsqueeze$ (strng$)
  .
  .
  .
END DEF
  .
  .
  .
PRINT FNsqueeze$(teststring$)
```

expression defines a value that is returned by the function. The
expression must be the same type (string or numeric) as FNname. For
example:

```
DEF FNsqueeze$ (strng$)
  .
  .
  .
  FNsqueeze$ = squeeze$
END DEF
```

EXIT DEF is an optional way to exit from the multiline function
definition. This is used for special conditions when the normal exit
(END DEF) is not desirable. However, the END DEF statement must
be present to show where the definition ends. A multiline function
must end with an END DEF statement.

Since the multiline function is essentially a definition, it must appear
in the program before any statement that uses the function. Therefore,
you should place function definitions near the beginning of a
program.

Program 4-6, STRING SQUEEZER TEST PROGRAM, demon-
strates a multiline function, called FNsqueeze\$, to remove all spaces
from a string.

Figure 4-6 shows a test run of the program. For each value of
teststring\$ entered the program prints the squeezed string with all
spaces removed.

The function FNsqueeze\$ is a string function of a string argu-
ment. The argument *strng\$* has meaning only within the function.
You can safely use *strng\$* as a variable elsewhere in the program.

```
REM ** STRING SQUEEZER **
' Program 4-6   7/22/87

REM ** DEFINE FUNCTION **
DEF FNsqueeze$ (strng$)
' FNsqueeze$ squeezes spaces out of a string
' and returns the squeezed string
  STATIC squeeze$, k%, char$
  squeeze$ = ""
  FOR k% = 1 TO LEN(strng$)
    char$ = MID$(strng$, k%, 1)
    IF char$ <> " " THEN squeeze$ = squeeze$ + char$
  NEXT k%
  FNsqueeze$ = squeeze$
END DEF

REM ** MAIN PROGRAM, TEST FNsqueeze$ **

CLS

getdata:
INPUT "String, please"; teststring$
PRINT FNsqueeze$(teststring$)
PRINT : GOTO getdata
```

Program 4-6. *STRING SQUEEZER TEST PROGRAM*

The variables *squeeze$*, *k%*, and *char$* are declared to be static
variables, as follows:

```
STATIC squeeze$, k%, char$
```

Static variables are local to the function and have no meaning outside
the function definition. You may use these same variables elsewhere in
your programs. Using this function does not change the values of
squeeze$, *k%*, or *char$* used elsewhere in a program, outside the
definition of FNsqueeze$.

Also note that *squeeze$* is used as part of the function name and
also as a variable in the definition. QuickBASIC has no trouble
distinguishing the function name FNsqueeze$ from the variable
squeeze$. This is especially evident in the statement that assigns the
value of *squeeze$* as the value of the function:

```
FNsqueeze$ = squeeze$
```

```
String, please? North Dakota
NorthDakota

String, please? R E M O V E   S P A C E S
REMOVESPACES

String, please? 800 999 9999
8009999999

String, please?
```

Figure 4-6.   *Output of Program 4-6*

Remember, a multiline function always ends with the statement END DEF.

In Program 2-1, STATES & ABBREVIATIONS, a subroutine named UPSQUEEZE was used to remove blank spaces from a string and also to change lowercase letters to uppercase. Here are two ways to create a QuickBASIC function to do the same task.

1. Use the previously defined function FNsqueeze$ in a single-line function definition:

```
DEF FNupsqueeze$ (strng$) = UCASE$(FNsqueeze$(strng$))
```

2. Define a multiline function, as shown below:

```
DEF FNupsqueeze$ (strng$)
  STATIC squeeze$, k%, char$
  squeeze$ = ""
```

```
  FOR k% = 1 to LEN(strng$)
    char$ = MID$(strng$, k%, 1)
    IF char$ <> " " THEN squeeze$ = squeeze$ + char$
  NEXT k%
  FNupsqueeze$ = UCASE$(squeeze$)
END DEF
```

In Chapter 2, subroutines created substrings by keeping characters from a source string (Program 2-2) or by purging characters from a source string (Program 2-3). These tasks can be done in QuickBASIC by defining multiline functions called FNafterkeep$ and FNafterpurge$.

The function FNafterkeep$ constructs a substring of the string called *before$*, using only characters in the string *keep$:*

```
DEF FNafterkeep$ (before$, keep$)
  STATIC after$, k%, char$, keep%
  after$ = ""
  FOR k% = 1 to LEN(before$)
    char$ = MID$(before$, k%, 1)
    keep% = INSTR(keep$, char$)
    IF keep% THEN after$ = after$ + char$
  NEXT k%
END DEF
```

The function FNafterpurge$ constructs a substring of the string called *before$*, using only characters that are not in the string *purge$.*

```
DEF FNafterpurge$ (before$, purge$)
  STATIC after$, k%, char$, purge%
  after$ = ""
  FOR k% = 1 TO LEN(before$)
    char$ = MID$(before$, k%, 1)
    purge% = INSTR(purge$, char$)
    IF NOT purge% THEN after$ = after$ + char$
  NEXT k%
  FNafterpurge$ = after$
END DEF
```

You may want to save these function definitions on your toolkit disk.

Control Structures

GW-BASIC has a set of control structures used to make decisions and to do repetitive operations. It is assumed that you are familiar with these GW-BASIC control structures:

FOR...NEXT loops

IF...THEN...ELSE

ON...GOSUB and ON...GOTO

WHILE...WEND loops

QuickBASIC has all of the control structures of GW-BASIC plus powerful structures not available in GW-BASIC, including the following structures:

Block IF...THEN...ELSE

SELECT CASE

DO...LOOP

These structures are powerful, flexible, and readable. In the remainder of this chapter each of these control structures is described and examples are provided.

Block IF...THEN...ELSE

The Block IF structure greatly expands the usefulness and readability of GW-BASIC's single-line IF...THEN...ELSE statement. Table 4-2 shows the syntax and a simple example. Three more simple examples follow on the next page.

```
1. IF number = INT(number) THEN        ' condition1
      PRINT "Integer"                   ' statementblock-1
   ELSE
      PRINT "Non-integer"               ' statementblock-2
   END IF

2. IF number < 0 THEN                   ' condition1
      nzp$ = "negative"                 ' statementblock-1 has
      flag% = -1                        ' two statements
   ELSEIF number = 0 THEN               ' condition2
      nzp$ = "zero"                     ' statementblock-2 has
      flag% = 0                         ' two statements
   ELSE
      nzp$ = "positive"                 ' statementblock-3 has
      flag% = 1                         ' two statements
   END IF

3. IF CorV$ = "C" THEN                  ' condition1
      word$ = word$ + consonant$        ' statementblock-1
   ELSEIF CorV$ = "V" THEN              ' condition2
      word$ = word$ + vowel$            ' statementblock-2
   END IF
```

In writing a Block IF structure, please note that

1. A line beginning with IF or ELSEIF must end with **THEN**.

2. A statement block (*statementblock*) can have any number of statements.

3. END IF includes a blank space, but ELSEIF does not.

4. The Block IF structure must end with END IF.

Syntax	Example

IF condition1 THEN
   [statementblock−1]
[ELSEIF condition2 THEN
   [statementblock−2]]
.
.
.
[ELSE
   [statementblock−n]]
END IF
	IF number = 1 THEN
	   PRINT "One"
	ELSEIF number = 2 THEN
	   PRINT "Two"
	ELSEIF number = 3 THEN
	   PRINT "Three"
	ELSE
	   PRINT "Not one, two, or three"
	END IF

Table 4-2.   *Block IF...THEN...ELSE Syntax and Example*

```
REM ** WORDMAKER NUMBER TWO **
' Program 4-7  7/25/87
' Used to test FNrndword$(wordform$)

REM ** DEFINE FUNCTION **
DEF FNrndword$ (wordform$)
' Returns a random word of the form defined by the
' value of wordform$.  For example, if wordform$
' is "CVCVC", the random word is of the form
' consonant, vowel, consonant, vowel, consonant.
  STATIC word$, k%, CorV$, rc%, consonant$, rv%, vowel$
  word$ = ""
  FOR k% = 1 TO LEN(wordform$)
    CorV$ = UCASE$(MID$(wordform$, k%, 1))
    IF CorV$ = "C" THEN
      rc% = INT(21 * RND(1)) + 1
      consonant$ = MID$("bcdfghjklmnpqrstvwxyz", rc%, 1)
      word$ = word$ + consonant$
    ELSEIF CorV$ = "V" THEN
      rv% = INT(6 * RND(1)) + 1
      vowel$ = MID$("aeiouy", rv%, 1)
      word$ = word$ + vowel$
    END IF
  NEXT k%
  FNrndword$ = word$
END DEF

REM ** MAIN PROGRAM **

CLS

INPUT "Word structure (string of C's and V's)"; structure$
INPUT "How many words (enter 0 to quit)"; numwords%
IF numwords% = 0 THEN END
PRINT
FOR word% = 1 TO numwords%
  PRINT FNrndword$(structure$),
NEXT word%
PRINT : END
```

Program 4-7. *WORDMAKER NUMBER 2*

Program 4-7, WORDMAKER NUMBER 2, puts the Block IF to work. With this program, you can enter the desired word structure and the number of words you want to have that structure. The word structure is a string consisting of only the letters C and V to specify consonants (C) or vowels (V).

Figures 4-7 and 4-8 show runs for two word structures: cvcvc and vccvcv.

```
Word structure (string of C's and V's)? cvcvc
How many words (enter 0 to quit)? 80

syvib      cotyk      gogug      yyvih      falas
kecuq      gikoj      fypat      jebak      tixan
tewuw      jodiz      dosew      detuc      wuvuv
dosyq      dasiv      pukec      jijeg      hamag
halon      cured      guxiq      dubyy      paclu
zodan      xuxyq      qiyex      higep      lumyr
coqey      dejik      decif      deroh      qyuyt
jabep      dubel      jewar      wuzix      loyyk
cyzar      doxod      rovoq      hafer      zegyu
dozyw      vixat      lakip      yobul      xomiv
jujur      podof      hejib      gabyd      byjiv
bovol      waqer      kugel      xemol      zopif
mujut      lavux      sybyn      gopir      dybeb
guxiy      yykoz      tepid      nilif      jezot
jiyig      kipet      weyid      fykus      wakyr
rezar      fijex      xuweb      tases      zexol




Press any key to continue
```

Figure 4-7. *First Output of Program 4-7*

The SELECT CASE Structure

SELECT CASE is a multiple-choice decision structure. Table 4-3 shows the syntax and a simple example.

The expression following SELECT CASE can be numeric or string. The *expressionlist* in each CASE clause must be the same type (numeric or string) as the expression following SELECT CASE.

The SELECT CASE example shown in Table 4-3 operates in this way:

■ If the value of a number is 1, 2, or 3, the corresponding string (*"One"*, *"Two"*, or *"Three"*) is printed.

■ If the value of a number is not 1, 2, or 3, the string *"Not 1, 2, or 3"* is printed.

```
Word structure (string of C's and V's)? vccvcv
How many words (enter 0 to quit)? 88

uzwiba      otyigo      evgyzu      ihfala      ukgavo
elkoje      ypduje      adkumy      antewu      ujqany
apsewa      etvawu      uvvapu      yqdasi      uptiga
ekjege      ambeha      innavo      edguxi      odsaxy
odclwy      odfixu      yzqomy      exhige      olsizo
arqeya      ejwide      akfafo      ohqywy      ujcaho
asbele      evfovu      ylxiry      ykcyza      odpypa
oqvoqe      afhoze      eyvaqy      yvvixa      ulfiko
yqbuly      ormuju      etropa      ofheji      agdaya
azjiva      owriwa      ofrive      elxeno      izpona
isjuti      avtysy      azneqo      irdybe      agvymy
yykozu      eplani      ikfegy      otjiyi      ekloju
ygylde      yksuwa      ixrojy      arfije      yxtufa
ufsesy      exriju      ubxufi      izjeyu      ayzevu
ybwuba      iqhagi      askyqe      ufnaga      ijqyfi
ygyyji      yrrita      egbiba      yxdusi      akbomu



Press any key to continue
```

Figure 4-8. *Second Output of Program 4-7*

Syntax	Example
SELECT CASE expression	SELECT CASE number
CASE expessionlist1	CASE 1
[statementblock−1]	PRINT "One"
[CASE expressionlist2	CASE 2
[statementblock−2]]	PRINT "Two"
.	CASE 3
.	PRINT "Three"
.	CASE ELSE
[CASE ELSE	PRINT "Not 1, 2, or 3"
[statementblock−n]]	END SELECT
END SELECT	

Table 4-3. *SELECT CASE Syntax and Example*

The converse of the example shown in Table 4-3 appears as follows:

```
SELECT ·CASE NumberName$
  CASE "One"
    PRINT 1
  CASE "Two"
    PRINT 2
  CASE "Three"
    PRINT 3
  CASE ELSE
    PRINT "Not One, Two, or Three"
END SELECT
```

A CASE clause can specify a list of values, as the following two examples show:

```
1. SELECT CASE number
      CASE 0, 2, 4, 6, 8
         PRINT "Even decimal digit"
         OddOrEven% = 0
      CASE 1, 3, 5, 7, 9
         PRINT "Odd decimal digit"
         OddOrEven% = 1
      CASE ELSE
         PRINT "Not a decimal digit"
   END SELECT

2. SELECT CASE UCASE$(LEFT$(month$,3))
      CASE "DEC", "JAN", "FEB"
         PRINT "Sleighbells ring, ..."
      CASE "MAR", "APR", "MAY"
         PRINT "Spring is bursting out ..."
      CASE "JUN", "JUL", "AUG"
         PRINT "Summertime, and the ..."
      CASE "SEP", "OCT", "NOV"
         PRINT "Oh, the days grow ..."
      CASE ELSE
         PRINT "Time on my hands ..."
   END SELECT
```

A CASE clause can depend on a relational expression. To signal this, CASE is followed by the word IS, as in this example:

```
SELECT CASE number
  CASE IS < 0
    PRINT "Negative number"
  CASE IS = 0
    PRINT "Zero"
  CASE IS > 0
    PRINT "Positive number"
END SELECT
```

Here the CASE ELSE clause is omitted since a number must be negative, zero, or positive. No other possibilities exist to be handled by the "catch-all" CASE ELSE clause.

Program 4-8, NUMBER OF DAYS IN A MONTH, uses SELECT CASE to differentiate months that contain different numbers of days. SELECT CASE is used in FNDaysInMonth%, a function definition that determines the number of days during a month in a common year. The extra February leap-year day is found by using FNleap%, a function defined earlier in this chapter.

```
REM ** NUMBER OF DAYS IN A MONTH **
' Program 4-8  7/24/87
' Used to test FNDaysInMonth%

REM ** DEFINE FUNCTIONS **

DEF FNleap% (yr%) = (yr% MOD 4 = 0 AND yr% MOD 100 <> 0) OR yr% MOD 400 = 0
' FNleap% returns values as follows:
' -1 if the argument is a leap year
'  0 if the argument is not a leap year

DEF FNDaysInMonth% (month%)
' FNDaysInMonth% returns the number of days in a
' month for values of month% 1 through 12.  Returns
' 28 for February (month% = 2) and zero for invalid month.
  STATIC days%
  SELECT CASE month%
    CASE 1, 3, 5, 7, 8, 10, 12
      days% = 31
    CASE 4, 6, 9, 11
      days% = 30
    CASE 2
      days% = 28
    CASE ELSE
      days% = 0
  END SELECT
  FNDaysInMonth% = days%
END DEF

REM ** MAIN PROGRAM **

CLS

getdata:
INPUT "Year"; year%
INPUT "Month (1 to 12)"; month%
numdays% = FNDaysInMonth%(month%)
IF FNleap%(year%) AND month% = 2 THEN numdays% = numdays% + 1
PRINT "Month #"; month%; "has"; numdays%; "days."
PRINT : GOTO getdata
```

Program 4-8.   *NUMBER OF DAYS IN A MONTH*

```
Year? 1939
Month (1 to 12)? 2
Month # 2 has 28 days.

Year? 1940
Month (1 to 12)? 2
Month # 2 has 29 days.

Year? 1941
Month (1 to 12)? 3
Month # 3 has 31 days.

Year? 1941
Month (1 to 12)? 4
Month # 4 has 30 days.

Year? 1941
Month (1 to 12)? 1
Month # 1 has 31 days.

Year?
```

Figure 4-9. *Output of Program 4-8*

Input a year and the number of any month in that year (1-12). The program prints the number of days in that month. Figure 4-9 gives a sample run of the program.

Program 4-9, NUMBER OF DAYS IN A MONTH, STRING VERSION, also uses SELECT CASE. However, instead of numbers for the months, it uses three-letter strings (JAN, FEB, MAR, and so on) Figure 4-10 shows a sample run.

DO...LOOP Structure

A DO...LOOP repeats a block of statements WHILE or UNTIL a condition is satisfied. The DO...LOOP is more versatile than WHILE...WEND or FOR...NEXT loops because of its ability to test for a condition either at the beginning or end of the loop.

```
REM ** NUMBER OF DAYS IN A MONTH **
' Program 4-9  7/24/87
' Used to test FNDaysInMonth%

REM ** DEFINE FUNCTIONS **

DEF FNleap% (yr%) = (yr% MOD 4 = 0 AND yr% MOD 100 <> 0) OR yr% MOD 400 = 0
' FNleap% returns values as follows:
' -1 if the argument is a leap year
'  0 if the argument is not a leap year

DEF FNDaysInMonth% (month$)
' FNDaysInMonth% returns the number of days in a
' month for values of month% = "JAN", "FEB", and so on.
' Returns 28 for "FEB" and 0 for invalid value of month$.
' Value of month$ can be lower case or upper case.
  STATIC days%
  SELECT CASE UCASE$(month$)
    CASE "JAN", "MAR", "MAY", "JUL", "AUG", "OCT", "DEC"
      days% = 31
    CASE "APR", "JUN", "SEP", "NOV"
      days% = 30
    CASE "FEB"
      days% = 28
    CASE ELSE
      days% = 0
  END SELECT
  FNDaysInMonth% = days%
END DEF

REM ** MAIN PROGRAM **

CLS

getdata:
INPUT "Year"; year%
INPUT "Month"; month$
numdays% = FNDaysInMonth%(LEFT$(month$, 3))
IF FNleap%(year%) AND UCASE$(LEFT$(month$, 3)) = "FEB" THEN numdays% = 29
PRINT month$; " has"; numdays%; "days."
PRINT : GOTO getdata
```

Program 4-9. *NUMBER OF DAYS IN A MONTH, STRING VERSION*

The DO...LOOP has two possible forms. One form tests for the condition at the beginning of the loop:

```
DO [{WHILE/UNTIL} booleanexpression]
  [statementblock]
  [EXIT DO]
  .
  .
  .
LOOP
```

```
Year? 1939
Month? February
February has 28 days.

Year? 1940
Month? February
February has 29 days.

Year? 1941
Month? March
March has 31 days.

Year? 2000
Month? february
february has 29 days.

Year? 1900
Month? February
February has 28 days.

Year?
```

Figure 4-10.   *Output of Program 4-9*

The *statementblock* consists of one or more BASIC statements. The *booleanexpression* is any expression that evaluates to true (nonzero) or false (zero).

The second form tests for the condition at the end of the loop:

```
DO
  [statementblock]
  [EXIT DO]
  .
  .
  .
LOOP [<WHILE/UNTIL> booleanexpression]
```

The condition is contained in either the WHILE or the UNTIL clause. For example:

```
DO WHILE INKEY$ = ""
  ' This is an empty loop that is
  ' executed WHILE no key has been pressed
LOOP

DO UNTIL INKEY$ <> ""
  ' This is an empty loop that is
  ' executed UNTIL a key is pressed
LOOP
```

Both forms produce the same result.

If you want to execute the loop at least once, put the test at the end of the loop. If the test is at the beginning, the condition may cause the statements within the loop to be skipped. For example, you may want a loop to balance your checkbook. Execution of at least one pass through the loop would be ensured by writing the loop in this form:

```
DO
  INPUT "Enter transaction"; amount
  balance = balance + amount
LOOP WHILE amount <> 0
```

The loop would be executed at least once. If your first entry is zero, the total would not change. An exit would be made after the zero entry. If you enter a nonzero value, the entry would be added to the balance and the loop executed again. Enter negative values for checks written and positive values for deposits.

An equivalent form is

```
DO
  INPUT "Enter transaction"; amount
  balance = balance + amount
LOOP UNTIL amount = 0
```

An exit from a DO...LOOP can be made from within the loop by using the optional EXIT DO clause. A DO...LOOP can contain any number of EXIT DO statements.

Program 4-10, COUNT CHARACTERS IN A STRING, uses a DO...LOOP with a WHILE clause at the beginning of the loop. This placement ensures that the loop will not be executed if the condition is not satisfied. EXIT DO is located within the loop to end the search for a character.

```
REM ** COUNT CHARACTERS IN A STRING **
' Program 4-10   7/24/87
' Used to test FNcountchr%

REM ** DEFINE FUNCTION **
DEF FNcountchr% (strng$, char$)
' FNcountchr% counts the number of occurrences
' of a single character (char$) in a string (strng$).
  STATIC count%, start%, found%
  count% = 0
  start% = 1
  DO WHILE start% <= LEN(strng$)
    found% = INSTR(start%, strng$, char$)
    IF found% = 0 THEN
      EXIT DO
    ELSE
      count% = count% + 1
      start% = found% + 1
    END IF
  LOOP
  FNcountchr% = count%
END DEF

REM MAIN PROGRAM **

CLS

getdata:
INPUT "String, please"; teststring$
INPUT "Character, please"; testchar$
occurs% = FNcountchr%(teststring$, testchar$)
PRINT "The character occurs"; occurs%; "times in the string."
PRINT : GOTO getdata
```

Program 4-10.   *COUNT CHARACTERS IN A STRING*

The DO...LOOP is a part of a multiline function definition that counts the number of times a character occurs within a string. Use the program to test the character-counting function. Enter a string at the first prompt. At the second prompt, enter the character you wish to count. The program then counts the number of times the character occurs in your string and prints the result. Figure 4-11 shows some typical results.

```
String, please? This string has four spaces,
Character, please? " "
The character occurs 4 times in the string,

String, please? "This string has five spaces, "
Character, please? " "
The character occurs 5 times in the string,

String, please? "11001010001010010000111110"
Character, please? "1"
The character occurs 11 times in the string,

String, please? "11001010001010010000111110"
Character, please? "11"
The character occurs 4 times in the string,

String, please?
```

Figure 4-11. *Output of Program 4-10*

Review

This chapter introduced the idea of building a kit of programming tools, saving them to disk, and merging them with later programs.

QuickBASIC variables were discussed, either as local to a particular unit of a program or as global to the whole program. Data types were explained. QuickBASIC program lines and line labels were discussed and demonstrated.

A discussion of built-in QuickBASIC functions led into user-defined functions. A variety of single-line function definitions were demonstrated. The powerful multiline function definition was discussed in detail and used in program demonstrations.

New QuickBASIC control structures—Block IF...THEN...ELSE, SELECT CASE, and DO...LOOP—were introduced and demonstrated.

5 *Editing: Honing Your Tools*

In Chapters 1 through 4 editing was limited to the cursor-control (arrows), BACKSPACE, and DEL keys. This chapter discusses more sophisticated editing methods and offers practice in their use. You will learn to move the cursor and scroll the screen in small and large steps. You will practice inserting and deleting text in small amounts. The use of the Edit menu commands used to manipulate large amounts of text is discussed. In addition, you will practice how to use the Cut, Undo, Paste, and Copy commands.

QuickBASIC automatically performs some editing functions, such as

■ Converting QuickBASIC keywords to uppercase letters if they have been entered in lowercase

■ Inserting blank spaces before and after all operators if they are not present

■ Checking for syntax, memory, and duplicate definition errors

■ Performing minor modifications, such as inserting spaces, so that QuickBASIC source code appears in a standard format

Moving Around in a File

When you start QuickBASIC you are taken to the editor. In the editor you can choose commands from menus; enter new text; move the cursor around a file; and insert, replace, or delete text.

Each editing task involves three steps:

1. Moving the cursor to the desired location

2. Selecting the text to be modified

3. Inserting, replacing, or deleting text

Table 5-1 describes various ways of moving the cursor through your text from the keyboard—from top to bottom, line to line, word to word, and character to character. It also describes ways to scroll the screen. Many cursor movements require holding down one key, pressing another, and then releasing both. In this book, the combined keystroke is indicated by the hold key, a plus sign, and the second key. For example, CTRL+END means "Hold down CTRL and press END." You will use STRING SQUEEZER, previously presented as Program 4-6, to practice moving the cursor and editing text. Program 4-6 is shown here again for your reference. You will begin by making small changes and progress to deleting, copying, and inserting blocks of text.

Moving to Start or End of a File

Load Program 4-6, STRING SQUEEZER, from the File menu. When the program is loaded, you can see that only the beginning portion of the program shows on the screen (see Figure 5-1). The cursor is positioned in the upper-left corner under *R* of the first REM state-

Movement of cursor	Keys to press
To beginning of file	CTRL+HOME
To end of file	CTRL+END
Up one line	Up arrow
Down one line	Down arrow
To beginning of line	HOME
To end of line	END
Left one word	CTRL+left arrow
Right one word	CTRL+right arrow
Left one character	Left arrow
Right one character	Right arrow

Scrolling	Keys to press
Left one window	CTRL+PGUP
Right one window	CTRL+PGDN
Up one window	PGUP
Down one window	PGDN
Up one line	CTRL+down arrow
Down one line	CTRL+up arrow

Table 5-1. *Cursor Movement and Scrolling*

```
REM ** STRING SQUEEZER **
' Program 4-6  7/22/87

REM ** DEFINE FUNCTION **
DEF FNsqueeze$ (strng$)
' FNsqueeze$ squeezes spaces out of a string
' and returns the squeezed string
  STATIC squeeze$, k%, char$
  squeeze$ = ""
  FOR k% = 1 TO LEN(strng$)
    char$ = MID$(strng$, k%, 1)
    IF char$ <> " " THEN squeeze$ = squeeze$ + char$
  NEXT k%
  FNsqueeze$ = squeeze$
END DEF

REM ** MAIN PROGRAM, TEST FNsqueeze$ **

CLS

getdata:
INPUT "String, please"; teststring$
PRINT FNsqueeze$(teststring$)
PRINT : GOTO getdata
```

Program 4-6. *STRING SQUEEZER*

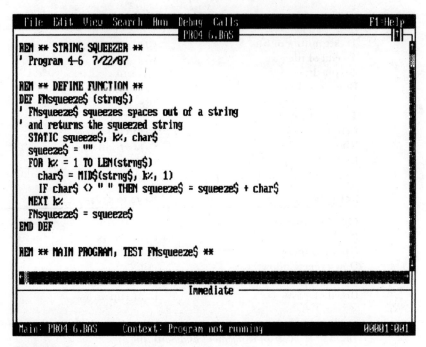

```
 File  Edit  View  Search  Run  Debug  Calls                          F1=Help
┌───────────────────────────── PRO4 6.BAS ────────────────────────────────┐
│REM ** STRING SQUEEZER **                                                 │
│' Program 4-6  7/22/87                                                     │
│                                                                          │
│REM ** DEFINE FUNCTION **                                                 │
│DEF FNsqueeze$ (strng$)                                                    │
│' FNsqueeze$ squeezes spaces out of a string                              │
│' and returns the squeezed string                                         │
│  STATIC squeeze$, k%, char$                                              │
│  squeeze$ = ""                                                            │
│  FOR k% = 1 TO LEN(strng$)                                                │
│    char$ = MID$(strng$, k%, 1)                                            │
│    IF char$ <> " " THEN squeeze$ = squeeze$ + char$                       │
│  NEXT k%                                                                  │
│  FNsqueeze$ = squeeze$                                                    │
│END DEF                                                                    │
│                                                                          │
│REM ** MAIN PROGRAM, TEST FNsqueeze$ **                                    │
│                                                                          │
├──────────────────────────── Immediate ──────────────────────────────────┤
│                                                                          │
└──────────────────────────────────────────────────────────────────────────┘
 Main: PRO4 6.BAS     Context: Program not running              00001:001
```

Figure 5-1. *First part of Program 4-6*

ment. In other words, it is at the beginning of the file.

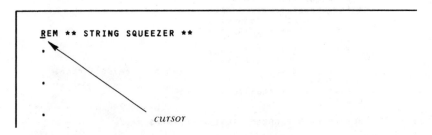

REM ** STRING SQUEEZER **

cursor

Press CTRL+END. The screen changes; it now shows the end of the program. The cursor is positioned below the last line of the program, at the end of the file:

```
INPUT "String, please"; teststring$
PRINT FNsqueeze$(teststring$)
PRINT: GOTO getdata
```

cursor

While the cursor is at the end of the file, press CTRL+HOME. The cursor moves back to its original position at the beginning of the file.

- CTRL+END moves the cursor to the end of a file.

- CTRL+HOME moves the cursor to the beginning of a file.

Moving Up or Down One Line

The cursor is at the the top line, or beginning of the file. Press the down arrow key. The cursor moves down one line, remaining in the same column.

```
REM ** STRING SQUEEZER **
_ Program 4-6  7/22/87
.

.

.
```

cursor

Press the down arrow key a few more times. The cursor moves down one line for each keystroke.

Press the up arrow key. The cursor moves up one line. Press it several more times until the cursor is back to the beginning of the file.

- The down arrow key moves the cursor down one line.

- The up arrow key moves the cursor up one line.

Moving to the Beginning or End of a Line

Using one of the methods just described, move the cursor to the beginning of the fourth line on the screen. This line is shown below:

```
REM ** DEFINE FUNCTION **
```

When you have done so, press the END key. The cursor moves to the column just to the right of the end of the same line:

```
         .
         .
         .
  REM ** DEFINE FUNCTION **_
         .
         .
         .
                              cursor
```

Press the HOME key to move the cursor back to the beginning of the line.

- END moves the cursor to the end of a line.

- HOME moves the cursor to the beginning of a line.

Moving Left or Right One Word

With the cursor at the beginning of the fourth line, press CTRL+right arrow. The cursor moves to the right by one word when this key combination is pressed. Note that the asterisks are not considered to be words.

Press CTRL+left arrow. The cursor moves one word to the left when this key combination is pressed. Press this combination enough times to move the cursor back to the beginning of the fourth line.

- CTRL+right arrow moves the cursor to the right by one word.
- CTRL+left arrow moves the cursor to the left by one word.

What happens if the cursor is already at the first word of the fourth line and you press CTRL+left arrow? Does the cursor move to the third line, which is blank? Does it disappear off the left edge of the screen? Does nothing happen at all because it can't move any farther to the left on the line? Try it and find out. (The cursor moves to the last word of the second line, since the third line is blank.)

Moving Left or Right One Character

Now that you have learned how to move around in your file by giant strides or inchworm creeps, move the cursor to the beginning of the REM statement of the MAIN PROGRAM block of Program 4-6. When you get there, press the right arrow key again and again. The cursor moves to the right by one character each time you press this key. Press the left arrow key several times. The cursor moves to the left by one character each time you press left arrow.

- The right arrow key moves the cursor to the right by one character.
- The left arrow key moves the cursor to the left by one character.

Can you predict what will happen if you are at the end of a line and press right arrow? Remember, QuickBASIC's physical line is 255 characters long. What happens when you are at the beginning of a line and press left arrow? Try both. (You will find that the cursor will not move past the end of the physical line.)

If you followed all these directions, you can now move the cursor anywhere in a file. See how few keystrokes you can use to move the cursor to the places shown in Table 5-2. A keystroke combination such as CTRL+HOME counts as one keystroke. No fair holding down keys

Cursor position		Number of keystrokes
1. ' and returns the squeezed string	*(line 7)*	
2. ' and returns the squeezed string		
3. squeeze$ = ""	*(line 9)*	
4. PRINT: GOTO getdata	*(last line)*	
5. END DEF	*(line 15)*	
6. ' Program 4-6 7/22/87	*(line 2)*	
7. getdata::	*(line 26)*	
8. PRINT FNsqueeze$(teststing$)	*(line 28)*	TOTAL

Table 5-2. *Cursor/Keystroke Exercise*

for repeated actions—those are multiple keystrokes. Positions in the table are for Program 4-6, so you may want to print a hard copy of the program to use as a guide. Begin with the cursor at position 1 of the table. Then move successively to positions 2, 3, 4, 5, 6, 7, and 8 with as few keystrokes as possible. Total your keystrokes to see how many it takes to complete the maze. Invite a friend over and see if he or she can do any better.

Scrolling Up or Down One Window

Scrolling means rolling the lines in the window up or down as if you were rolling or unrolling a scroll. Place the cursor on the letter g in the second line of the DEFINE FUNCTION block of Program 4-6. This is the fifth line in the window (including blank lines and REMs).

```
REM ** STRING SQUEEZER **
' Program 4-6  7/22/87

REM ** DEFINE FUNCTION **
DEF FNsqueeze$ (strng$)
    .
    .
    .
```

cursor

Press PGDN. The screen scrolls down to the second window of the program. The cursor is now on the fifth line of the second window of the program.

```
CLS

getdata:
INPUT "String please"; teststring$
PRINT FNsqueeze$(teststring$)
PRINT: GOTO getdata
```
cursor

Now press PGUP. The display scrolls back to the first window of the program. The cursor is still in the same relative position (fifth line, twenty-first column). The cursor hasn't moved, only the window being displayed.

- PGDN scrolls the display down one window.

- PGUP scrolls the display up one window.

Scrolling Up or Down One Line

With the cursor still on the letter *g* of the word *strng$* in the DEFINE FUNCTION block, press CTRL+down arrow. The cursor stays where it was (under the letter *g*) but the lines on the screen scroll up one line. The top line scrolls off the screen and a new line appears at the bottom, as shown here:

```
' Program 4-6  7/22/87

REM ** DEFINE FUNCTION **
DEF FNsqueeze$ (strng$)
  .
  .
  .
```
cursor

Now press the CTRL+up arrow. All lines on the screen scroll down one line. The bottom line scrolls off the screen, and a new line appears at the top of the screen. The screen is back where it was before CTRL+down arrow was pressed.

■ CTRL+down arrow scrolls the text down one line.

■ CTRL+up arrow scrolls the text up one line.

Scrolling Left or Right One Window

You can scroll horizontally as well as vertically. Scrolling the screen left or right is like rolling and unrolling a scroll sideways. Place the cursor once again below the letter *g* in the second line of the DEFINE FUNCTION block. Press CTRL+PGDN. You are confronted by a blank window. The display has been scrolled to the right by one window. Since the lines in the program do not extend beyond the original window, nothing appears in this window. Press CTRL+PGUP. The display scrolls to the left by one window. You are back at the original position.

■ CTRL+PGDN scrolls the display to the right by one window.

■ CTRL+PGUP scrolls the display to the left by one window.

The cursor can be placed anywhere within the file by one or more of these two actions: cursor movement and screen scrolling. Go back to Table 5-2 and see if you can improve your keystroke total now that you have added scrolling to your list of skills.

Inserting and Deleting Text

The QuickBASIC editor includes two modes of operation: insert mode and overtype mode, both controlled by the INS key. The INS key acts as a toggle switch. When you first enter the editor the insert mode is active. The cursor is the underscore character (___).

To start a new line	Keys to press
At current cursor position	ENTER

To insert	Keys to press
A line above current line	CTRL+N
A line below current line	ENTER

To delete	Keys to press
The entire current line	CTRL+Y
To the end of current line	CTRL+Q, Y
The character to the left of cursor	BACKSPACE
The character under the cursor	DEL

Table 5-3.   *Inserting and Deleting Text*

When the cursor is in insert mode, characters typed at the cursor position are displayed at that position. The character above the cursor and all characters to the right of the cursor are pushed one position to the right to make room for the new character.

Pressing the INS key toggles the mode. When the insert mode is active, pressing the INS key causes the editor to enter the overtype mode. The cursor changes to a flashing solid block (■). When the editor is in overtype mode, the character under the cursor is replaced by the character typed. Other characters in the line remain as they are.

Remember, the cursor is a solid block when the overtype mode is active. It is an underscore character when the insert mode is active. Pressing INS deactivates the current mode and activates the other mode.

Table 5-3 shows ways to insert and delete a character, a line, or part of a line of text. It also shows how to start a new line of text at the current cursor position.

Starting a New Line

In entering previous programs you have started new lines by pressing the ENTER key. The ENTER key can also be used to start a new line from any cursor position. Suppose you have typed in a program line and decide to break it into parts. The line is

```
start: CLS
```

Programs in this book usually place line labels on a separate line. Therefore the CLS statement should be moved to a new line. To do so, move the cursor to the *C* in CLS and press the ENTER key. A new line space opens up, and the new line moves there. The cursor also moves to the beginning of the new line, as shown below:

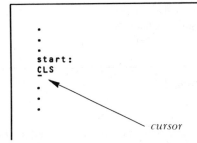

Inserting Text

You can insert text when you are in the editor's insert mode in this way:

1. Move the cursor to the position at which you want to start the insertion.

2. Type in the text to be inserted.

This method works well when you want to make a short insertion, such as a few characters or a word or two. As you type in the insertion, all characters on the line under and to the right of the cursor are shifted to the right one place for each character inserted. The editor reformats the lines following the insertion.

Program 4-6 will be used to demonstrate short insertions and later to show two ways to make longer insertions. You may want to format a new disk for the programs you will use in the rest of this chapter to practice your editing techniques. Copy Program 4-6 to this practice disk, making sure you have retained the original program elsewhere.

You are going to edit Program 4-6, STRING SQUEEZER, to

```
REM ** STRING SQUEEZER WITH STRING VARIABLES DESCRIBED **
' Program 5-1  7/22/87

REM ** DEFINE FUNCTION **
DEF FNsqueeze$ (strng$)
' FNsqueeze$ squeezes spaces out of a string
' and returns the squeezed string
  STATIC squeeze$, k%, char$
  squeeze$ = ""
  FOR k% = 1 TO LEN(strng$)
    char$ = MID$(strng$, k%, 1)
    IF char$ <> " " THEN squeeze$ = squeeze$ + char$
  NEXT k%
  FNsqueeze$ = squeeze$
END DEF

REM ** STRING VARIABLES USED **
' squeeze$        string with spaces removed
' char$           one character of the string entered
' teststring$     string entered for testing FNsqueeze$

REM ** MAIN PROGRAM, TEST FNsqueeze$ **

CLS

getdata:
INPUT "String, please"; teststring$
PRINT FNsqueeze$(teststring$)
PRINT : GOTO getdata
```

Program 5-1. *String Squeezer with String Variable Described*

create Program 5-1, STRING SQUEEZER WITH STRING VARIA-
BLES DESCRIBED. The following editing steps will be taken:

1. Changing the title to STRING SQUEEZER WITH STRING
VARIABLES DESCRIBED

2. Changing the program number to Program 5-1

3. Inserting a block of program lines titled STRING VARIABLES
USED

When you have prepared the practice disk, access Program 4-6.
Move the cursor to the first asterisk following the word *SQUEEZER*
in the top line of Program 4-6.

```
REM ** STRING SQUEEZER _**
    •
    •
    •
```

Press INS to activate the insert mode of the editor if it is not already active. The cursor should be the underline character. Type in the words **WITH VARIABLES DESCRIBED** and add a blank space.

```
REM ** STRING SQUEEZER WITH VARIABLES DESCRIBED _**
    •
    •
    •
```

Now, still in insert mode, move the cursor to the number 4 in the second line of the program.

```
REM ** STRING SQUEEZER WITH VARIABLES DESCRIBED **
' Program 4-6   7/22/87
    •
    •
    •
```

Type **5-1**. The screen now shows

```
REM ** STRING SQUEEZER WITH VARIABLES DESCRIBED **
' Program 5-14-6   7/22/87
    •
    •
    •
```

Press the DEL key three times to delete 4-6. The program is now ready to be modified by a longer insertion. Leave it in memory.

If you have long insertions, such as several lines, a paragraph, or more, it is practical to use one of the insertion methods shown in Table 5-3.

To insert a line above another line, activate the insert mode of the editor (if it is not already active). Move the cursor to the beginning of the line that is to follow your insertion. Press CTRL+N. This opens up a blank line above the line on which you placed the cursor. Then type in the insertion.

For example, suppose you decide to add a section that describes the string variables used in the program. You wish to place it between the **DEFINE FUNCTION** block and the **MAIN PROGRAM** block. The string variable descriptions are to be

squeeze$	String with spaces removed
char$	One character of the string entered
teststring$	String entered for testing FNsqueeze$

Move the cursor to the letter *R* at the start of the REM statement of the MAIN PROGRAM.

```
   .
   .
   .
END DEF

REM ** MAIN PROGRAM, TEST FNsqueeze$ **
   .
   .
   .
```

Press CTRL+N to open a new line above the REM statement. The REM statement is moved down one line. The cursor is now at the beginning of the new blank line, ready for the insertion.

```
   .
   .
   .
END DEF


REM ** MAIN PROGRAM, TEST FNsqueeze$ **
   .
   .
   .
```

Insert the following lines:

```
REM ** STRING VARIABLES USED **
' squeeze$      string with spaces removed
' char$         one character of the string entered
' teststring$   string entered for testing FNsqueeze$
```

You now have completed Program 5-1, STRING SQUEEZER WITH STRING VARIABLES DESCRIBED. It contains the insertions described. Modify the title of the file and save it to your practice disk for later use, but also leave it in memory. It will be used to demonstrate the second method for making long insertions.

To use the second method, activate the insert mode of the editor, if it is not already active. Move the cursor to the beginning of the line above which you wish to enter an insertion. Press ENTER. This opens up a blank line below the line at which you placed the cursor. Now type the insertion. For example, suppose you want to add another section to describe the numeric variables used in the program. There is only one:

```
k%            character counter in FOR-NEXT loop
```

Using Program 5-1, move the cursor to the beginning of the blank line between the STRING VARIABLES USED block and the MAIN PROGRAM block:

```
    .
    .
    .
' teststring$  string entered for testing FNsqueeze$

REM ** MAIN PROGRAM, TEST FNsqueeze$ **
    .
    .
    .
```

Press ENTER to open a new line below the cursor position. All the program lines below move down one line. The cursor is now at the beginning of the second blank line, ready for the insertion. The lines look like this:

```
    .
    .
    .
' teststring$  string entered for testing FNsqueeze$


REM ** MAIN PROGRAM, TEST FNsqueeze$ **
    .
    .
    .
```

Type in the following lines, pressing ENTER at the end of each line:

```
REM ** NUMERIC VARIABLES USED **
' k%               character counter in FOR-NEXT loop
```

Modify the title and program number to complete Program 5-2, STRING SQUEEZER WITH ALL VARIABLES DESCRIBED. Save Program 5-2 to disk and also leave it in memory. You will use it in the next section to delete text demonstrations.

```
REM ** STRING SQUEEZER WITH ALL VARIABLES DESCRIBED **
' Program 5-2  7/22/87

REM ** DEFINE FUNCTION **
DEF FNsqueeze$ (strng$)
' FNsqueeze$ squeezes spaces out of a string
' and returns the squeezed string
  STATIC squeeze$, k%, char$
  squeeze$ = ""
  FOR k% = 1 TO LEN(strng$)
    char$ = MID$(strng$, k%, 1)
    IF char$ <> " " THEN squeeze$ = squeeze$ + char$
  NEXT k%
  FNsqueeze$ = squeeze$
END DEF

REM ** STRING VARIABLES USED **
' squeeze$       string with spaces removed
' char$          one character of the string entered
' teststring$    string entered for testing FNsqueeze$

REM ** NUMERIC VARIABLES USED **
' k%             character counter in FOR-NEXT loop

REM ** MAIN PROGRAM, TEST FNsqueeze$ **

CLS

getdata:
INPUT "String, please"; teststring$
PRINT FNsqueeze$(teststring$)
PRINT : GOTO getdata
```

Program 5-2. *STRING SQUEEZER WITH ALL VARIABLES DESCRIBED*

Deleting Text

One way to delete individual characters is to move the cursor to the character to be deleted and press the DEL key. Another way is to move the cursor to the character that is one position to the right of the character to be deleted and press the BACKSPACE key.

With Program 5-2 in memory, move the cursor to the apostrophe that is two spaces to the left of *k%* in the NUMERIC VARIABLES USED block:

```
   .
   .
   .
REM ** NUMERIC VARIABLES USED **
' k%            character counter in FOR-NEXT loop
   .
   .
   .
```

Press DEL 15 times. Each press of the key deletes one character or space. All characters or spaces to the right of the cursor shift to the left by one place. The result is

```
   .
   .
   .
character counter in FOR-NEXT loop
   .
   .
   .
```

Now press CTRL+BACKSPACE three times. The result of this keystroke combination is the same as that of the DEL key, as follows:

```
   .
   .
   .
racter counter in FOR-NEXT loop
   .
   .
   .
```

Now move the cursor to the position just to the right of the letter *p* in the word *loop*.

```
    .
    .
    .
racter counter in FOR-NEXT loop_
    .
    .
    .
```

Each press of the BACKSPACE key deletes the character to the left of the cursor. Press BACKSPACE until only the cursor remains on the line.

```
    .
    .
    .
REM ** NUMERIC VARIABLES USED **
_.
    .
    .
```

Press BACKSPACE one more time, and the blank line disappears. The cursor moves to the end of the line above:

```
    .
    .
    .
REM ** NUMERIC VARIABLES USED **_
    .
    .
```

Move the cursor to the left to the *U* of *USED*. Press CTRL+Q. Notice the ^Q characters appear on the bottom line of the screen at the right.

```
Main: PRO5-2.BAS    Context: Program not running    ^Q   00017:025
```

Now press Y. CTRL+Q, followed by Y, erases everything from the cursor position to the end of the line.

```
    .
    .
    .
REM ** NUMERIC VARIABLES _
    .
    .
    .
```

With the cursor in its present position, press CTRL+Y. This key combination deletes the entire line on which the cursor is positioned.

```
      .
      .
      .
' teststring$  = string entered for testing FNsqueeze$
  _
      .
      .
      .
```

With these deletions, the program is the same as Program 5-1, except for the first two lines, which identify the program title, program number, and date.

Edit Menu Commands

The Edit menu commands shown in Figure 5-2 are used to delete or insert long sections of text. Portions of text may be deleted from one place and inserted at another place by combining the delete and insert commands from the Edit menu.

Selecting Text

Before deleting or inserting text using the Edit menu, you must first select the text to be erased or moved. While in the editor, move the cursor to the beginning of the block to be edited. Then hold down the SHIFT key while using any of the cursor-movement keys (left arrow, right arrow, CTRL+right arrow, PGUP, and so on) to move the highlight to the end of the block.

To demonstrate this process, load Program 5-1, which you saved earlier. Figure 5-3 shows the Edit window containing part of the program.

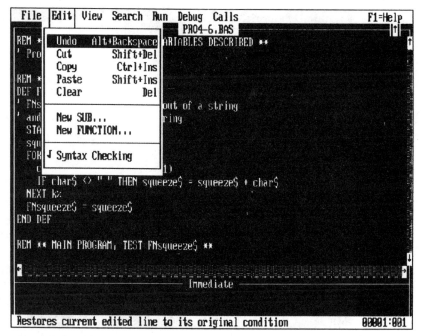

Figure 5-2. *Edit menu*

Suppose you wish to select the **STRING VARIABLES USED** block from Program 5-1. The first step would be to select all the lines in the block from the editor. To do this, move the cursor to the *R* of the REM statement at the beginning of the block.

```
        .
        .
        .
REM ** STRING VARIABLES USED **
' squeeze$      string with spaces removed
        .
        .
        .
```

Press SHIFT+down arrow. The REM statement is displayed in reverse video, showing that it has been selected. The cursor moves down one line.

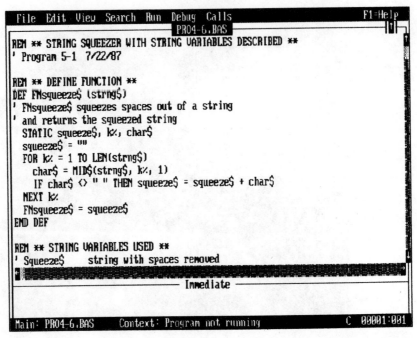

Figure 5-3.   *First part of Program 5-1*

Press SHIFT+down arrow again. The second line of the block is also displayed in reverse video. The cursor has moved to the third line of the block.

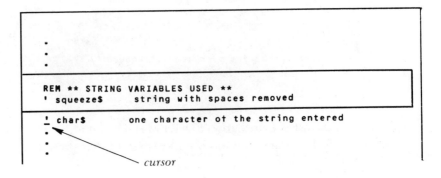

Press SHIFT+down arrow two more times. You have now selected four lines, which is the complete STRING VARIABLES USED block.

```
        •
        •
        •
REM ** STRING VARIABLES USED **
' squeeze$      string with spaces removed
' char$         one character of the string entered
' teststring$   string entered for testing FNsqueeze

 ̄
        •
        •
        •                        cursor
```

Using the Cut Command

To delete the text just selected, you must move from the editor to the Edit menu. Press ALT+E to do so. Use the down arrow key to move the highlight to the Cut command, as shown in Figure 5-4.

Press ENTER to carry out the Cut command, and the STRING VARIABLES USED block is deleted. Even though the block is deleted from the program, it is still within reach. It has been saved on the Clipboard and can be recovered, as you will see later.

If you are sure you want to delete a block of text, you may select the block of text and simply press the DEL key. However, there is no way to recover text when you delete it in this way. Another way to delete text is to activate the Clear command from the Edit menu. Text deleted by the Clear command also is unrecoverable.

After deleting the STRING VARIABLES USED block, the program is the same as Program 4-6 except for the first two lines. Therefore, it is unnecessary to save the result; you have saved Program 4-6 on disk.

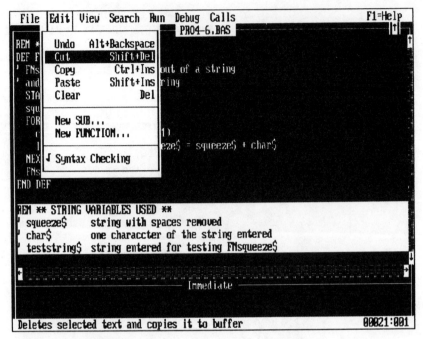

Figure 5-4. *Edit menu with Cut Command highlighted*

Using the Undo Command

The Undo command of the Edit menu is disabled until the current line is modified. Undo restores the current line to its original state, provided the cursor is still on that line. Be aware that Undo has no effect if the cursor has moved from the modified line.

Load the original Program 5-2 so that you can see how the Undo command works. Suppose you decide to remove the word *USED* from the REM line of the STRING VARIABLES USED block. You select the REM line of that block by positioning the cursor at the beginning of the word *USED* and pressing SHIFT+right arrow until each letter of the word *USED* is highlighted, as shown here:

Press ALT+E to access the Edit menu. Delete the word *USED* by selecting the Cut command from the menu and pressing ENTER.

REM ** STRING VARIABLES _**

Since you have modified the current line and the cursor is still on the line, you can restore the line to its original condition by selecting the Undo command from the Edit menu and pressing ENTER.

_REM ** STRING VARIABLES USED **

The cursor moves to the beginning of the restored line.

Cutting and Pasting

When text is deleted by the Cut command, the deleted text is placed on the Clipboard. You still have access to it. Furthermore, you can insert the deleted text anywhere in the file that is in memory. The Paste command inserts text from the Clipboard at the position before the cursor. The Cut and Paste commands are used together to move a block of text from one place in a program to another.

Suppose you wish to exchange the order of the STRING VARIA-BLES USED block and the NUMERIC VARIABLES USED block. You can move either block you wish. Since you have already practiced using the Cut command with the STRING VARIABLES USED block, use that process again.

Select the STRING VARIABLES USED block from the editor using SHIFT+down arrow. Include the blank line following the block.

```
                .
                .
                .
REM ** STRING VARIABLES USED **
' squeeze$        string with spaces removed
' char$           one character of the string entered
' teststring$     string entered for testing FNsqueeze

REM ** NUMERIC VARIABLES USED **
                .
                .
                .
```

cursor

Go to the Edit menu and use the Cut command. This will delete the **STRING VARIABLES USED** block and place it on the Clipboard. From the editor, move the cursor to the *R* that begins the MAIN PROGRAM REM statement:

```
REM ** MAIN PROGRAM, TEST FNsqueeze$ **
```

Enter the Edit menu again and move the highlight to the Paste command, as shown in Figure 5-5. Press ENTER, and the STRING VARIABLES USED block is inserted into its new position.

```
        .
        .
        .
END DEF

REM ** NUMERIC VARIABLES USED **
' k%              character counter

REM ** STRING VARIABLES USED **
' squeeze$        string with spaces removed
' char$           one character of the string entered
' teststring$     string entered for testing FNsqueeze

REM ** MAIN PROGRAM, TEST FNsqueeze$ **
        .
        .
        .
```

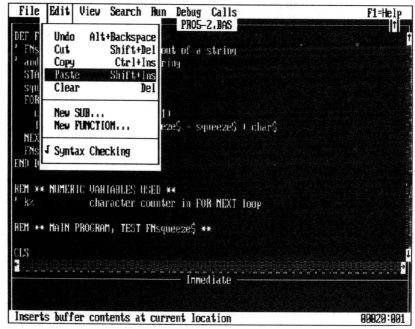

Figure 5-5. *Edit menu with Paste command highlighted*

Using the Copy Command

When it is active, the Copy command makes a copy of the selected text and places it on the Clipboard. The text is left in its original place in the file.

As before, select the text and press ALT+E to move to the Edit menu. Position the highlight on the Copy command and press ENTER. This places a copy of the selected text on the Clipboard, a temporary storage area. The original text remains in place in the file.

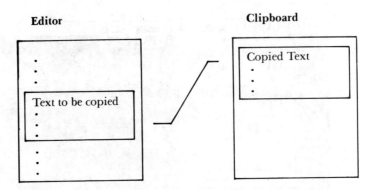

Reload Program 5-2 for the demonstration that follows. Suppose you decide to move the NUMERIC VARIABLES USED block from Program 5-2 to Program 5-1. You can copy the block to the Clipboard with these steps:

1. Select the complete NUMERIC VARIABLES USED block from the editor by moving the cursor to the *R* of the REM statement at the beginning of the block. Press SHIFT+down arrow three times, highlighting both lines of the block and the blank line that follows the block.

2. Access the Edit menu.

3. Use the Copy command to copy the block to the Clipboard.

When these steps have been completed, access the File menu and load Program 5-1. Even though a new program has been loaded, the text that was copied from Program 5-2 is still on the Clipboard.

When Program 5-1 has been loaded, move the cursor to the *R* at the beginning of the MAIN PROGRAM REM statement. Access the Edit menu and select the Paste command. Press ENTER, and the text from the Clipboard is inserted just ahead of the cursor position.

```
   .
   .
   .
' teststring$  = string entered for testing FNsqueeze
REM ** NUMERIC VARIABLES USED **
' kX             character counter in FOR-NEXT loop

REM ** MAIN PROGRAM, TEST FNsqueeze$ **
   .
   .
   .
```

The NUMERIC VARIABLES USED block has been copied from
Program 5-2 to Program 5-1.

Clear Command

The Clear command works like the Cut command except that the
selected text is not placed on the Clipboard. The selected text is erased
and cannot be recovered.

Other Edit Menu Commands

■ The New SUB. . . command allows you to add a new subprogram
to your program. This command will be discussed in detail in Chapter 6.

■ The New FUNCTION. . . command allows you to add a new
FUNCTION to your program. This command will be discussed in
detail in Chapter 6.

■ The Syntax Checking command turns the editor's automatic syntax checking on or off.

Review

A small amount of text can be edited by

- Moving the cursor, scrolling the display window to locate the text to be edited, or a combination of both

- Inserting new text or deleting existing text

Methods of moving the cursor, scrolling the display window, and editing small amounts of text were discussed in this chapter and demonstrated with a familiar, previously used program. You moved the cursor by as little as one character to as much as the complete file. You scrolled the text in the file by as little as one line to as much as a complete display window.

Larger chunks of data were edited by choosing commands from the Edit menu. First the text to be edited is selected. Then an edit command (Cut, Copy, Clear, or Paste) is chosen to delete, copy, or insert blocks of text. The Clipboard, a temporary storage area, is used to hold blocks of data that are to be inserted in a new location of the file.

You can now manipulate text within a file in many different ways. You have also learned how to move a block of text from one file to another.

6 Power Tools: SUB Program and FUNCTION Procedures

This chapter introduces procedures that are external to a QuickBASIC program's main module. A procedure is a subprogram or a function that is defined in these ways:

- A subprogram defined by a SUB...END SUB statement pair

- A function defined by a FUNCTION...END FUNCTION statement pair

A QuickBASIC program consists of one or more modules. A module is equivalent to a source file. Every QuickBASIC program has a main module. The main module contains the program's entry point—the place at which the execution of the program begins.

The QuickBASIC editor is more than a text editor. It is also designed to edit and manage multiple-module programming. Modules can contain lower levels of code organized into procedures, such as those defined by SUB...END SUB or FUNCTION...END FUNCTION statements. QuickBASIC organizes these lower levels of code alphabetically and keeps them separate from the rest of the program. Procedures are entered from the Edit menu; once entered, they are accessible from the View menu.

Procedures

The SUB...END SUB procedure is similar to a GOSUB...RE-TURN subroutine, and a FUNCTION...END FUNCTION procedure is similar to a DEF FN...END DEF function. However, procedures have a number of advantages over the older style of subroutine and function definition structures. The three major benefits of programming with procedures are these:

1. They allow you to break your programs into discrete logical units. Each unit can be tested and corrected more easily than an entire program that does not use procedures.

2. Once procedures have been debugged (tested and corrected), they can be used as building blocks in other programs.

3. They are generally more reliable because they have one and only one entry point and because any variables declared inside them are, by default, local to that particular procedure.

FUNCTION...END FUNCTION has the syntax

```
FUNCTION procedurename [(parameterlist)] [STATIC]
    .
    .
    .
    definition: a block of statements
    that tell what the procedure does
    .
    .
    .
    [EXIT FUNCTION]
    .
    .
    .
END FUNCTION
```

where

FUNCTION marks the beginning of the FUNCTION procedure.

procedurename is any valid variable name up to 40 characters. The same procedure name cannot be used for both a subprogram (SUB) and a FUNCTION.

parameterlist is a list of variables separated by commas. The parameter list shows the number and type of arguments to be passed to the FUNCTION.

STATIC indicates that the FUNCTION's local variables are to be saved between calls to the FUNCTION. If STATIC is omitted, local variables are automatic. That is, they are initialized to zero (or null strings) at the start of each call to the FUNCTION.

END FUNCTION marks the end of the FUNCTION and causes an exit from the FUNCTION. A return is made to the statement immediately following the statement that called the FUNCTION.

One or more EXIT FUNCTION statements may be placed within the body of the definition as an alternate way to exit from the FUNCTION.

SUB...END SUB has a similar syntax:

```
SUB procedurename [(parameterlist)] [STATIC]
   .
   .
   .
   a block of statements that tell
   what the procedure does
   .
   .
   .
   [EXIT SUB]
   .
   .
   .
END SUB
```

where

SUB marks the beginning of the SUB procedure.

procedurename is any valid variable name up to 40 characters. The same procedure name cannot be used for both a subprogram (SUB) and a FUNCTION.

parameterlist is a list of variables separated by commas. The parameter list shows the number and type of arguments to be passed to the SUB. An argument that is to be passed back to the calling module should also be included.

STATIC indicates that the SUB's local variables are saved between calls to the subprogram. If STATIC is omitted, local variables are automatic—they are initialized to zero (or null strings) at the start of each call to the subprogram.

END SUB marks the end of the SUB procedure and causes an exit from the SUB. A return is made to the statement immediately following the statement that called the SUB.

One or more EXIT SUB statements may be placed within the body of the definition as an alternate way to exit from the SUB.

FUNCTION...END FUNCTION

You call a FUNCTION the same way you call QuickBASIC's built-in functions such as INT, ABS, etc. You use its name in an expression as follows:

Built-in function:

```
PRINT UCASE$(teststring$)
```

Prints each character in teststring$ in upper case

Defined function:

```
PRINT Squeezer$(teststring$)
```

Prints the value of teststring$ with all spaces removed in the FUNCTION named Squeezer$

Program 6-1, STRING SQUEEZER WITH FUNCTION, is similar to Program 4-6, STRING SQUEEZER. However, Program 6-1 uses FUNCTION instead of the multiline DEF FN of Program 4-6. It is not a complete program until the FUNCTION Squeezer$ is added.

The main module of Program 6-1 is

```
REM ** STRING SQUEEZER WITH FUNCTION **
' Program 6-1   8/4/87

REM ** MAIN PROGRAM **

CLS

getdata:
LINE INPUT "String, please "; teststring$
PRINT Squeezer$(teststring$)
PRINT : GOTO getdata
```

The FUNCTION to be added is named Squeezer$. The function is called, along with its argument (*teststring$*), in a PRINT statement in the next-to-last line of the program's main module.

```
PRINT Squeezer$(teststring$)
```

```
DECLARE FUNCTION Squeezer$ (strng$)
REM ** STRING SQUEEZER WITH FUNCTION **
' Program 6-1   8/4/87

REM ** MAIN PROGRAM **

CLS

getdata:
LINE INPUT "String, please "; teststring$
PRINT Squeezer$(teststring$)          'FUNCTION called
PRINT : GOTO getdata
FUNCTION Squeezer$ (strng$) STATIC
  squeeze$ = ""
  FOR k% = 1 TO LEN(strng$)
    char$ = MID$(strng$, k%, 1)
    IF char$ <> " " THEN squeeze$ = squeeze$ + char$
  NEXT k%
  Squeezer$ = squeeze$                ' assign return value
END FUNCTION
```

Program 6-1. *STRING SQUEEZER WITH FUNCTION*

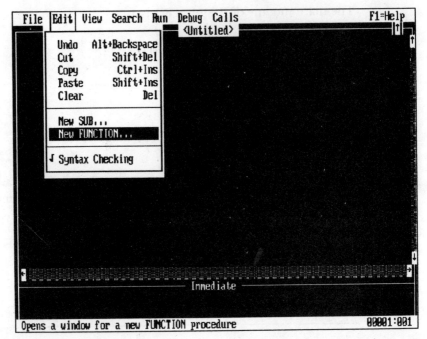

Figure 6-1. *Edit menu*

The function does not appear as part of the main module shown but is entered after the main module has been entered and saved. Enter the part of Program 6-1 that is shown and save it as PRO6-1.BAS.

After the partial program has been saved, access the Edit menu and move the highlight down to the New FUNCTION... command, as shown in Figure 6-1. Press the ENTER key. A dialog box, shown in Figure 6-2, is displayed.

Type in the name of the new FUNCTION, which is Squeezer$. A new screen is displayed with the beginning and ending of the FUNCTION provided for you, as shown in Figure 6-3. Note that the cursor is just to the right of the name of the FUNCTION. This allows you easily to add the argument that is being passed (*strng$*) and the keyword STATIC to the name of the FUNCTION:

```
FUNCTION Squeezer$ (strng$) STATIC
```

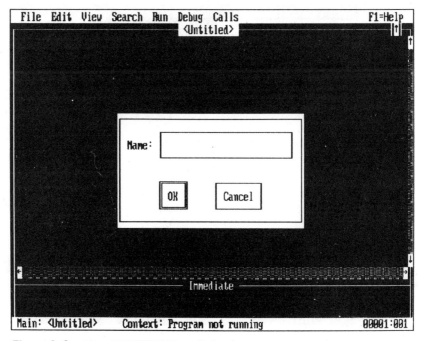

Figure 6-2. *New FUNCTION... dialog box*

Press ENTER and type in the balance of the FUNCTION definition, shown below. Each time you press ENTER a new blank line opens, ready for the next statement.

```
FUNCTION Squeezer$ (strng$) STATIC
  squeeze$ = ""
  FOR k% = 1 to LEN(strng$)
    char$ = MID$(strng$, k%, 1)
    IF char$ <> " " THEN squeeze$ = squeeze$ + char$
  NEXT k%
  Squeezer$ = squeeze$              ' assign return value
END FUNCTION
```

When you have finished entering the FUNCTION, access the File menu and move the highlight down to the Save All command. When you press ENTER with the Save All command highlighted, the main program and the FUNCTION are saved together as PRO6-1.BAS. This completes Program 6-1.

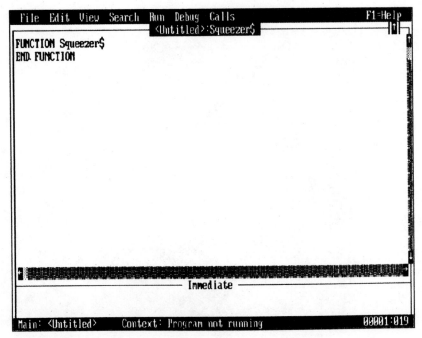

Figure 6-3. *Beginning and end of Squeezer$ FUNCTION*

Access the File menu again, select the Open Program... command, and type in the name of the main program:

```
File Name:  PRO6-1.BAS
```

Press ENTER and the program appears on the screen. Notice that QuickBASIC has automatically added the following line to the beginning of the program:

```
DECLARE FUNCTION Squeezer$ (strng$)
```

The DECLARE statement is necessary for your program to call procedures that are defined later in the module, such as FUNCTION...END FUNCTION or SUB...END SUB, or that are defined in another module altogether. The DECLARE statement remains as a part of the main program.

Run Program 6-1 to assure yourself that it works in the same way as Program 4-6.

SUB...END SUB

A defined subprogram is called in a different way than a defined function. Actually, there are two ways to call a defined subprogram. You can

1. Put its name in a CALL statement, such as

```
CALL Squeezer(teststring$)
```

2. Use its name as a statement by itself, as in

```
Squeezer teststring$
```

where Squeezer is the subprogram's name and *teststring$* is the argument being passed to the subprogram.

If the CALL keyword is used (as in number 1), parentheses must be placed around the argument(s) being passed. If CALL is omitted (as in number 2), do not put parentheses around the argument(s). In the rest of this book, all calls to subprograms will use a CALL statement to indicate clearly that a subprogram is being used.

Program 6-2, STRING SQUEEZER WITH SUBPROGRAM, has a main module that illustrates the use of a subprogram in place of the FUNCTION...END FUNCTION, as used in Program 6-1.

```
REM ** STRING SQUEEZER WITH SUBPROGRAM
' Program 6-2   8/5/87

REM ** MAIN PROGRAM **

CLS

getdata:
LINE INPUT "String, please "; teststring$
CALL Squeezer(teststring$, squeeze$)
PRINT squeeze$
PRINT : GOTO getdata
```

```
DECLARE SUB Squeezer (strng$, squeeze$)
REM ** STRING SQUEEZER WITH SUBPROGRAM **
' Program 6-2   8/5/87

REM ** MAIN PROGRAM **

CLS

getdata:
LINE INPUT "String, please "; teststring$
CALL Squeezer(teststring$, squeeze$)
PRINT squeeze$
PRINT : GOTO getdata
SUB Squeezer (strng$, squeeze$) STATIC
  squeeze$ = ""
  FOR k% = 1 TO LEN(strng$)
    char$ = MID$(strng$, k%, 1)
    IF char$ <> " " THEN squeeze$ = squeeze$ + char$
  NEXT k%
END SUB
```

Program 6-2. *STRING SQUEEZER WITH SUBPROGRAM*

Notice the difference in the way the subprogram is called, compared to the way FUNCTION is called in Program 6-1. First comes the CALL keyword, then the subprogram's name, followed by the argument to be passed to the subprogram (*teststring$*) and the argument to be passed back by the subprogram (*squeeze$*). The argument to be passed back is then printed by a separate statement. Notice that you do not use data-type declaration symbols (such as $) in the subprogram's name.

Enter the main module of Program 6-2 and save it as PRO6-2.BAS in text format. When it has been saved, access the Edit menu, as you did for Program 6-1. This time move the highlight down to the New SUB... command and press ENTER. A dialog box will appear, requesting the name of the subprogram. Enter the name:

```
Name:  Squeezer
```

Press ENTER and the beginning and ending of the subprogram appear. Finish typing the first line of the program:

```
SUB Squeezer (strng$, squeeze$) STATIC
```

Now type in the balance of the subprogram:

```
SUB Squeezer (strng$, squeeze$)  STATIC
  squeeze$ = ""
  FOR k% = 1 TO LEN(strng$)
    char$ = MID$(strng$, k%, 1)
    IF char$ <> " " THEN squeeze$ = squeeze$ + char$
  NEXT k%
END SUB
```

When you have finished entering the subprogram, access the File menu, move the highlight to Save All, and press ENTER. This completes Program 6-2 under the file name PRO6-2.BAS.

Access the File menu, move the highlight to Open Program..., and press ENTER. Type **PRO6-2.BAS** in the Open... dialog box and press ENTER. When the program appears, notice that a DECLARE statement has been added as the beginning line. If you are using the QuickBASIC editor to write your programs, the DECLARE statement will automatically be supplied for procedures. If you are not using the QuickBASIC editor to write your programs and you do not use the CALL statement to call a subprogram that is used, you must supply your own DECLARE statement. This is another good reason to include the CALL keyword to call a subprogram.

Run Program 6-2 a few times to assure yourself that the output works in the same way as that of Program 6-1.

Using Arrays

Original Dartmouth BASIC had only one-dimensional and two-dimensional arrays. In the documentation, one-dimensional arrays were called lists or vectors, and two-dimensional arrays were called tables or matrices. The DIM statement was used to specify the upper bound for subscripts; the lower bound was always 1. If no DIM statements were used, BASIC set the upper bound to 10 by default.

QuickBASIC allows you to use numeric or string arrays with up to 63 dimensions. Numeric arrays can be of any numeric type: integer, long integer, single precision, or double precision.

Dimensioning Arrays

In QuickBASIC, default values for subscripts are 0 for the lower bound and 10 for the upper bound. You can change these, of course, by using the DIM statement. You can also change the lower bound by using the OPTION BASE statement:

OPTION BASE 1 sets the lower bound for subscripts to 1.
OPTION BASE 0 sets the lower bound for subscripts to 0.

Remember: The default value for the lower bound is 0. Don't use the OPTION BASE statement to change it unless you have a good reason to do so.

The DIM statement initializes all elements of numeric strings to zero and all elements of string arrays to the null, or empty, string (""). A DIM statement should be used before the array it dimensions is referenced. It is good practice to put all DIM statements near the beginning of a program, outside any loops. Otherwise, you are likely to encounter an "array already dimensioned" error.

You may dimension an array as STATIC (allocated when the program is translated) or DYNAMIC (allocated when the program is run). Arrays that are dimensioned with only numeric constants are STATIC. Arrays that are dimensioned with variables are DYNAMIC.

STATIC arrays are fixed in size at the time the program is translated by QuickBASIC. Table 6-1 shows some examples of DIM statements used to dimension STATIC arrays. Note the use of the keyword TO to define both the lower bound and the upper bound for a subscript in *State$*(1 TO 60) and *TicTacToe%*(1 TO 3, 1 TO 3).

DYNAMIC arrays use variables as subscripts in a DIM statement. Table 6-2 shows examples of DIM statements used to dimension DYNAMIC arrays.

QuickBASIC has two functions that make it easy to find the upper and lower bounds of an array. The LBOUND and UBOUND functions allow you to write general subprograms and FUNCTIONS that can be used by any program that uses arrays.

DIM statement	Description of STATIC array
DIM *price*(100)	One-dimensional, single-precision array with 101 elements, *price*(0) to *price*(100)
DIM State$(1 TO 60)	One-dimensional string array with 60 elements, *State$*(1) to *State$*(60). Note the use of TO to set both the lower and upper bounds
DIM *TicTacToe%*(1 TO 3, 1 TO 3)	Two-dimensional integer array with nine elements. You can think of this array as being arranged in three rows and three columns
DIM *Hyperspace#*(99, 99, 99, 99)	Four-dimensional double-precision array with 100 * 100 * 100 * 100 elements. Oops— out of memory

Table 6-1. *DIM Statements Used to Dimension STATIC Arrays*

DIM statement	Description of DYNAMIC array
DIM *price*(*Last%*)	One-dimensional, single-precision array with elements from *price*(0) to *price*(*Last%*)
DIM *price*(1 TO *Last%*)	One-dimensional, single-precision array with elements from *price*(1) to *price*(*Last%*)
DIM *price*(10 TO *Last%*)	One-dimensional, single-precision array with elements from *price*(10) to *price*(*Last%*)
DIM *Gomoku%*(1 TO *n%*, 1 TO *n%*)	Two-dimensional integer array with elements from *Gomoku%*(1, 1) to *Gomoku%*(*n%*, *n%*)
DIM *airmiles%*(*n%*, *n%*)	Two-dimensional integer array with elements from *airmiles%*(0, 0) to *airmiles%*(*n%*, *n%*)

Table 6-2. *DIM Statements Used to Dimension DYNAMIC Arrays*

LBOUND returns the lower bound (smallest available subscript for an array). It is used in the form

```
LBOUND (array [, dimension])
```

where   •

array is the name of the array.

dimension is an integer from 1 to the number of dimensions in the array (maximum of 63). The number used indicates which dimension of the array you want returned.

UBOUND returns the upper bound (largest available subscript for an array). It is used in the following form:

```
UBOUND (array [, dimension])
```

where

array is the name of the array.

dimension is an integer from 1 to the number of dimensions in the array (maximum of 63). The number used indicates which dimension of the array you want returned.

For example, suppose an array has been dimensioned as follows:

```
DIM Filedrawer (1 TO 100, 0 TO 25, -5 TO 5)
```

Table 6-3 shows the value that would be returned for the specified LBOUND and UBOUND statements. You may use the shortened form of LBOUND or UBOUND for one-dimensional arrays, since the default value for dimension is 1 (one-dimensional array):

```
LBOUND (array)   instead of LBOUND (array, 1)
UBOUND (array)   instead of UBOUND (array, 1)
```

Statement	Value returned
LBOUND (*Filedrawer*, 1)	1
LBOUND (*Filedrawer*, 2)	0
LBOUND (*Filedrawer*, 3)	−5
UBOUND (*Filedrawer*, 1)	100
UBOUND (*Filedrawer*, 2)	25
UBOUND (*Filedrawer*, 3)	5

Table 6-3. *Value Returned for LBOUND and UBOUND Statements*

If an array has not been dimensioned, LBOUND is 0 by default unless you have used an OPTION BASE statement to set the lower bound to 1. The upper bound of a nondimensioned array is 10.

It is recommended that you use a DIM statement for any array you are using so that no confusion about the array's subscripts will result. QuickBASIC makes it easy to state a dimension's upper and lower bounds clearly. Use every method available to make your programs easy to read and understand. The next section will use the tools discussed so far in several examples and will introduce some new tools.

Passing Arrays to FUNCTION Procedures

You can pass an entire array to a FUNCTION or SUB procedure by putting the name of the array, followed by an "empty" pair of parentheses, in the argument list. An array name followed by a pair of parentheses must also appear in the parameter list of the FUNCTION or SUB statement. Program 6-3, SUM AND AVERAGE FOR ONE-DIMENSIONAL STATIC ARRAYS, uses a FUNCTION procedure to calculate the sum of the elements in an array.

```
DECLARE FUNCTION ArraySum! (array!())
REM ** SUM AND AVERAGE FOR ONE-DIMENSIONAL STATIC ARRAYS **
' Program 6-3  8/9/87
' Computes the sum and average of elements of two arrays

' Dimension arrays Celsius & Fahrenheit as STATIC
DIM Celsius(1 TO 7), Fahrenheit(1 TO 12)

' Read data for Celsius array
FOR k% = 1 TO 7
  READ Celsius(k%)
NEXT k%
DATA 20, 18, 23, 22, 19, 21, 24

' Read data for Fahrenheit array
FOR k% = 1 TO 12
  READ Fahrenheit(k%)
NEXT k%
DATA 68, 67, 73, 71, 79, 82, 89, 85, 80, 75, 76, 74

' Print sum and average for Celsius array
CLS
PRINT "Celsius sum: "; ArraySum(Celsius())
PRINT "Celsius average: "; ArraySum(Celsius()) / 7

' Print sum and average for Fahrenheit array
PRINT "Fahrenheit sum: "; ArraySum(Fahrenheit())
PRINT "Fahrenheit average: "; ArraySum(Fahrenheit()) / 12

END
FUNCTION ArraySum (array()) STATIC
' Returns the sum of the elements of a one-dimensional array
  sum = 0
  FOR k% = LBOUND(array) TO UBOUND(array)
    sum = sum + array(k%)
  NEXT k%
  ArraySum = sum
END FUNCTION
```

Program 6-3. *SUM AND AVERAGE FOR ONE-DIMENSIONAL STATIC ARRAYS*

Two arrays are created in the main module of Program 6-3. *Celsius( )* is a one-dimensional array with 7 elements. *Fahrenheit( )* is a one-dimensional array with 12 elements. The elements in the two arrays are passed to the FUNCTION ArraySum by the statements

```
PRINT "Celsius sum: "; ArraySum(Celsius())

PRINT "Fahrenheit sum: "; ArraySum(Fahrenheit())
```

Note that the **PRINT** statements contain the name of the FUNC-TION (ArraySum) and the array name (*Celsius* or *Fahrenheit*), followed by an empty pair (left and right) of parentheses. The empty parentheses are essential to pass the elements of the array.

An array name also appears in the FUNCTION statement, followed by an empty pair of parentheses. The parentheses are necessary to pass the elements of the array:

```
FUNCTION ArraySum(array())
```

The sum of the elements in the array is passed back from the FUNC-TION to the main module by the assignment

```
ArraySum = sum
```

In addition to printing the sum of the elements of each array, the main module prints the average of the elements of each array:

```
PRINT "Celsius average: "; ArraySum(Celsius ()) / 7
PRINT "Fahrenheit average: "; ArraySum(Fahrenheit ()) / 12
```

The FUNCTION is called twice for each array. The first time the FUNCTION is called, the sum of the elements is printed. The second time the FUNCTION is called, the sum of the elements is used to find the average of the elements. If the arrays were large, you would want to call each function once to get the sum of the elements, assign that value to a variable, and compute the average of the elements from the variable. Note that by using LBOUND and UBOUND the FUNC-TION can handle arrays of different sizes.

Figure 6-4 shows how Program 6-3 prints the sum of the temperatures and their averages. The averages are printed as single-precision numbers. The expressions in the PRINT statements that calculate the averages do not specify a data type. Single precision is the default type in such a case. Look at the DECLARE statement that QuickBASIC added to the beginning of Program 6-3. Notice that the default data type appears in the DECLARE statement:

```
DECLARE FUNCTION ArraySum! (array!())
```

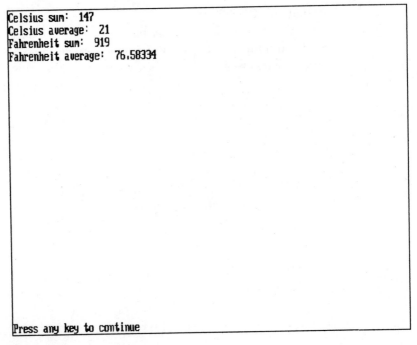

```
Celsius sum: 147
Celsius average: 21
Fahrenheit sum: 919
Fahrenheit average: 76.58334
```

```
Press any key to continue
```

Figure 6-4. *Output of Program 6-3*

The data type (!) specified in the DECLARE statement appears after both the FUNCTION name (ArraySum) and the array name (*array*).

Program 6-4, SUM OF ELEMENTS OF A ONE-DIMENSIONAL DYNAMIC ARRAY, demonstrates the use of dynamic arrays and the REDIM statement that allows you to resize an array anytime during a program.

When a program is compiled by QuickBASIC, all arrays declared in a REDIM statement are treated as dynamic arrays. When the program is run and a REDIM statement is executed, the array is deallocated (if it has been previously allocated). The REDIM statement reallocates the array with the new dimensions specified in the REDIM statement. Previous array element values are lost because all numeric

```
DECLARE FUNCTION ArraySum! (array!())
REM ** SUM AND AVERAGE OF ELEMENTS OF A ONE-DIMENSIONAL DYNAMIC ARRAY **
' Program 6-4  8/9/87
' Computes the sum and average of the elements of an array
' entered from the keyboard

' Enter the number of elements in the array

CLS
INPUT "How many elements"; size%

' Redimension the dynamic array.
REDIM array(1 TO size%)

' Enter the elements array(1) to array(size%)
FOR k% = 1 TO UBOUND(array)
   PRINT "Array element #"; k%; : INPUT array(k%)
NEXT k%

' Print sum and average of elements
PRINT
PRINT "Sum of elements: "; ArraySum(array())
PRINT "Average element: "; ArraySum(array()) / size%

END
FUNCTION ArraySum (array()) STATIC
' Returns the sum of the elements of a one-dimensional array
   sum = 0
   FOR k% = LBOUND(array) TO UBOUND(array)
     sum = sum + array(k%)
   NEXT k%
   ArraySum = sum
END FUNCTION
```

Program 6-4. *SUM AND AVERAGE OF A ONE-DIMENSIONAL DYNAMIC ARRAY*

elements are reset to zero and all string elements are reset to null (empty) strings. Figures 6-5*a* and 6-5*b* show typical runs of 6-4.

Program 6-5, **GROSS VALUE OF STOCKS,** demonstrates the use of the function SubTotal#, which computes the sum of the products of corresponding elements of two arrays. You can probably think of several other uses for this function.

```
How many elements? 3
Array element # 1 ? 13
Array element # 2 ? 17
Array element # 3 ? 24

Sum of elements:  54
Average element:  18




Press any key to continue
```

Figure 6-5a. *Output of Program 6-4 (#1)*

```
How many elements? 4
Array element # 1 ? 14.2
Array element # 2 ? 17.65
Array element # 3 ? 22
Array element # 4 ? 33

Sum of elements:  86.85
Average element:  21.7125




Press any key to continue
```

Figure 6-5b. *Output of Program 6-4 (#2)*

```
DECLARE FUNCTION SubTotal# (Qty&(), PriceEach#())
REM ** GROSS VALUE OF STOCKS **
' Program 6-5  8/11/87

' Enter the number of elements in arrays
CLS
INPUT "How many items (pairs of numbers)"; size%

' Redimension dynamic arrays, Shares& and SharePrice#
REDIM Shares&(1 TO size%), SharePrice#(1 TO size%)

' Enter stock data: number of shares and price per share
FOR k% = 1 TO UBOUND(Shares&)
   PRINT
   INPUT "Number of shares"; Shares&(k%)
   INPUT "Price per share"; SharePrice#(k%)
NEXT k%
PRINT
PRINT "Gross value is "; SubTotal#(Shares&(), SharePrice#())
END
FUNCTION SubTotal# (Qty&(), PriceEach#()) STATIC
   ' Returns the sum of the products of corresponding elements
   ' Assumes both arrays have the same LBOUND, UBOUND
   First% = LBOUND(Qty&)
   Last% = UBOUND(Qty&)
   sum# = 0
   FOR k% = First% TO Last%
     sum# = sum# + Qty&(k%) * PriceEach#(k%)
   NEXT k%
   SubTotal# = sum#
END FUNCTION
```

Program 6-5. *GROSS VALUE OF STOCKS*

Passing Arrays to SUB Procedures

You can pass an array to a SUB procedure by putting the name of the array, followed by an empty pair of parentheses, in the argument list of a CALL statement. A corresponding array must also appear in the parameter list in the SUB statement that begins the procedure. A SUB procedure can return an entire array to the calling module.

Program 6-6, **CREATE SCRAMBLED NUMERIC ARRAY**, creates an array of integers from 1 to n, and then scrambles the array by using a subprogram called Shuffle%. This method creates a scrambled array in which each element is known (integers from 1 to n). Thus, it is useful in testing searching and sorting procedures, as you will see.

```
DECLARE SUB Shuffle (array%())
REM ** CREATE SCRAMBLED NUMERIC ARRAY **
' Program 6-6   8/11/87
' Generate an array of integers 1 to n, then shuffle it.
CLS

getdata:
PRINT "Starting array is an ordered list, 1 to n."
INPUT "What value of n do you want"; n%

' Redimension Numbers as a one-dimensional DYNAMIC integer array
REDIM Numbers%(1 TO n%)

' Create ordered array with element #k equal to k.
FOR k% = 1 TO n%
  Numbers%(k%) = k%
NEXT k%

' Shuffle the array
CALL Shuffle(Numbers%())

' Print the scrambled array.
PRINT
PRINT "Here are your mixed-up numbers:"
PRINT
FOR k% = 1 TO n%
  PRINT Numbers%(k%),
NEXT k%
PRINT : PRINT : GOTO getdata
SUB Shuffle (array%()) STATIC
  ' Randomizes a numeric array.  Assumes lower bound is one (1).
  RANDOMIZE (TIMER)

  ' Find size of array (number of elements)
  size% = UBOUND(array%)

  ' Swap each element with a randomly selected element
  FOR k% = 1 TO size%
    rndindex% = INT(size% * RND(1)) + 1
    SWAP array%(k%), array%(rndindex%)
  NEXT k%
END SUB
```

Program 6-6.   *CREATE SCRAMBLED NUMERIC ARRAY*

Figure 6-6 illustrates a test run for two values of n. Note that for each value of n every integer from 1 to n appears in the shuffled list of numbers.

A subprogram to sort an integer array is shown below. It is a variation of the bubble sort shown in Program 1-4*a* in Chapter 1. Note

```
Starting array is an ordered list, 1 to n,
What value of n do you want? 15

Here are your mixed-up numbers:

9          10          12          3          6
7          2           11          13         4
15         5           8           1          14


Starting array is an ordered list, 1 to n,
What value of n do you want? 25

Here are your mixed-up numbers:

9          5           2           17         11
12         4           21          19         6
13         7           3           23         25
15         18          14          22         16
18         1           20          8          24


Starting array is an ordered list, 1 to n,
What value of n do you want?
```

Figure 6-6.   *Output of two runs of Program 6-6*

the use of a DO...LOOP with a WHILE clause and a Block
IF...THEN structure.

```
SUB BubbleSort (array%()) STATIC
  ' Sorts an integer array from top to bottom
  top% = LBOUND(array%)
  bottom% = UBOUND(array%)
  DO WHILE top% < bottom%
    FOR here% = top% TO bottom% - 1
      IF array%(here%) > array%(here% + 1) THEN
        SWAP array%(here%), array%(here% + 1)
      END IF
    NEXT here%
  LOOP
END SUB
```

Program 6-7, BUBBLE SORT TEST PROGRAM, sets up an array of
integers 1 to n, shuffles this array, prints the shuffled array, sorts the
shuffled array, prints the sorted array, and prints the time required to
sort the array.

```
DECLARE SUB Shuffle (array%())
DECLARE SUB ArrayPrint (array%())
DECLARE SUB BubbleSort (array%())
REM ** BUBBLE SORT TEST PROGRAM **
' Program 6-7   8/11/87
CLS

getdata:
INPUT "How many numbers in array"; n%

' Redimension Numbers as a STATIC integer array
REDIM numbers%(1 TO n%)

' Create shuffled array containing integers 1 to n.
FOR k% = 1 TO n%
  numbers%(k%) = k%
NEXT k%
CALL Shuffle(numbers%())

' Print shuffled array
PRINT : PRINT "Shuffled array:"
CALL ArrayPrint(numbers%())

' Sort shuffled array.  Time the sort.
start = TIMER
CALL BubbleSort(numbers%())
finish = TIMER

' Print sorted array and sorting time
PRINT "Sorted array:"
CALL ArrayPrint(numbers%())
PRINT "Sorting time:"; finish - start; "seconds"

GOTO getdata

REM ** PROCEDURES **

SUB ArrayPrint (array%()) STATIC
  ' Prints an integer array using comma spacing.
  FOR k% = LBOUND(array%) TO UBOUND(array%)
    PRINT array%(k%),
  NEXT k%
  PRINT : PRINT
END SUB
SUB BubbleSort (array%()) STATIC
  ' Sorts an integer array from top to bottom
  top% = LBOUND(array%)
  bottom% = UBOUND(array%)
  DO WHILE top% < bottom%
    FOR here% = bottom% TO top% + 1 STEP -1
      IF array%(here%) < array%(here% - 1) THEN
        SWAP array%(here%), array%(here% - 1)
      END IF
    NEXT here%
    top% = top% + 1
```

Program 6-7.   *BUBBLE SORT TEST PROGRAM*

```
  LOOP
END SUB
SUB Shuffle (array%()) STATIC
  ' Randomizes a numeric array.   Assumes lower bound is one (1).

  RANDOMIZE (TIMER)

  ' Find size of array (number of elements)
  size% = UBOUND(array%)

  ' Swap each element with a randomly selected element
  FOR k% = 1 TO size%
    rndindex% = INT(size% * RND(1)) + 1
    SWAP array%(k%), array%(rndindex%)
  NEXT k%
END SUB
```

Program 6-7. *BUBBLE SORT TEST PROGRAM (continued)*

Using More than One Procedure

QuickBASIC programs are not limited to one procedure, as Program 6-7 demonstrated. You may add procedures to expand an existing program. You might have a notepad program with the following subprogram that prints the notes:

```
CALL Prnt(Note$())
  .                                        ' pass entire array
  .
  .
SUB Prnt(Item$()) STATIC
  CLS
  FOR num% = 1 to UBOUND(Item$)            ' one element at a time
    PRINT Item$(num%)                      ' is printed from 1 to
    PRINT                                  ' UBOUND(ItemS)
  NEXT num%
END SUB
```

Program 6-8, NOTE PRINTER, uses the above example as a subprogram to input five short text items. The items are placed in an array named Note$. The subprogram Prnt, shown above, is then added.

```
DECLARE SUB Prnt (Item$())
REM ** NOTE PRINTER **
' Program 6-8  8/10/87


CLS
INPUT "How many notes "; numb%
DIM Note(1 TO numb%) AS STRING


FOR numb% = 1 TO UBOUND(Note$)
  PRINT numb%;
  LINE INPUT "> "; Note$(numb%)
  PRINT
NEXT numb%
CALL Prnt(Note$())

END
SUB Prnt (Item$()) STATIC
  CLS
  FOR num% = 1 TO UBOUND(Item$)      ' one element at a time
    PRINT Item$(num%)                ' is printed from 1 to
    PRINT                            ' UBOUND(Item$)
  NEXT num%
END SUB
```

Program 6-8. *NOTE PRINTER*

Enter the main module of Program 6-8 and save it with the Save As... command from the File menu, giving it the name PRO6-8.BAS. Then add the subprogram by using the New SUB... command from the Edit menu. As a final step, save the two together by using the Save All command from the File menu. Figure 6-7 shows five typical notes printed by the subprogram after they had been entered in the main module.

You can change the DIM statement to increase or decrease the size of the array. Nothing in the subprogram would have to be changed, since LBOUND and UBOUND take care of the upper and lower limits of the FOR...NEXT loop that prints the notes.

You can add a second subprogram to Program 6-8. Use the Open Program... command from the File menu to access Program 6-8 if it is not already on display. Move the cursor down to the blank line just above the END statement. Type the following line and press ENTER:

```
CALL CountChars(Note$())
```

```
All the elements in an array can be passed to a subprogram as follows:

The array's name is followed by empty parentheses (),

The name and parentheses are used in an argument list,

They are also used in the subprogram's parameter list,

LBOUND and UBOUND are useful for determining the size of an array,




Press any key to continue
```

Figure 6-7. *Output of Program 6-8*

This statement will pass the array Note$ to the CountChars subprogram.

Now access the New SUB... command from the Edit menu. Type in the name of the subprogram, as shown below, and press ENTER:

```
Name:   CountChars
```

Enter the following subprogram:

```
SUB CountChars (Rec$()) STATIC
  char% = 0
  FOR num% = 1 TO UBOUND(Rec$)
    char% = char% + LEN(Rec$(num%))
  NEXT num%
  PRINT "Number of characters in array is:"; char%
END SUB
```

When you have entered the subprogram, access the dialog box from the SUBs... command of the View menu, as shown in Figure 6-8.

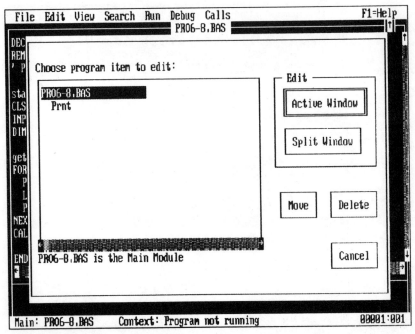

Figure 6-8. *SUBs... dialog box*

Make sure the highlight is on the main module name and press ENTER. The main module then appears on the display. Change the name and number of the program to Program 6-9, NOTE PRINTER AND CHARACTER COUNTER, as shown below:

```
REM ** NOTE PRINTER AND CHARACTER COUNTER **
' Program 6-9  8/10/87
```

Now access Save As... from the File menu and press ENTER. At the file name prompt enter

```
File Name:  PRO6-9.BAS
```

The CountChars subprogram is now a part of Program 6-8, along with the Prnt subprogram. Figure 6-9 shows the output of Program 6-9, using the same five notes shown in Figure 6-7.

```
DECLARE SUB CountChars (Rec$())
DECLARE SUB Prnt (Item$())
REM ** NOTE PRINTER AND CHARACTER COUNTER **
' Program 6-9   8/10/87


CLS
INPUT "How many notes "; numb%
DIM Note(1 TO numb%) AS STRING

FOR numb% = 1 TO UBOUND(Note$)
  PRINT numb%;
  LINE INPUT "> "; Note$(numb%)
  PRINT
NEXT numb%
CALL Prnt(Note$())
CALL CountChars(Note$())

END
SUB CountChars (Rec$()) STATIC
  char% = 0
  FOR num% = 1 TO UBOUND(Rec$)
    char% = char% + LEN(Rec$(num%))
  NEXT num%
  PRINT "Number of characters in array is:"; char%
END SUB
SUB Prnt (Item$()) STATIC
  CLS
  FOR num% = 1 TO UBOUND(Item$)        ' one element at a time
    PRINT Item$(num%)                  ' is printed from 1 to
    PRINT                              ' UBOUND(Item$)
  NEXT num%
END SUB
```

Program 6-9.   *NOTE PRINTER AND CHARACTER COUNTER*

Viewing Subprograms

When you load a QuickBASIC program, all files that contain modules belonging to the program are placed in memory. However, only the main module is displayed. The View menu, shown in Figure 6-10, lets you open new windows, display program output, look at modules in memory, and customize your screen's appearance.

Move the highlight down to the Split command. Notice the message at the bottom of the screen: "Divides screen into two View windows." Press ENTER. The screen is split into two windows with

```
All the elements in an array can be passed to a subprogram as follows:

The array's name is followed by empty parentheses (),

The name and parentheses are used in the argument list,

They are also used in the subprogram's parameter list,

LBOUND and UBOUND are useful for determining the size of an array,

Number of characters in array is: 298




Press any key to continue
```

Figure 6-9. *Output of Program 6-9*

the cursor in the upper window. Parts of the main module are shown in each window.

Access the View menu again. While the highlight is on the SUBs... command, press the ENTER key. The large box on the lefthand side of the screen displays a list of the main module and the procedures that now make up Program 6-9, as Figure 6-11 shows.

The main module, PRO6-9.BAS, is highlighted. You can move the highlight between the main module and the subprograms by pressing the down or up arrow keys. The highlighted module is described beneath the box that lists the modules.

Press the down arrow key once. The highlight moves down to CountChars, and this subprogram is described beneath the listing box: "CountChars is a SUB in PRO6-9.BAS."

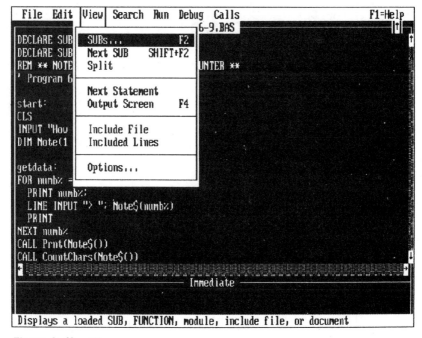

Figure 6-10.   *View menu*

Press the down arrow key again. The highlight moves down to Prnt. This subprogram is now described beneath the listing box: "Prnt is a SUB in PRO6-9.BAS." Leave the highlight on Prnt.

Press the TAB key twice. You see the cursor move, first to the Active Window box and then to the Split Window box. The Split Window box is shown with a double outline after the second TAB keystroke. Press ENTER. This sends you back to the editor's View window, which is now split into two windows, as shown in Figure 6-12. The subprogram Prnt has been placed in the lower window. The cursor is in the lower window because you selected Prnt in the large dialog box and Split Window as the active window. Since the cursor is in the area of the subprogram, you can now edit Prnt if you wish.

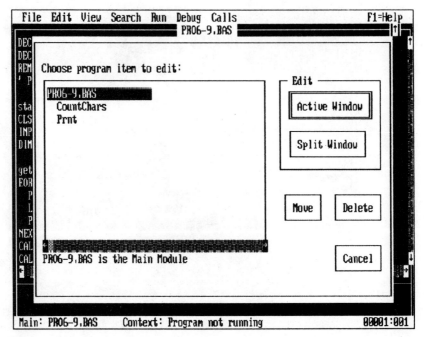

Figure 6-11. *SUBs... dialog boxes*

Press the F6 key. The cursor moves down to the small Immediate window at the bottom of the screen. An immediate command, such as RUN, may be entered when the cursor is in this window. Type **BEEP** and press ENTER. Immediately you will hear a beep.

Press F6 again. The cursor moves to the upper View window where the main module is. You can now scan the main module. Although it doesn't all show in the short window, you can scroll the module by using the arrow keys. You can also edit the main module while the cursor is in its window.

Only two View windows (plus the Immediate window) appear on the screen at one time. To rotate between any of these two—the main module, subprogram CountChars, and subprogram Prnt—access Next SUB on the View menu and press ENTER.

Press CTRL+F10 to expand the active window to fill the screen.

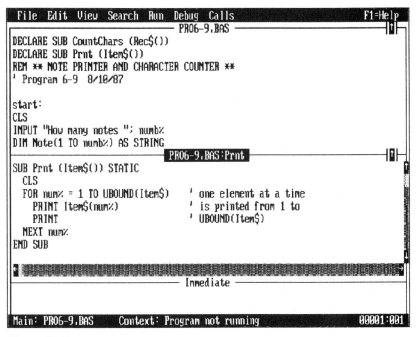

```
 File  Edit  View  Search  Run  Debug  Calls                    F1=Help
┌───────────────────────── PRO6-9.BAS ─────────────────────────────┐↑├┐
│DECLARE SUB CountChars (Rec$())                                    │
│DECLARE SUB Prnt (Item$())                                         │
│REM ** NOTE PRINTER AND CHARACTER COUNTER **                       │
│' Program 6-9  8/10/87                                             │
│                                                                   │
│start:                                                             │
│CLS                                                                │
│INPUT "How many notes "; numb%                                     │
│DIM Note(1 TO numb%) AS STRING                                     │
├───────────────────────── PRO6-9.BAS:Prnt ────────────────────────┤
│SUB Prnt (Item$()) STATIC                                          │
│  CLS                                                              │
│  FOR num% = 1 TO UBOUND(Item$)    ' one element at a time         │
│    PRINT Item$(num%)              ' is printed from 1 to          │
│    PRINT                          ' UBOUND(Item$)                 │
│  NEXT num%                                                        │
│END SUB                                                            │
│                                                                   │
├───────────────────────────  Immediate  ──────────────────────────┤
│                                                                   │
│                                                                   │
└───────────────────────────────────────────────────────────────────┘
 Main: PRO6-9.BAS     Context: Program not running          00001:001
```

Figure 6-12. *Split View window*

Review

This chapter has emphasized modular programming by using the procedures SUB...END SUB and FUNCTION...END FUNCTION. Subprograms and this type of function are procedures that are outside of the main program. QuickBASIC organizes these lower levels of code alphabetically and keeps them separate from the rest of the program.

Procedures are entered from the Edit menu and can be viewed from the View menu.

QuickBASIC arrays were introduced. Methods for passing data in arrays to subprogram and function procedures were discussed and demonstrated in several programs.

7 Sequential Unstructured Files

In previous chapters you have used many files. For instance, you copied files from MS-DOS and QuickBASIC disks to create a work disk. You created, stored, and used program files containing Quick-BASIC programs and modules that can be merged into programs. These programs use data that is supplied from the keyboard or that is included in the program as assignment statements (*start% = 1*) or in DATA statements.

When you are working with small amounts of information, DATA statements provide a good method for storing data. DATA statements are stored in memory along with the program that uses the information contained in them. However, when you need to handle large amounts of data, DATA statements become cumbersome to edit, are prone to error, and fill up much memory space in the computer. A better way to store large amounts of information is in data files on disks. Data files stored on disks can be conveniently used by more than one program, and one program can use data from more than one file.

QuickBASIC supports two types of data files: sequential files and random-access files. In this book, sequential files are subdivided into unstructured and structured files. In this chapter, you will learn how to create and use unstructured sequential files. Chapter 8 covers structured sequential files and Chapter 9 discusses random access files.

Types of Data Files

A data file is a collection of records; it is usually stored on magnetic tape or disk. Sequential files hark back to the days before disk drives were invented, when data files were stored on magnetic tape — rooms full of magnetic tape! A sequential file has a first record, a second record, a third record, and so on.

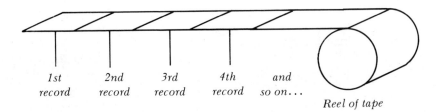

1st   *2nd*   *3rd*   *4th*   *and*

record *record* *record* *record* *so on...*

Reel of tape

Today, magnetic tape is used mostly for archival or backup purposes. Current files are stored on disks. Even on disk, sequential files act as if they were on tape. To get record 7, the computer reads, sequentially, record 1, record 2, and so on, until the desired record, number 7, appears.

Sequential files have their advantages and disadvantages:

Advantages
Variable-length records. Records can be any length: very short, very long, or in between.

Efficient use of space. Since records can be of variable length, each record is as short or as long as it needs to be.

Excellent for information that doesn't change or changes infrequently, for example, historical data.

Disadvantages
In a large data file, looking up information is serial and slow.

Editing a sequential file is cumbersome, usually requiring a file to be rewritten.

Although adding records to the end of a file is easy, inserting records into the file requires rewriting the entire file. Deleting records may also require a complete rewrite.

Sorting a large sequential file is a difficult process, considerably more difficult than sorting a random-access file.

A sequential file is like music stored on a cassette: first song, second song, third song, and so on. Songs can be different lengths. To get to song 7, you must move the tape through each song starting from song 1. To delete or add a song in the middle of the tape would require making a new tape. Imagine the difficulty of creating a tape in which the songs appear in an entirely different order.

In this book, sequential files are either unstructured or structured:

Unstructured

Free form; one record is one string. A record can be any length a string can be, either very short or quite long. You can even have an empty string (*" "*) as a record.

Structured

A record consists of two or more parts, called fields. Each record has the same fields. A field can be string or numeric. String fields can be any length up to the maximum length for a string (32,767 characters). Numeric fields are stored in ASCII format, one byte per digit. Numeric fields are limited in length by the numeric variables used to write to or read from the files.

Most of this chapter is devoted to the creation and use of an unstructured sequential file called NotePad. This file consists of free-form records that are, well, notes. A record can be anything you wish, as long as it is typed as a single string, including any ASCII characters — for example, notes about how to use QuickBASIC.

If you looked into the NotePad file, you might see

```
First Record:   This is the NotePad.Dat File.
Second Record:  NotePad.Dat is an unstructured sequential file.
Third Record:   Use it for notes about how to use QuickBASIC.
Fourth Record:  Each record is one string, commas OK, semicolons OK.
Fifth Record:   Call Bob about stuff for Chapter 8.
Sixth Record:   Call dentist for appointment soon.
```

For an example of a structured sequential file, recall Program 2-1, STATES AND ABBREVIATIONS, which found the two-letter abbreviation for a state. In Chapter 8, you will create a data file with the same information. Each record in the file will have two fields:

	First field	**Second field**
First Record:	Alabama	AL
Second Record:	Alaska	AK
Third Record:	American Samoa	AS
.	.	.
.	.	.
.	.	.
Last Record:	Wyoming	WY

In this file, each record has two fields. The first field (perhaps called *State$*) has a variable length. The second field (perhaps called *Abbrev$*) has a fixed length (two characters).

Another example of a structured file is inspired by browsing through a catalog of camping equipment. In this file, each record is divided into fields, as follows:

Page%	Page number, a numeric field
CatNum$	Catalog number, a string field
Description$	Brief description of item, a string field
Price	Price, a numeric field
Grams%	Weight in grams, a numeric field

Here are a few records:

Page%	*CatNum$*	*Description$*	*Price*	*Grams%*
5	33-972	Backpack	129.95	1824
10	47-865	Tent	199.95	3175
19	50-336	Sleeping bag	99.95	1653
25	40-027	Stove	41.95	379
27	40-115	Cooking kit	29.95	884
31	45-820	Compass	25.95	86
44	47-322	Swiss army knife	13.95	57

Now suppose the entire catalog is on a disk. It would be easy to write a program to browse through and assemble various configurations of gear, complete with total price and total weight. Since the catalog information usually changes only a few times a year, this would be an appropriate application for a sequential file.

Sequential files are stored as ASCII text files. This means that they can be used by word processors and other application programs that accept ASCII text. You could use a word processor to view or modify a sequential file.

The invention of the disk file in the 1950s made large random-access files possible. In a random-access file, any record can be obtained directly and quickly without reading any other file. If you want record 237, you can get it immediately, without first reading the first 236 records.

Random-access files are highly structured. All records must be the same length. You can set the record size. If you don't specify the record size, QuickBASIC assigns a default size of 128 characters.

Records can be divided into fields. Fields must have a fixed size. That is, corresponding fields in all records must be the same size. Fields must occur in the same order within each record.

Random-access files have advantages and disadvantages:

Advantages

Fast access to any record.

Easy to edit. You can change any record without rewriting the entire file.

Easier to delete or insert records than with sequential files.

Easier to sort than sequential files.

Disadvantages

Fixed record length and fixed field length. Some records or fields may be partially "empty."

Requires more work to design the file, specifying the structure and size of fields.

A random-access file of states and two-letter abbreviations would contain 60 records, one for each state or territory in the United States that has a two-letter abbreviation assigned to it. The longest name in the file is Federated States of Micronesia, which has 30 characters. Therefore, each record could contain two fields:

State$	Name of state or territory, 30 characters
Abbrev$	Two-letter abbreviation, 2 characters

This file would provide fast access to any state or territory, but would be inefficient in its use of space. For example, Iowa has only 4 letters but would occupy a 30-character field.

The use that you plan to make of information determines the type of data file that should be used. Keep in mind how often the file will be used to alter, add, or delete information. Generally, sequential files are best for data that doesn't change frequently. Random-access files are best for information that you will frequently change or for information to which you need fast access. When you finish this and the next two chapters, you should be able to choose and design the file type best suited to your application.

Naming a File

Sequential files are named just like any other kind of MS-DOS file and must conform to MS-DOS file-naming conventions. File names are limited to eight characters plus a three-letter extension. The following example, used in a program later in this chapter, contains seven characters plus a three-letter extension:

NotePad.Dat

The three-letter extension (Dat) was chosen to indicate that this is a data file.

File names may be composed of the following characters:

- The letters *a-z* (lower- or uppercase)

- The decimal digits 0-9

- These special characters: ( ) { } @ # $ % ^ & ! — _ ' / "

MS-DOS converts all lowercase letters in file names to uppercase. Therefore, do not rely on mixing lowercase and uppercase letters to distinguish between files.

Since a file name is essential to locating a file, make your file names as descriptive as possible, within the eight-character description. You might want to set up a separate file listing the rather terse file names and describing their contents. An unstructured sequential file can be used for this purpose. You might call this file Filenote.Dat. For example:

Record 1: NotePad.Dat holds notes of any type.

Record 2: States.Abr holds names of states and abbreviations.

Record 3: Food.Dat has nutritional information.

Record 4: Address.Dat has names, addresses, and phone numbers.

Record 5: Camping.Cat is a catalog of camping equipment.

Record 6: Scratch.Pad is for doodling and experimenting.

Once a file has been given a name, that name will remain the same unless you change it with the MS-DOS Rename command or a QuickBASIC NAME statement. The NAME statement has the form

```
NAME oldfilename AS newfilename
```

where *oldfilename* is the current name of the file, and *newfilename* is the new name to be given to the file.

You cannot rename a file with a new drive designation. The file you wish to rename must be closed before using a NAME statement. After a NAME statement is used, the file exists on the same disk and in the same disk space, but with a new name.

Creating a Sequential File

A simple example of a sequential file is a notepad file. Think of each record in the file as a 3- by 5-inch card. The records are not structured into fields. Hence the file is free form. On each card you might have a note on the use of QuickBASIC.

To create a file called NotePad.Dat you must

- Open the file so that information can be entered into it.

- Enter records from the keyboard and put them into the file.

- Close the file after all records have been entered.

To accomplish these steps, use the following QuickBASIC statements:

OPEN   To open the file
LINE INPUT   To obtain a record from the keyboard
PRINT #   To write the record into the file
CLOSE   To close the file

These statements are described below as they appear later in the program used to create a notepad file.

1. Create the new file and open it for output so that records can be written into the file. In the OPEN statement, the file is called Note-Pad.Dat and assigned the file number 1. Disk Drive B is selected.

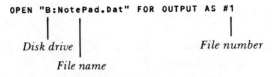

If you are using a hard disk, substitute its file specification in the OPEN statement.

Note that NotePad.Dat is used as the file name. This conforms to conventions for variable names and line labels. QuickBASIC recognizes NotePad.Dat and NOTEPAD.DAT as the same file name.

Caution: If there is already a file named NotePad.Dat on the disk, the output mode shown in the OPEN statement would erase the existing contents of NotePad.Dat before writing any new data to it. If you want to add new data to the end of an existing file without erasing what is already in it, be sure to use the append mode in the OPEN statement, as described later in this chapter.

Before you use an OPEN...FOR OUTPUT statement, check the directory of the disk to be used. Make sure you are using a new file name when creating a new file. The append mode is always a safe alternative to output mode since the append mode also allows you to create a file. If a file named NotePad.Dat does not reside on disk, opening it in the append mode makes a new file with that name.

2. The LINE INPUT statement is aptly suited for entering records in an unstructured sequential data file. LINE INPUT allows you to enter up to 255 characters, including punctuation marks. When the ENTER key is pressed, the entered information is stored as a single string (one record). The LINE INPUT statement looks like this:

```
LINE INPUT "> "; record$
```

3. The PRINT # statement is used to write one string as one record to a file, as shown below:

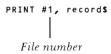

File number

In the next chapter, you will see another way to write information to a file, using the WRITE # statement.

4. After all records have been entered from the keyboard and written to a file, the file is closed.

```
CLOSE #1
```

The above statement closes file number 1, the only file used in the program in the next section to create the NotePad file.

A Program to Create the NotePad File

Program 7-1, CREATE A FILE, consists of a main program and a subprogram. The main program is short because it does only two things: It calls the subprogram (where the file is created) and it ends the program.

```
REM ** CREATE A FILE **
' Program 7-1  8/20/87

REM ** CALL FILE CREATOR **
CALL CreateFile

REM ** END PROGRAM **
END
```

The subprogram CreateFile creates a free-form data file to hold records that you enter from the keyboard. Each record is restricted to the number of characters allowed by the LINE INPUT statement — up to 255 characters.

The subprogram uses the VIEW PRINT statement to create a text viewport, restricting the area where output appears. The format is

```
VIEW PRINT [topline TO bottomline]
```

where *topline* is the first line of the viewport, and *bottomline* is the last line of the viewport.

Information contained in a PRINT statement is displayed in the normal way if it is executed before a VIEW PRINT statement. The CreateFile subprogram prints the instructions for its use before a VIEW PRINT statement is used. The instructions are placed in a fixed area at the bottom of the screen.

Viewport

Information in this area scrolls

Instructions in this area

```
DECLARE SUB CreateFile ()
REM ** CREATE A FILE **
' Program 7-1  8/19/87

REM ** CALL FILE CREATOR **
CALL CreateFile
              Dim TEXT$ (5)

REM ** END PROGRAM **
END
SUB CreateFile STATIC
' Create NotePad.Dat file.  Each record is a string.

   ' Put instructions in lines 21 to 25.
   Text$(1) = STRING$(74, 196)
   Text$(2) = "Create a new file called NotePad.Dat."
   Text$(3) = "Put the data disk in drive B and press any key."
   Text$(4) = "At the prompt (>), type one record and press ENTER."
   Text$(5) = "To end the file, press ENTER without typing data."
   CLS
   FOR row% = 1 TO 5
     LOCATE row% + 20, 3: PRINT Text$(row%);
   NEXT row%

   ' Wait for a keypress to begin.
   LOCATE 10, 28: PRINT "Press a key to begin."
   anykey$ = INPUT$(1)
   CLS 2

   ' Define rows 1 to 20 as a viewport.  Used for entering records.
   VIEW PRINT 1 TO 20

   ' Open the file NotePad.Dat on drive B for output as file #1.
   OPEN "B:NotePad.Dat" FOR OUTPUT AS #1

   ' Enter records from keyboard and write to file.
   DO
     LINE INPUT "> "; record$
     PRINT
     IF record$ = "" THEN EXIT DO
     PRINT #1, record$
   LOOP

   ' Close the file and end the subprogram.
   CLOSE #1

END SUB
```

Program 7-1. *CREATE A FILE*

Lines 21 through 25 of the display, at the bottom of the screen, are outside the viewport area. These lines stay fixed on the screen and are not affected by lines printed in the viewport, which is set by a VIEW PRINT statement.

```
VIEW PRINT 1 TO 20
```

After the VIEW PRINT statement is executed, all output to the screen appears in the area defined by the topline (1) and bottomline (20) of the VIEW PRINT statement.

The CreateFile subprogram opens the NotePad.Dat file for output on Drive B. Records are entered, one at a time, in a DO...LOOP using LINE INPUT, and are written to the file by a PRINT # statement. If the ENTER key is pressed without entering a record at the LINE INPUT prompt (>), an exit is made from the loop.

```
      .
      .
      .
OPEN "B:NotePad.Dat" FOR OUTPUT AS #1
      .
      .
      .
DO
   LINE INPUT "> "; record$
   PRINT
   IF record$ = "" THEN EXIT DO
   PRINT #1, record$
LOOP
```

When an exit is made from the DO...LOOP, the file is closed and the subprogram ends.

```
      .
      .
      .
   CLOSE #1
END SUB
```

Control passes back to the main program.

Using the Sequential File Creator

To use the sequential file creator, you must hook the main program to the subprogram. First enter the main program. Save it to disk, if you

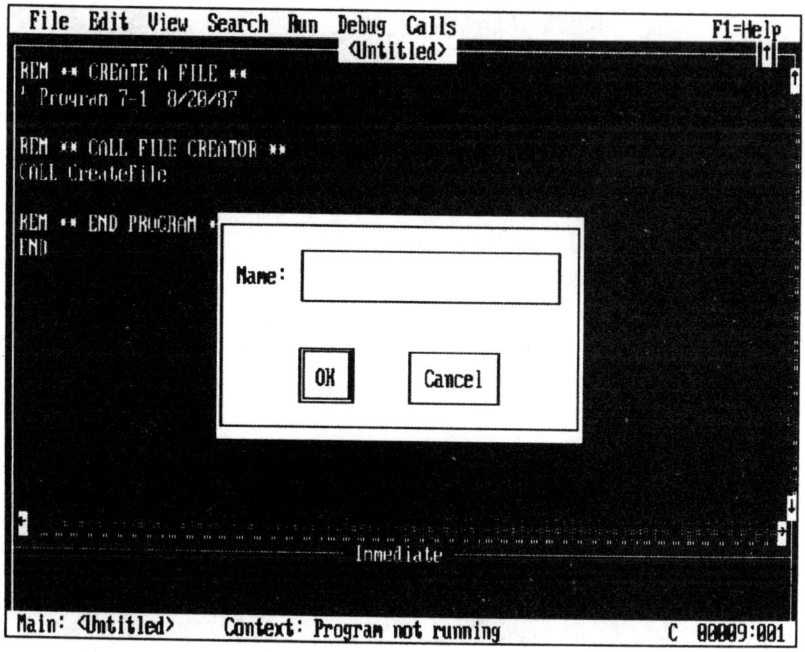

Figure 7-1. *New SUB... dialog box*

wish, as **CREATEFI.BAS**. Then enter the subprogram using these steps:

1. Access the Edit menu and move the highlight down to the New SUB... command.

2. Press ENTER when New SUB... is highlighted. A dialog box is displayed, as shown in Figure 7-1.

3. Type in the name of the subprogram, CreateFile, and press ENTER. The screen shown in Figure 7-2 is displayed. QuickBASIC automatically provides the opening and closing lines of the subprogram.

4. Finish entering the first line of the subprogram:

```
SUB CreateFile STATIC
```

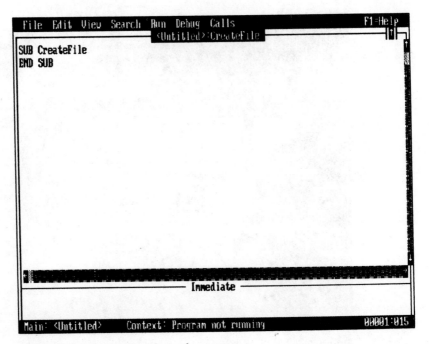

Figure 7-2. *Start and end of subprogram*

5. Enter the other lines of the subprogram:

```
SUB CreateFile STATIC
' Create NotePad.Dat file.  Each record is a string.

  ' Put instructions in lines 21 to 25.
  Text$(1) = STRING$(74,196)                'separates screen areas
  Text$(2) = "Create a new file called NotePad.Dat."
  Text$(3) = "Put the data disk in drive B and press any key."
  Text$(4) = "At the prompt (>), type one record and press ENTER."
  Text$(5) = "To end the file, press ENTER without typing data."
  CLS
  FOR row% = 1 TO 5
    LOCATE row% + 20, 3: PRINT Text$(row%);
  NEXT row%

  ' Define rows 1 to 20 as a viewport.  Used for entering records.
  VIEW PRINT 1 TO 20

  ' Open the file NotePad.Dat on drive B for output as file #1.
  OPEN "B:NotePad.Dat" FOR OUTPUT AS #1
```

```
' Enter records from keyboard and write to file.
DO
  LINE INPUT "> "; record$
  PRINT
  IF record$ = "" THEN EXIT DO
  PRINT #1, record$
LOOP

' Close the file and end the subprogram.
CLOSE #1

END SUB
```

6. When you have entered the complete subprogram, access the File menu. Move the highlight down to the Save All command and press ENTER. The subprogram CreateFile is saved along with the main program as Program 7-1, CREATE A FILE.

When the program has been saved, the subprogram remains on the screen. Access the View menu. While the highlight is on the SUBs... command, press ENTER. The dialog box shown in Figure 7-3 is displayed.

From the dialog box, you can choose whether you want to view and edit the main program, CREATEFI.BAS, or the subprogram, CreateFile. While the highlight is on CREATEFI.BAS, press the ENTER key. QuickBASIC returns to the View window with the main program displayed.

Notice the first line of the main program. QuickBASIC has automatically inserted the line

```
DECLARE SUB CreateFile ()
```

The DECLARE statement allows your program to call procedures that are defined later in the module or in another module altogether.

The main program and the subprogram are now ready to use. Access the Run menu with the Start command highlighted and press ENTER. The screen shown in Figure 7-4 is displayed.

Type in the notes shown in Table 7-1. Press ENTER only after each complete record (which may continue onto more than one line). The number of characters printed on your screen will not correspond with the lines in the table.

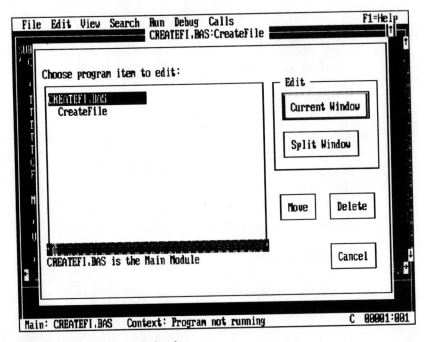

Figure 7-3. *SUBs... dialog box*

When you have entered the notes in Table 7-1, press the ENTER key at the last prompt without entering text. The subprogram then leaves the DO...LOOP and closes the file. Control passes back to the driver program, which is considered the main module. Execution ends there with the END statement.

Files are created to be used. The next step is to write a subprogram .that will read the records from the data file that has been created.

Reading the NotePad File

Once again, a short main program is used to access a new subprogram called ScanFile. The main program calls the subprogram and ends the program. Enter the main program and save it to the same disk as Program 7-1. Name it SCANFI.BAS.

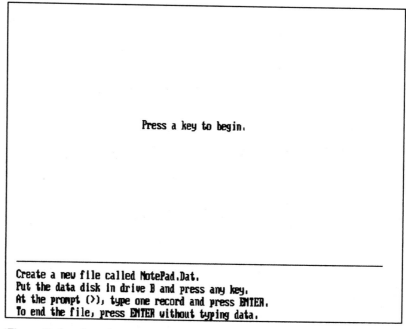

Figure 7-4. *Opening output screen for Program 7-1*

```
REM ** SCAN A FILE **
' Program 7-2  8/21/87

REM ** CALL FILE SCANNER **
CALL ScanFile

REM ** END PROGRAM **
END
```

The subprogram ScanFile prints instructions on lines 21 through 25 on the display. It then sets up a viewport (lines 1 through 20) for scanning the file. The subprogram then opens NotePad.Dat (the data file previously created) for input as file number 1:

```
OPEN "B:NotePad.Dat" FOR INPUT AS #1
```

LINE INPUT # is used in a DO...LOOP to read one record at a time from the file. The records are printed one at a time on the screen. Press any key except Q to scan the next record. The DO...LOOP has

File names in OPEN statements are string expressions.

OPEN statements may contain letters *a-z*, digits 0-9, and special characters.

Special characters are ( ) { } @ # $ % ^ & ! – _ ' / "

The OPEN statement can also contain a disk drive specification.

Your program can work with data files on another drive.

An OPEN statement with FOR OUTPUT is used to create a new file.

APPEND can be used in an OPEN statement to add records.

APPEND adds records to the end of the file.

An existing file is read by using FOR INPUT in an OPEN statement.

You may enter punctuation in a LINE INPUT statement. You may include characters that are delimiters in a regular INPUT statement (such as commas).

LINE INPUT # reads characters in a sequential file.

Use the CLOSE statement within a program to close a file.

CLOSE frees the file number for use by another OPEN statement.

Table 7-1. *Notes to Enter in CreateFile*

two possible exits:

- Press the Q key to force an exit.

- When all records have been read and you press a key other than Q, the End Of File (EOF) marker is encountered. This will cause an exit because of the DO UNTIL EOF(1) statement at the top of the loop:

```
    .
    .
    .
DO UNTIL EOF(1)
    LINE INPUT #1, record$
    PRINT record$
    PRINT
    nextkey$ = INPUT$(1)
    IF UCASE$(nextkey$) = "Q" THEN EXIT DO
LOOP
```

When an exit is made from the loop, the file is closed and the subprogram ends. Control passes back to the main program, where it also ends.

Using the Sequential File Scanner

If you have not yet entered the main program, do so now.

If you entered the main program previously and it is not now in the View window, access it from the Open Program... command of the File menu. When the main program is in the View window, you are ready to enter the subprogram.

Select the New SUB... command from the Edit menu. Press ENTER and the dialog box shown in Figure 7-1 appears. Type in the name **ScanFile** and press ENTER. A mostly blank screen appears. The start and end lines of the new subprogram are near the top of the screen:

```
SUB ScanFile_
END SUB
```

Type in the rest of the ScanFile subprogram, as shown below. When you have finished, use the Save All command from the File menu to save the ScanFile subprogram along with the main program.

```
SUB ScanFile STATIC
' Scan the NotePad.Dat File, one record at a time

   ' Put instructions in line 21 to 25.
   Text$(1) = STRING$(74,196)
   Text$(2) = "Scan the Note Pad file, one record at a time."
   Text$(3) = "Put the data disk in drive B and press any key."
   Text$(4) = "Starts with the 1st record in the viewport."
   Text$(5) = "Press space bar to get next record, Q to quit."
   CLS
   FOR row% = 1 TO 5
      LOCATE row% + 20, 3: PRINT Text$(row%);
   NEXT row%

   ' Define rows 1 to 20 as a viewport, used for scanning records.
   VIEW PRINT 1 TO 20

   ' Open the file NotePad.Dat on drive B for input as file #1.
   OPEN "B:NotePad.Dat" FOR INPUT AS #1

   ' Read one record each time a key other than Q is pressed.
   DO UNTIL EOF(1)
      LINE INPUT #1, record$
      PRINT record$
      PRINT
      nextkey$ = INPUT$(1)
      IF UCASE$(nextkey$) = "Q" THEN EXIT DO
   LOOP

   ' Close the file and end the subprogram.
   CLOSE #1

END SUB
```

```
DECLARE SUB ScanFile ()
REM ** SCAN A FILE **
' Program 7-2  8/21/87

REM ** CALL FILE SCANNER **
CALL ScanFile

REM ** END PROGRAM **
END
SUB ScanFile STATIC
' Scan the NotePad.Dat File, one record at a time.

    ' Put instructions in lines 21 to 25.
    Text$(1) = STRING$(74, 196)
    Text$(2) = "Scan the Note Pad file, one record at a time."
    Text$(3) = "Put the data disk in drive B and press any key."
    Text$(4) = "Starts with the 1st record in the viewport."
    Text$(5) = "Press space bar to get next record, Q to quit."
    CLS
    FOR row% = 1 TO 5
      LOCATE row% + 20, 3: PRINT Text$(row%);
    NEXT row%

    ' Define rows 1 to 20 as a viewport, used for scanning records.
    VIEW PRINT 1 TO 20

    ' Wait for a key press to begin.
    LOCATE 10, 28: PRINT "Press a key to begin."
    anykey$ = INPUT$(1)
    CLS 2                                   'Clears only viewport

    ' Open the file NotePad.Dat on drive B for input as file #1.
    OPEN "B:NotePad.Dat" FOR INPUT AS #1

    ' Read one record each time a key other than Q is pressed.
    DO UNTIL EOF(1)
      LINE INPUT #1, record$
      PRINT record$
      PRINT
      nextkey$ = INPUT$(1)
      IF UCASE$(nextkey$) = "Q" THEN EXIT DO
    LOOP

    ' Close the file and end the subprogram
    CLOSE #1

END SUB
```

Program 7-2.   *SCAN A FILE*

This completes Program 7-2, SCAN A FILE.

When the subprogram has been saved with the main program, access the Start command of the Run menu and press ENTER. A screen similar to the screen shown in Figure 7-4 is displayed. Press any key

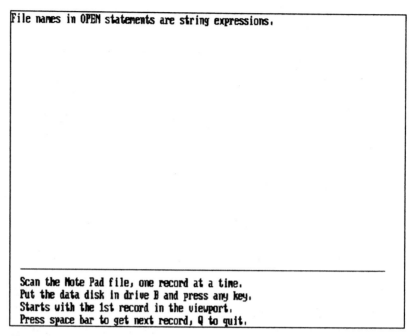

Figure 7-1. *First note of Program 7-2*

and the display shown in Figure 7-5 appears.

Press any key and the next record is printed on the screen. Each time you press a key other than Q, a new record is added to the display. When you have scanned as many records as you want, press Q to quit. Otherwise, keep going until all the records have been read.

You now have programs to create and to scan an unstructured sequential data file. Next, you need a program to send the records to your printer for printing a hard copy.

Printing the NotePad File

The main program to output the records of the NotePad file to your printer is much like that used with Programs 7-1 and 7-2. It looks like the program on the next page.

```
REM ** PRINT A FILE **
' Program 7-3   8/21/87

REM ** CALL PRINTER **
CALL PrintFile

REM ** END PROGRAM **
END
```

Enter the main program and save it as PRINTFI.BAS.

Using the Sequential File Printer

The subprogram PrintFile does not halt after printing each record. It keeps printing until the end of the file is reached or until you hold down the Q key to quit. The records are printed on the screen as well as being sent to the printer. Enter the subprogram in the usual manner and save it, along with the main program, to the same disk on which the previous data file subprograms are saved.

Study Program 7-3, PRINT A FILE. Notice the similarities and differences when compared to Program 7-2.

Caution: Be sure your printer is on and ready to print before running the program.

When your printer is ready, access the Start command of the Run menu. Press ENTER and your printer is on its way. Notice that the records are printed on the screen as well as being sent to the printer. Figure 7-6 shows a printed version of the notes shown in Table 7-1.

Appending the NotePad File

As you learn new things about QuickBASIC, you will probably want to add notes to the NotePad file. This can be done by using the append mode in an OPEN statement:

```
OPEN "B:NotePad.Dat" FOR APPEND AS #1
```

```
DECLARE SUB PrintFile ()
REM ** PRINT A FILE **
' Program 7-3  8/21/87

REM ** CALL PRINTER **
CALL PrintFile

REM ** END PROGRAM **
END
SUB PrintFile STATIC
' Print NotePad.Dat File

  ' Put instructions in lines 21 to 25.
  Text$(1) = STRING$(74, 196)
  Text$(2) = "Print the Note Pad File to the printer."
  Text$(3) = "Put the data disk in drive B."
  Text$(4) = "Make sure the printer is ready.  Press any key."
  Text$(5) = "To interrupt, hold down the Q key."
  CLS
  FOR row% = 1 TO 5
    LOCATE row% + 20, 3: PRINT Text$(row%);
  NEXT row%

  ' Define rows 1 to 20 as a viewport.  Records displayed during printing.
  VIEW PRINT 1 TO 20

  ' Wait for a key press to begin.
  LOCATE 10, 28: PRINT "Press a key to begin."
  anykey$ = INPUT$(1)
  CLS 2                                  'Clears only viewport

  ' Open the file NotePad.Dat on drive B for input as file #1.
  OPEN "B:NotePad.Dat" FOR INPUT AS #1

  ' Read records, print to screen, print to printer.
  DO UNTIL EOF(1)
    kbd$ = INKEY$: IF UCASE$(kbd$) = "Q" THEN EXIT DO
    LINE INPUT #1, record$
    PRINT record$
    LPRINT record$
    LPRINT
  LOOP

  ' Close file and end subprogram
  CLOSE #1

END SUB
```

Program 7-3. *PRINT A FILE*

The append mode will automatically set the file's pointer to the end of the NotePad file so that the records you enter will be added to the end of the file.

```
File names in OPEN statements are string expressions.

OPEN statements may contain letters a-z, digits 0-9, and special characters.

Special characters are: ( ) { } @ # $ % ^ & ! - _ ' / "

The OPEN statement can also contain a disk drive specification.

Your program can work with files on another drive.

An OPEN statement with FOR OUTPUT is used to create a new file.

APPEND can be used in an OPEN statement to add records.

APPEND adds records to the end of the file.

An existing file is read by using FOR INPUT in an OPEN statement.

You may enter punctuation in a LINE INPUT statement.  You may include characters
   that are delimiters in a regular INPUT statement (such as commas).

LINE INPUT # reads characters in a sequential file

LINE INPUT # reads a line at a time from a text file.

Use the CLOSE statement within a program to close a file.

CLOSE frees the file number for use by another OPEN statement.
```

Figure 7-6.   *Printed output of Program 7-3*

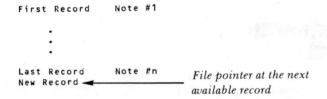

The main program is similar to the previous ones. The subprogram AppendFile is similar to the CreateFile subprogram of Program 7-1. In fact, either program can be used to create a new file.

Using Sequential File Append

Enter only the main program of Program 7-4, APPEND TO A FILE. Save it as APPENDFI.BAS. Then use the New SUB... command from

```
DECLARE SUB AppendFile ()
REM ** APPEND TO A FILE **
' Program 7-4   8/22/87

REM ** CALL APPEND **
CALL AppendFile

REM ** END PROGRAM **
END
SUB AppendFile STATIC
' Append information to the NotePad.Dat file.

  ' Put instructions in lines 21 to 25
  Text$(1) = STRING$(74, 196)
  Text$(2) = "Append records to the Note Pad file."
  Text$(3) = "Put data disk in drive B and press any key."
  Text$(4) = "At the prompt (>), type one record and press the ENTER key."
  Text$(5) = "To end the file, press ENTER without typing data."
  CLS
  FOR row% = 1 TO 5
    LOCATE row% + 20, 3: PRINT Text$(row%);
  NEXT row%

  ' Define rows 1 to 20 as a viewport.  Used for appending records.
  VIEW PRINT 1 TO 20

  ' Wait for a key press to begin.
  LOCATE 10, 28: PRINT "Press a key to begin."
  anykey$ = INPUT$(1)
  CLS 2                                  'Clears only viewport

  ' Open the file NotePad.Dat on drive B for append as file #1.
  OPEN "B:NotePad.Dat" FOR APPEND AS #1

  ' Enter records from keyboard and append to file.
  DO
    LINE INPUT "> "; record$
    PRINT
    IF record$ = "" THEN EXIT DO
    PRINT #1, record$
  LOOP

  ' Close the file and end the subprogram.
  CLOSE #1

END SUB
```

Program 7-4. *APPEND TO A FILE*

the Edit menu to enter the subprogram as you have done with the other subprograms. Name the subprogram AppendFile. Save it, along with the main program, with the Save All command from the File menu.

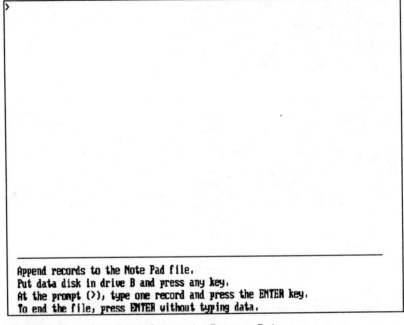

```
>
```

```
Append records to the Note Pad file.
Put data disk in drive B and press any key.
At the prompt (>), type one record and press the ENTER key.
To end the file, press ENTER without typing data.
```

Figure 7-7.   *Append record screen for Program 7-4*

Run the program from the Start command of the Run menu. The similar display shown in Figure 7-4 appears. Press any key and the screen displayed in Figure 7-7 appears, ready for you to add new records.

Notice the similarity to Figure 7-4. Type in any new notes. When you have added all the notes you want, press ENTER at the input prompt without entering any text.

With the completion of Program 7-4, you have the following programs to manipulate text in an unstructured sequential file:

To create a file:	Program 7-1, CREATEFI.BAS
To scan a file:	Program 7-2, SCANFI.BAS
To print a file:	Program 7-3, PRINTFI.BAS
To append to a file:	Program 7-4, APPENDFI.BAS

Each program performs a distinct function. However, the programs are related: They all work with the same disk file, NotePad.Dat. It would be convenient to tie them together into a single program that provides a choice of which function to perform. The next section describes one way to do this.

Making an Integrated NotePad File

You have been learning many tools in past chapters. Combining the four NotePad file programs discussed in this chapter will give you a chance to exercise some of the editing skills learned in Chapter 5. To create an integrated notepad program, you need a main driver program and the four subprograms used in Programs 7-1, 7-2, 7-3, and 7-4.

Each of these four programs has a short main program that calls the necessary subprogram. The main program for an integrated notepad will be a little longer. You need a way to make a selection from a list of functions that the program can perform. A menu is a good way to display the selections. Items on the menu are

```
        Create a File

        Scan a File

        Print a File

        Append to a File

        Quit
```

This simple menu of five items can be displayed using the following strings:

Menu$(1) = "Create a File"
Menu$(2) = "Scan a File"
Menu$(3) = "Print a File"
Menu$(4) = "Append to File"
Menu$(5) = "Quit"

You can print the text and draw a simple border around the selections. If you wish, you can get fancy and add color and even graphics.

A short message should tell how to use the menu:

Menu$(6) = "Type first letter of your choice (C, S, P, A, or Q)."

The selection made should call the appropriate subprogram. QuickBASIC's **SELECT CASE** structure is ideal for this task:

```
pictkey$ = UCASE$(INPUT$(1))                    'gets the menu choice
                                                 (C, S, P, A, or Q)
SELECT CASE pictkey$
   CASE "C"
     CALL CreateFile
   CASE "S"
     CALL ScanFile
   CASE "P"
     CALL PrintFile
   CASE "A"
     CALL AppendFile
   CASE "Q"
     END
   CASE ELSE
     LOCATE 21, 5: PRINT "Entry not a C, S, P, A, or Q."
     LOCATE WW, 5: PRINT "Press any key to try again."
     reptkey$ = INPUT$(1)
END SELECT
```

The menu and **SELECT CASE** compose the major part of the main program shown here. Enter the main program. Then save it as NOTEFI.BAS.

Putting the Pieces Together

After saving the program, you will need to merge each of the previous programs—CREATEFI.BAS, SCANFI.BAS, PRINTFI.BAS, and APPENDFI.BAS—and perform some editing operations.

The subprograms CreateFile, ScanFile, PrintFile, and Append-File are needed for the integrated program. However, the individual main programs attached to them need to be deleted. The steps to be performed for each of the four programs are

1. Merge the previous individual program with the new combined main program.

2. Move the DECLARE statement of the merged program to the top of the integrated main program.

3. Delete the short main program that previously called the subprogram.

Merging CREATEFI.BAS into NOTEFI.BAS

With the main program of NOTEFI.BAS in the View window, move the cursor down to a position two lines below the last line of the program:

```
        .
        .
        .
END SELECT
CLS 2: GOTO start
```

 *cursor*

This is the place where CREATEFI.BAS will be merged into NOTEFI.BAS.

With the cursor at the position shown above, access the Merge... command from the File menu. Press ENTER and a dialog box appears. Type in the name **CREATEFI**, as shown in Figure 7-8. Press the ENTER key to merge the program.

CREATEFI.BAS has been merged at the bottom of the main program, NOTEFI.BAS. Now, it's time to apply the editing skills you acquired in Chapter 5.

Notice that the DECLARE statement for the subprogram is below the main program.

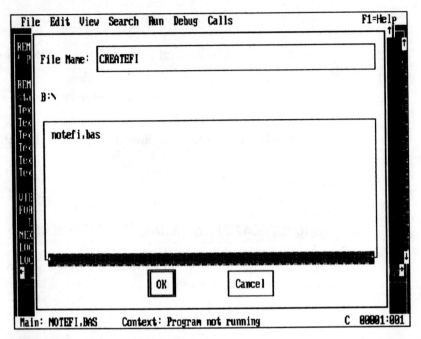

Figure 7-8. *Merge... dialog box*

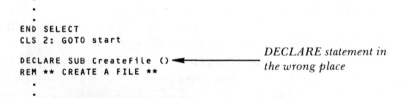

The DECLARE statement needs to be moved to the top of the file. Do you remember the Cut command of the Edit menu from Chapter 5? If you do, use it to cut the DECLARE statement. Then proceed to step 3 below. The Cut command moves the selected text to the Clipboard.

If you don't remember how to use the Cut command, follow these steps:

1. Move the cursor to the letter *D* of the DECLARE statement and press the SHIFT+down arrow key combination to highlight (select) the statement:

```
DECLARE SUB CreateFile ()
```

2. While the statement is highlighted, go to the Edit menu. Select the Cut command and press ENTER. Presto! The line is gone from the program. It has been magically transported to the Clipboard where you can't see it.

3. Press CTRL+HOME to move to the top of the file (the first line of the main program):

```
REM ** NOTE PAD WITH MENU **
' Program 7-5  8/22/87
       .
       .
       .
```

4. Access the Paste command from the Edit menu and press ENTER. Presto again! The DECLARE statement is transported — this time from the Clipboard to the top line of the main program:

```
DECLARE SUB CreateFile ()
REM ** NOTE PAD WITH MENU **
' Program 7-5  8/22/87
       .
       .
       .
```

One more editing task remains: to delete the merged main program of CREATEFI.BAS. Press the PGDN key twice to bring the merged program into view. Now move the cursor down to the R of REM ** CREATE A FILE **. Press SHIFT+down arrow eight times. The undesired lines should all be highlighted.

```
REM ** CREATE A FILE **
' Program 7-1  8/20/87

REM ** CALL FILE CREATOR **
CALL CreateFile

REM ** END PROGRAM **
END
```

Go to the Edit menu once more while the lines shown are highlighted. Select the Clear command and press ENTER. Zap! The lines are gone from the display. They did not go to the Clipboard this time; they are gone forever.

The same process needs to be repeated for each of the other three programs: SCANFI.BAS, PRINTFI.BAS, and APPENDFI.BAS:

1. Merge the program.

2. Move the DECLARE statement to the top of the file.

3. Delete the balance of the merged program.

When you finish these steps for each program, you have the complete Program 7-5, NOTEPAD WITH MENU. The four necessary subprograms are now included. Use Save All from the File menu to save the complete package.

```
DECLARE SUB AppendFile ()
DECLARE SUB PrintFile ()
DECLARE SUB ScanFile ()
DECLARE SUB CreateFile ()
REM ** NOTEPAD WITH MENU **
' Program 7-5  8/22/87

REM ** SET UP MENU **
start:
Menu$(1) = "Create a File"
Menu$(2) = "Scan a File"
Menu$(3) = "Print a File"
Menu$(4) = "Append to a File"
Menu$(5) = "Quit"
Menu$(6) = "Type first letter of choice (C, S, P, A, or Q)"
```

Program 7-5. *NOTEPAD WITH MENU*

```
VIEW PRINT 1 TO 25: CLS
FOR row% = 1 TO 5
  LOCATE row% + 5, 25: PRINT Menu$(row%);
NEXT row%
LOCATE 21, 5: PRINT Menu$(6)
LOCATE 4, 20: PRINT CHR$(218); STRING$(29, 196); CHR$(191);
LOCATE 12, 20: PRINT CHR$(192); STRING$(29, 196); CHR$(217);
FOR row% = 5 TO 11
  LOCATE row%, 20: PRINT CHR$(179);
  LOCATE row%, 50: PRINT CHR$(179);
NEXT row%

REM ** ACCESS THE MENU CHOICE **
pictkey$ = UCASE$(INPUT$(1))

SELECT CASE pictkey$
  CASE "C"
    CALL CreateFile
  CASE "S"
    CALL ScanFile
  CASE "P"
    CALL PrintFile
  CASE "A"
    CALL AppendFile
  CASE "Q"
    END
  CASE ELSE
    LOCATE 21, 5: PRINT "Entry not a C, S, P, A, or Q."
    LOCATE 22, 5: PRINT "Press any key to try again."
    reptkey$ = INPUT$(1)
END SELECT
CLS 2: GOTO start
SUB AppendFile STATIC
' Append information to the NotePad.Dat file.

  ' Put instructions in lines 21 to 25
  Text$(1) = STRING$(74, 196)
  Text$(2) = "Append records to the Note Pad file."
  Text$(3) = "Put data disk in drive B and press any key."
  Text$(4) = "At the prompt (>), type one record and press the ENTER key."
  Text$(5) = "To end the file, press ENTER without typing data."
  CLS
  FOR row% = 1 TO 5
    LOCATE row% + 20, 3: PRINT Text$(row%);
  NEXT row%

  ' Define rows 1 to 20 as a viewport.  Used for appending records.
  VIEW PRINT 1 TO 20

  ' Wait for a key press to begin.
  LOCATE 10, 28: PRINT "Press a key to begin."
  anykey$ = INPUT$(1)
  CLS 2                                'Clears only viewport

  ' Open the file NotePad.Dat on drive B for append as file #1.
  OPEN "B:NotePad.Dat" FOR APPEND AS #1
```

Program 7-5. *NOTEPAD WITH MENU (continued)*

```
' Enter records from keyboard and append to file.
DO
   LINE INPUT "> "; record$
   PRINT
   IF record$ = "" THEN EXIT DO
   PRINT #1, record$
LOOP

' Close the file and end the subprogram.
CLOSE #1

END SUB
SUB CreateFile STATIC
' Create NotePad.Dat file.  Each record is a string.

   ' Put instructions in lines 21 to 25.
   Text$(1) = STRING$(74, 196)
   Text$(2) = "Create a new file called NotePad.Dat."
   Text$(3) = "Put the data disk in drive B and press any key."
   Text$(4) = "At the prompt (>), type one record and press ENTER."
   Text$(5) = "To end the file, press ENTER without typing data."
   CLS
   FOR row% = 1 TO 5
      LOCATE row% + 20, 3: PRINT Text$(row%);
   NEXT row%

   ' Define rows 1 to 20 as a viewport.  Used for entering records.
   VIEW PRINT 1 TO 20

   ' Wait for a key press to begin.
   LOCATE 10, 20: PRINT "Press a key to begin."
   anykey$ = INPUT$(1)
   CLS 2                                    'Clears only viewport

   ' Open the file NotePad.Dat on drive B for output as file #1.
   OPEN "B:NotePad.Dat" FOR OUTPUT AS #1

   ' Enter records from keyboard and write to file.
   DO
      LINE INPUT "> "; record$
      PRINT
      IF record$ = "" THEN EXIT DO
      PRINT #1, record$
   LOOP

   ' Close the file and end the subprogram.
   CLOSE #1

END SUB
SUB PrintFile STATIC
' Print NotePad.Dat File

   ' Put instructions in lines 21 to 25.
   Text$(1) = STRING$(74, 196)
   Text$(2) = "Print the Note Pad File to the printer."
   Text$(3) = "Put the data disk in drive B."
```

Program 7-5. *NOTEPAD WITH MENU (continued)*

You hold a special place in my Heart

I Love You

© 1991 BOB SIEMON DESIGNS, INC.

```
Text$(4) = "Make sure the printer is ready.  Press any key."
Text$(5) = "To interrupt, hold down the Q key."
CLS
FOR row% = 1 TO 5
  LOCATE row% + 20, 3: PRINT Text$(row%);
NEXT row%

' Define rows 1 to 20 as a viewport.  Records displayed during printing.
VIEW PRINT 1 'TO 20

' Wait for a key press to begin.
LOCATE 10, 28: PRINT "Press a key to begin."
anykey$ = INPUT$(1)
CLS 2                                    'Clears only viewport

' Open the file NotePad.Dat on drive B for input as file #1.
OPEN "B:NotePad.Dat" FOR INPUT AS #1

' Read records, print to screen, print to printer.
DO UNTIL EOF(1)
  kbd$ = INKEY$: IF UCASE$(kbd$) = "Q" THEN EXIT DO
  LINE INPUT #1, record$
  PRINT record$
  LPRINT record$
  LPRINT
LOOP

' Close file and end subprogram
CLOSE #1

END SUB
SUB ScanFile STATIC
' Scan the NotePad.Dat File, one record at a time.

  ' Put instructions in lines 21 to 25.
  Text$(1) = STRING$(74, 196)
  Text$(2) = "Scan the Note Pad file, one record at a time."
  Text$(3) = "Put the data disk in drive B and press any key."
  Text$(4) = "Starts with the 1st record in the viewport."
  Text$(5) = "Press space bar to get next record, Q to quit."
  CLS
  FOR row% = 1 TO 5
    LOCATE row% + 20, 3: PRINT Text$(row%);
  NEXT row%

  ' Define rows 1 to 20 as a viewport, used for scanning records.
  VIEW PRINT 1 TO 20

  ' Wait for a key press to begin.
  LOCATE 10, 28: PRINT "Press any key to begin."
  anykey$ = INPUT$(1)
  CLS 2                                    'Clears only viewport

  ' Open the file NotePad.Dat on drive B for input as file #1.
  OPEN "B:NotePad.Dat" FOR INPUT AS #1
```

Program 7-5. *NOTEPAD WITH MENU (continued)*

```
' Read one record each time a key other than Q is pressed.
DO UNTIL EOF(1)
   LINE INPUT #1, record$
   PRINT record$
   PRINT
   nextkey$ = INPUT$(1)
   IF UCASE$(nextkey$) = "Q" THEN EXIT DO
LOOP

' Close the file and end the subprogram
CLOSE #1

END SUB
```

Program 7-5.   *NOTEPAD WITH MENU (continued)*

Review

This chapter presented a general discussion of data files, followed by specific information on sequential data files. The major portion of the chapter was devoted to unstructured sequential data files.

Detailed information was given on the construction of subprograms to perform four functions of an unstructured sequential data file called NotePad. The functions were

- To create the NotePad file

- To scan records in the NotePad file

- To print records in the NotePad file

- To append notes to the NotePad File

The chapter concluded with the use of editing skills to merge the four programs containing the subprograms into one integrated program. The integrated program performs any of the four functions selected from a menu.

8 Sequential Structured Files

The previous chapter discussed and demonstrated the use of sequential files that are not structured, in which each record is a single string. This chapter discusses structured sequential files, in which each record consists of two or more fields. You will use several file statements and functions, including these:

Opening and closing files: OPEN   CLOSE
Putting information into a file: PRINT #   WRITE #
Reading information from a file:
INPUT #   INPUT$ LINE INPUT #
Getting the length of a file: LOF

The chapter begins with a simple file; each record consists of two fields, both strings. A program is shown to create and scan this file. Then three variations illustrate different ways of reading information from a structured file. The chapter concludes with some short programs that you can experiment with to learn more about how output statements send information to data files and how input statements receive information from data files.

States and Abbreviations

Way back in Chapter 2, you saw a GW-BASIC program to look up the two-letter postal abbreviation for any state or territory of the United States. This is a good sequential file application. The file is short and the information is not likely to change.

Program 8-1, STATES AND ABBREVIATIONS, creates and scans a sequential file of states and territories, along with the two-letter postal abbreviation for each one. Each record has two fields:

State$ The name of a state or territory. It is a variable-length field with field length ranging from 4 characters (Iowa, Utah) to 30 characters (Federated States of Micronesia).

Abbr$ The postal abbreviation. It is a fixed-length field that is 2 characters long (IA, UT).

If you saved Program 7-2, SCAN A FILE, you can load it, delete its main program, edit the subprogram, and add the main program of Program 8-1. This will save lots of time and typing. If you didn't save Program 7-2, enter both the main program and subprogram of Program 8-1.

The information to be put into the file is in DATA statements in the main program:

```
DATA Alabama,AL,  Alaska,AK,  American Samoa,AS
DATA Arizona,AZ,  Arkansas,AR,  California,CA
DATA Colorado,CO,  Connecticut,CT,  Deleware,DE
   .
   .
   .
DATA Wisconsin,WI,  Wyoming,WY
DATA End of data,ZZ
```

If you enter this program, feel free to use only part of the data base, perhaps only three or four DATA statements — the ones you want. However, be sure to include the last DATA statement, the one that looks like this:

```
DATA End of data,ZZ
```

```
DECLARE SUB ScanFile ()
REM ** STATES AND ABBREVIATIONS - CREATE & PROOF FILE **
' Program 8-1  8/25/87

REM ** CREATE THE FILE **
' Create StateAbr.Dat file with state names and abbreviations
' Sequential file with two fields: State$, Abbr$

OPEN "B:StateAbr.Dat" FOR OUTPUT AS #1

DO
  READ State$, Abbr$                  'Read data for one record.
  IF Abbr$ = "ZZ" THEN EXIT DO        'Exit on end of data record.
  WRITE #1, State$, Abbr$             'Print one record to file.
LOOP

CLOSE #1

DATA  Alabama,AL,  Alaska,AK,  American Samoa,AS
DATA  Arizona,AZ,  Arkansas,AR,  California,CA
DATA  Colorado,CO,  Connecticut, CT,  Delaware,DE
DATA  District of Columbia,DC,  Federated States of Micronesia,TT
DATA  Florida,FL,  Georgia,GA,  Guam,GU
DATA  Hawaii,HI,  Idaho,ID,  Illinois,IL
DATA  Indiana,IN,  Iowa,IA,  Kansas,KS
DATA  Kentucky,KY,  Louisiana,LA,  Maine,ME
DATA  Mariana Islands,CM,  Marshall Islands,TT,  Maryland,MD
DATA  Massachusetts,MA,  Michigan,MI,  Micronesia,TT
DATA  Minnesota,MN,  Mississippi,MS,  Missouri,MO
DATA  Montana,MT,  Nebraska,NE,  Nevada,NV
DATA  New Hampshire,NH,  New Jersey,NJ,  New Mexico,NM
DATA  New York,NY,  North Carolina,NC,  North Dakota,ND
DATA  Northern Mariana Islands,CM,  Ohio,OH,  Oklahoma,OK
DATA  Oregon,OR,  Palau,TT,  Pennsylvania,PA
DATA  Puerto Rico,PR,  Rhode Island,RI,  South Carolina,SC
DATA  South Dakota,SD,  Tennessee,TN,  Texas,TX
DATA  Utah,UT,  Vermont,VT,  Virgin Islands,VI
DATA  Virginia,VA,  Washington,WA,  West Virginia,WV
DATA  Wisconsin,WI,  Wyoming,WY
DATA  End of data,ZZ

REM ** SCAN THE FILE & PROOF READ IT
CALL ScanFile
END
SUB ScanFile STATIC
' Scan the StateAbr.Dat file, one record at a time.
  ' Put instructions in lines 21 to 25.
  Text$(1) = STRING$(74, 196)
  Text$(2) = "Scan the States & Abbreviations file, one record at a time."
  Text$(3) = "Put the data disk in drive B."
  Text$(4) = "Press a key to begin.  First record will open a viewport."
  Text$(5) = "Press space bar to get next record, Q to quit."
  CLS
  FOR row% = 1 TO 5
    LOCATE row% + 20, 3: PRINT Text$(row%);
  NEXT row%
```

Program 8-1. *STATES AND ABBREVIATIONS, CREATE AND PROOF FILE*

```
' Define rows 1 to 20 as a viewport, used for scanning records.
VIEW PRINT 1 TO 20

' Wait for a key press to begin.
PRINT "Press a key to begin."
anykey$ = INPUT$(1)
CLS 2                                      'Clears only viewport

' Open the file StateAbr.Dat on drive B for input as file #1.
OPEN "B:StateAbr.Dat" FOR INPUT AS #1

' Read one record each time a key other than Q is pressed.
DO UNTIL EOF(1)
  LINE INPUT #1, record$
  PRINT record$
  PRINT
  nextkey$ = INPUT$(1)
  IF UCASE$(nextkey$) = "Q" THEN EXIT DO
LOOP

' Close the file and the subprogram
VIEW PRINT 1 TO 25: CLS
CLOSE #1

END SUB
```

Program 8-1.   *STATES AND ABBREVIATIONS, CREATE AND PROOF FILE*
(continued)

Program 8-1 creates a file by reading records from DATA statements and printing them to the file. This is done in a DO...LOOP
structure that terminates after reading the fictitious state and abbreviation End of data,ZZ. The DO...LOOP is shown below:

```
DO
  READ State$, Abbr          ' Read data for one record.
  IF Abbr$ = "ZZ" THEN EXIT DO  ' Exit on end of data record.
  WRITE #1, State$, Abbr$    ' Print one record to file.
LOOP
```

The name of the state or territory is assigned to the variable *State$*.
The abbreviation is assigned to *Abbr$*. The values of the two variables
are read from DATA statements and written to the file as a single
record with two fields, *State$* and *Abbr$*.

The WRITE # statement, shown below, inserts commas between
fields as they are written to the file. It also encloses strings in quotation marks. Finally, it puts carriage-return and line-feed characters
following the last field in a record.

```
WRITE #1, State$, Abbr$
```

Write a record   *The record consists of*
to file opened as #1 *these two fields*

Therefore, in the file created by Program 8-1, one record consists of the following:

- The value of *State$*, enclosed in quotation marks.

- A comma.

- The value of *Abbr$*, enclosed in quotation marks.

- Carriage-return and line-feed characters to mark the end of the record.

You will see the strings enclosed in quotation marks and the comma between the fields when you run Program 8-1 and scan the file.

After reading the records and writing them to the file, the program calls the ScanFile subprogram, which begins as shown in Figure 8-1.

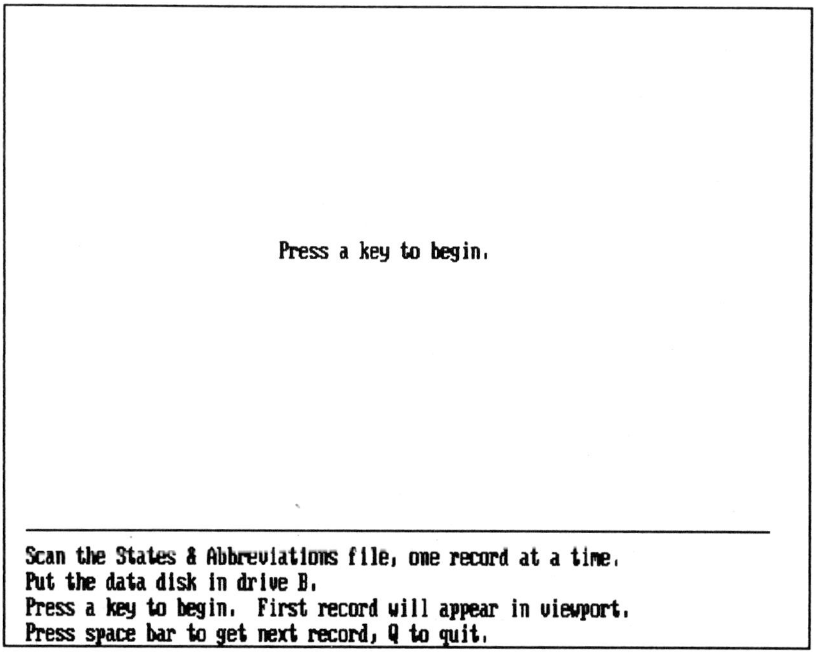

```
                        Press a key to begin.




Scan the States & Abbreviations file, one record at a time.
Put the data disk in drive B.
Press a key to begin. First record will appear in viewport.
Press space bar to get next record, Q to quit.
```

Figure 8-1. *Opening screen—ScanFile subprogram*

```
"Alabama","AL"

"Alaska","AK"

"American Samoa","AS"

"Arizona","AZ"

"Arkansas","AR"

"California","CA"

"Colorado","CO"

"Connecticut","CT"

"Delaware","DE"
```

```
Scan the States & Abbreviations file, one record at a time.
Put the data disk in drive B.
Press a key to begin.  First record will appear in viewport.
Press space bar to get next record, Q to quit.
```

Figure 8-2. *Scan in progress—nine records*

Press any key to begin, then scan and proofread the file. Figure 8-2 shows a proofreading session in progress with the first nine records on the screen.

The subprogram ScanFile reads a complete record composed of both fields (*State$*, *Abbr$*) with a LINE INPUT # statement, and prints them as a single string (*record$*):

```
      .
      .
      .
LINE INPUT #1, record$
PRINT record$
      .
      .
      .
```

The LINE INPUT # statement reads everything, including quotation marks, until it encounters the carriage-return and line-feed characters that mark the end of a record. Therefore, when you scan the file,

```
"Texas","TX"

"Utah","UT"

"Vermont","VT"

"Virgin Islands","VI"

"Virginia","VA"

"Washington","WA"

"West Virginia","WV"

"Wisconsin","WI"

"Wyoming","WY"
```

Scan the States & Abbreviations file, one record at a time.
Put the data disk in drive B.
Press a key to begin. First record will appear in viewport.
Press space bar to get next record, Q to quit.

Figure 8-3. *End of ScanFile*

you will see the quotation marks and the comma inserted by the WRITE # statement in creating the file. That is, you see an image of the record as it exists in the file.

Continue pressing the SPACEBAR and new states (or territories) and their abbreviations appear on the screen. When the viewport is full, the next press on the SPACEBAR will scroll the text in the viewport upward to make room for the new data.

The instructions remain fixed at the bottom of the screen. Only text in the viewport scrolls. Figure 8-3 shows the screen as the end of the file is reached. If you press either the SPACEBAR or the letter *Q*, the program ends. The screen is clear except for this message: **Press any key to continue**. Press a key and you return to the Edit screen.

Now change only two lines in the ScanFile subprogram so that a record will be read as two fields by an INPUT # statement and printed to the screen as two separate strings. The changes are in the DO...LOOP.

```
Original DO...LOOP

  ' Read one record each time a key other than Q is pressed.
  DO UNTIL EOF(1)
    LINE INPUT #1, record$
    PRINT record$
    PRINT
    nextkey$ = INPUT$(1)
    IF UCASE$(nextkey$) = "Q" THEN EXIT DO
  LOOP

Modified DO...LOOP

  ' Read one record each time a key other than Q is pressed.
  DO UNTIL EOF(1)
    INPUT #1, State$, Abbr$
    PRINT State$, Abbr$
    PRINT
    nextkey$ = INPUT$(1)
    IF UCASE$(nextkey$) = "Q" THEN EXIT DO
  LOOP
```

The INPUT# statement shown above will read the first field of the record as the value of *State$* and the second field as the value of *Abbr$*. Remember that in the record the two fields are separated by a comma. The INPUT# statement recognizes this comma as a field separator. However, it doesn't read the comma, nor does it read the quotation marks that enclose each field.

Figure 8-4 shows the first nine states and their abbreviations from a run of the modified program. Compare this figure with the output of Program 8-1 in Figure 8-2.

Note that the PRINT statement uses comma spacing in printing to the screen. Change the PRINT statement, as shown in the DO...LOOP below:

```
' Read one record each time a key other than Q is pressed.
DO UNTIL EOF(1)
  INPUT #1, State$, Abbr$
  PRINT State$; Abbr$
  PRINT
  nextkey$ = INPUT$(1)
  IF UCASE$(nextkey$) = "Q" THEN EXIT DO
LOOP
```

Again run the modified program. Figure 8-5 shows the first nine records. Note that no spaces are printed between the state and its abbreviation.

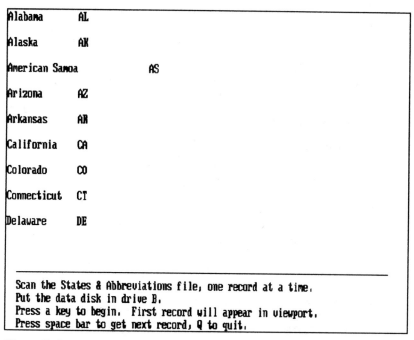

Figure 8-4. *Modified program output; comma spacing*

One more variation. Use TAB to print the states and abbreviations in neat columns. Change the DO...LOOP, as shown here:

```
' Read one record each time a key other than Q is pressed.
DO UNTIL EOF(1)
   INPUT #1, State$, Abbr$
   PRINT State$; TAB(35); Abbr$
   PRINT
   nextkey$ = INPUT$(1)
   IF UCASE$(nextkey$) = "Q" THEN EXIT DO
LOOP
```

Figure 8-6 shows the output during a run.

You may wish to save this as the final version of Program 8-1. If the list of states and territories or the two-letter abbreviations should change, just edit the program and make a new file.

```
AlabamaAL

AlaskaAK

American SamoaAS

ArizonaAZ

ArkansasAR

CaliforniaCA

ColoradoCO

ConnecticutCT

DelawareDE
```

```
Scan the States & Abbreviations file, one record at a time.
Put the data disk in drive B.
Press a key to begin.  First record will appear in viewport.
Press space bar to get next record, Q to quit.
```

Figure 8-5. *Modified program output; semicolon spacing*

You can perform another series of experiments as follows:

1. Change the WRITE # statement in the main program to PRINT #. For example, in the main program of Program 8-1:

Change   `WRITE #1, State$, Abbr$`

To   `PRINT #1, State$, Abbr$`

Then try this variation with some or all of the ways to read information from the file, shown previously.

2. Use explicit delimiters in the PRINT # statement. Add one line above the DO. . .LOOP in Program 8-1 and change the DO. . .LOOP as follows:

```
Q$ = CHR$(34)
DO
  READ State$, Abbr$
  IF Abbr$ = "ZZ" THEN EXIT DO
  PRINT #1, Q$ State$ Q$, Q$ Abbr$ Q$
LOOP
```

```
Alabama                         AL

Alaska                          AK

American Samoa                  AS

Arizona                         AZ

Arkansas                        AR

California                      CA

Colorado                        CO

Connecticut                     CT

Delaware                        DE



_____

Scan the States & Abbreviations file, one record at a time.
Put the data disk in drive B.
Press a key to begin.  First record will appear in viewport.
Press space bar to get next record, Q to quit.
```

Figure 8-6. *Program output using* TAB

When you move the cursor off the line containing the PRINT #
statement, you will see QuickBASIC reformat the line as

```
PRINT #1, Q$; State$; Q$, Q$; Abbr$; Q$
```

Don't be alarmed, but be aware that QuickBASIC sometimes changes
the format of program entries. Try this with various variations of the
ScanFile subprogram.

3. You can experiment further by removing the comma from the
PRINT # statement.

```
PRINT #1, Q$ State$ Q$ Q$ Abbr$ Q$
```

QuickBASIC will change the format of the statement to

```
PRINT #1, Q$; State$; Q$; Q$; Abbr$; Q$
```

Also try this with some or all of the ScanFile variations.

This section has discussed several ways to put information into a states and abbreviations file and read information out of the file. These ways are summarized below.

■ Putting information into the file:

```
WRITE #1, State$, Abbr$

PRINT #1, State$, Abbr$

PRINT #1, Q$; State$; Q$, Q$; Abbr$; Q$ (where Q$ = CHR$(34))

PRINT #1, Q$; State$; Q$; Q$; Abbr$; Q$
```

■ Reading information from the file:

```
LINE INPUT #1, record$

INPUT #1, State$, Abbr$
```

Experiment with various combinations of the above.

Finding Information in the StateAbr.Dat File

Program 8-2, FIND POSTAL ABBREVIATION, searches the State-Abr.Dat file for any state or territory record in the file, using a search key entered from the keyboard. This is done by the following lines in the main program:

```
' Get search key.  Empty string ends program.
getdata:
INPUT "State or Territory"; LookFor$
IF LookFor$ = "" THEN VIEW PRINT 1 TO 25: CLS: END   'Program can end here
```

You can end the program by entering the empty string as the search key. Just press ENTER without typing anything. In this event, the full screen is cleared, except for a message at the bottom of the screen: **Press any key to continue.** Press a key and QuickBASIC returns you to the Edit screen. If you enter a search key, the State-Abr.Dat file is opened and the SearchFile subprogram is called:

```
' Find and print records that match LookFor$
OPEN "B:StateAbr.Dat" FOR INPUT AS #1
CALL SearchFile(LookFor$)
```

The variable *LookFor$*, which holds your search key, is passed when the subprogram is called. It becomes the value of *SearchKey$* in the subprogram and is immediately converted to uppercase letters:

```
SearchKey$ = UCASE$(SearchKey$)
```

SearchFile then computes the length of *SearchKey$* and sets the match flag to zero to indicate no match as yet:

```
LenKey% = LEN(SearchKey$)
Match% = 0                              'No match yet
```

A DO...LOOP reads records from the StateAbr.Dat file and compares your search key with the variable *Maybe$*. *Maybe$* is comprised of the leftmost characters of each state, equal in length to your search key. If the state read from the record is beyond (greater than) the search key alphabetically, the search ends.

```
DO UNTIL EOF(1)
   INPUT #1, State$, Abbr$              'Read one record
   Maybe$ = UCASE$(LEFT$(State$, LenKey%))
   IF Maybe$ = SearchKey$ THEN
      Match% = -1                       'Match found
      PRINT State$; TAB(35); Abbr$
   ELSEIF Maybe$ > SearchKey$ THEN      'If true, more matches not possible
      EXIT DO                           'because file is alphabetical order.
   END IF
LOOP
IF Match% = 0 THEN PRINT "State not found."
```

The DO...LOOP prints every record that matches the search key. If no match is found, the value of *Match%* remains zero. In this case, the message "State not found." is printed when exiting from the DO...LOOP.

On completion of the subprogram, control is returned to the main program, where the file is closed and the program loops back to permit entry of another search key:

```
' Get search key.  Empty key ends program.
getdata.
INPUT "State or Territory"; LookFor$
IF LookFor$ = "" THEN VIEW PRINT 1 TO 25: CLS: END  'Program can end here
```

```
' Find and print records that match LookFor$
OPEN "B:StateAbr.Dat" FOR INPUT AS #1
CALL SearchFile(LookFor$)
CLOSE #1
PRINT: GOTO getdata
```

To use Program 8-2, enter the name of the state or territory whose abbreviation you desire, and the computer will find the state and its abbreviation. If you enter only the first letter of the state, the program will print all the states and territories that begin with that letter. You can enter the first two letters or the first three letters of the name of the state. Try it. The program will find all records for which the left part of the name of the state or territory matches your entry. Figure 8-7 shows the opening screen when Program 8-2 is run.

Press a key and the program begins. You are prompted for a state or territory at the top of the screen:

```
State or Territory?
```

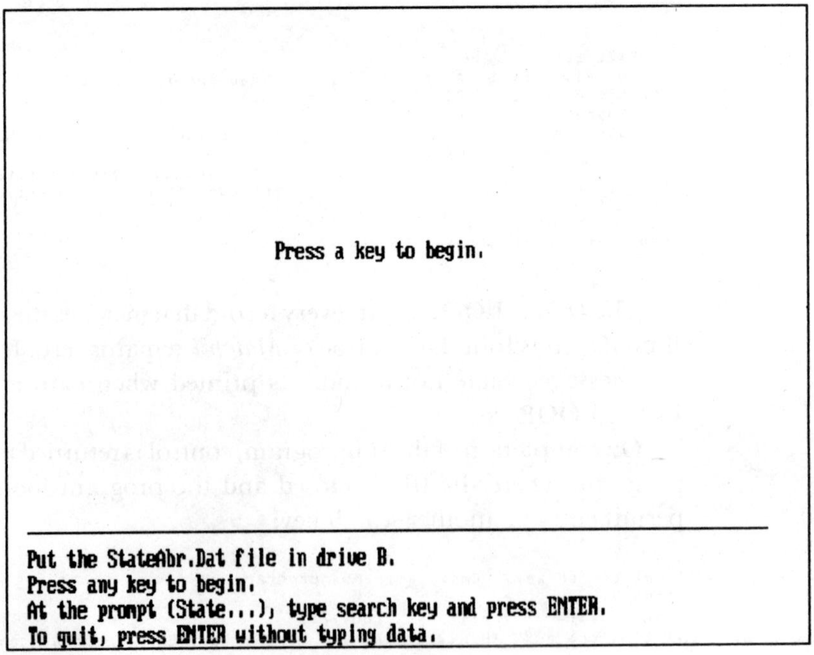

Press a key to begin.

Put the StateAbr.Dat file in drive B.
Press any key to begin.
At the prompt (State...), type search key and press ENTER.
To quit, press ENTER without typing data.

Figure 8-7. *Opening screen of Program 8-2*

```
DECLARE SUB SearchFile (SearchKey$)
REM ** FIND POSTAL ABBREVIATION **
' Program 8-2  8/25/87
' Finds postal abbreviation for any state or territory in
' StateAbr.Dat file.  Search key can be left part of the
' name of the state or territory.  Finds all records that
' match search key.  For example, enter the letter C to find
' California, Colorado, and Connecticut.  Search key can be
' upper case, lower case, or mixed upper and lower case.

' Put instructions in lines 21 to 25
Text$(1) = STRINGS$(74, 196)
Text$(2) = "Put the StateAbr.Dat file in drive B."
Text$(3) = "Press any key to begin."
Text$(4) = "At the prompt (State...), type search key and press ENTER."
Text$(5) = "To quit, press ENTER without typing data."
CLS
FOR row% = 1 TO 5
  LOCATE row% + 20, 3: PRINT Text$(row%);
NEXT row%

' Define rows 1 to 20 as a viewport
VIEW PRINT 1 TO 20

' Wait for a key press
LOCATE 10, 28: PRINT "Press a key to begin."
anykey$ = INPUT$(1)
CLS 2

' Get search key.  Empty key ends program.
getdata:
INPUT "State or Territory"; LookFor$
IF LookFor$ = "" THEN VIEW PRINT 1 TO 25: CLS : END    'Program can end here

' Find and print records that match LookFor$
OPEN "B:StateAbr.Dat" FOR INPUT AS #1
CALL SearchFile(LookFor$)
CLOSE #1
PRINT : GOTO getdata
SUB SearchFile (SearchKey$) STATIC
' Searches StateAbr.Dat file and prints all records for which left
' part of State$ matches SearchKey$.  If no match is found, prints
' the message: State not found.
  SearchKey$ = UCASE$(SearchKey$)
  Lenkey% = LEN(SearchKey$)
  Match% = 0                              'No match yet
  DO UNTIL EOF(1)
    INPUT #1, State$, Abbr$               'Read one record
    Maybe$ = UCASE$(LEFT$(State$, Lenkey%))
    IF Maybe$ = SearchKey$ THEN
      Match% = -1                         'Match found
      PRINT State$; TAB(35); Abbr$
    ELSEIF Maybe$ > SearchKey$ THEN       'If true, more matches not possible
      EXIT DO                             'because file is alphabetical order.
    END IF
  LOOP
  IF Match% = 0 THEN PRINT "State not found."

END SUB
```

Program 8-2. *FIND POSTAL ABBREVIATION*

You enter	The computer prints
C	California CA
	Colorado CO
	Connecticut CT
nor	North Carolina NC
	North Dakota ND
	Northern Mariana Islands CM
VIRGIN	Virgin Islands VI
	Virginia VA
Ioway	State not found
Iowa	Iowa IA

Table 8-1. *Samples from Program 8-2*

```
State or Territory? a
Alabama                       AL
Alaska                        AK
American Samoa                AS
Arizona                       AZ
Arkansas                      AR

State or Territory? z
State not found.

State or Territory? nor
North Carolina               NC
North Dakota                 ND
Northern Mariana Islands     CM

State or Territory?




Put the StateAbr.Dat file in drive B.
Press any key to begin.
At the prompt (State...), type search key and press ENTER.
To quit, press ENTER without typing data.
```

Figure 8-8. *Run of Program 8-2*

The instructions for use of the program are shown at the bottom of the screen:

```
Put the StateAbr.Dat file in Drive B.
Press any key to begin.
At the prompt (State...), type search key and press ENTER.
To quit, press ENTER without typing data.
```

The name to search for may be entered in any mixture of upper- and lowercase letters. Examples of entries and the printed result are shown in Table 8-1. Figure 8-8 shows a run of the program.

Learning by Doodling

You can use Program 8-3, FILE I/O EXPERIMENTS, to learn more about how information is stored in files. Program 8-3 uses two files called Doodle.One and Doodle.Two. The program operates as follows:

- Both files are opened for OUTPUT.

- One record is entered as a single string from the keyboard by means of a LINE INPUT statement.

- The record is written to Doodle.One by means of a PRINT # statement.

- The record is written to Doodle.Two by means of a WRITE # statement.

- The LOF function is used in PRINT statements to print the length of each file. The length of a file is the number of characters in the file.

- Both files are closed with the statement CLOSE #1, #2.

- Both files are opened for INPUT.

- The record in Doodle.One is read with a LINE INPUT # statement and printed to the screen.

■ The record in Doodle.Two is read with a LINE INPUT # statement and printed to the screen.

■ Both files are closed with CLOSE #1, #2.

■ You can press any key to do another.

In the examples that follow, note the number of characters in each file and the similarities and differences in the way records are stored in the two files.

```
REM ** FILE I/O EXPERIMENTS **
' Program 8-3   8/29/87
' Input/output experiments using two files, Doodle.One & Doodle.Two

start:
OPEN "B:Doodle.One" FOR OUTPUT AS #1
OPEN "B:Doodle.Two" FOR OUTPUT AS #2

' Get data from keyboard. Put same data in two files in two ways.
CLS
LINE INPUT "String, please? "; strng$
PRINT #1, strng$
WRITE #2, strng$

' Print the length of file (LOF) for each file and close the files.
PRINT
PRINT "Doodle.One has"; LOF(1); "characters."
PRINT "Doodle.Two has"; LOF(2); "characters."
CLOSE #1, #2

' Read information from both files and print to screen.
OPEN "B:Doodle.One" FOR INPUT AS #1
OPEN "B:Doodle.Two" FOR INPUT AS #2

PRINT : PRINT "Stuff from Doodle.One using LINE INPUT # :"
LINE INPUT #1, record$
PRINT record$

PRINT : PRINT "Stuff from Doodle.Two using LINE INPUT # :"
LINE INPUT #2, record$
PRINT record$

CLOSE #1, #2

' Tell how to do again.
PRINT : PRINT "To do another, press a key."
anykey$ = INPUT$(1): GOTO start
```

Program 8-3.   *FILE I/O EXPERIMENTS*

Run Program 8-3 and enter only a single letter as the string to be written to both files. An example is shown below:

```
String, please? a

Doodle.One has 3 characters.
Doodle.Two has 5 characters.

Stuff from Doodle.One using LINE INPUT # :
a

Stuff from Doodle.Two using LINE INPUT # :
"a"

To do another, press a key.
```

Examine these results and note the following:

■ In Doodle.One, the PRINT # statement wrote the string (a) to the file without enclosing it in quotation marks. The file contains three characters: the letter *a* and the carriage-return and line-feed characters that mark the end of the record.

■ In Doodle.Two, the WRITE # statement wrote the string (a) to the file enclosed in quotation marks. The file contains five characters: quotation marks, the letter *a*, quotation marks, carriage-return character, and line-feed character.

Another example is shown below:

```
String, please? 123

Doodle.One has 5 characters.
Doodle.Two has 7 characters.

Stuff from Doodle.One using LINE INPUT # :
123

Stuff from Doodle.Two using LINE INPUT # :
"123"

To do another, press a key.
```

This time three characters were entered: (123) and

■ Doodle.One contains five characters: 123, a carriage return, and a line feed.

■ Doodle.Two contains seven characters: quotation marks, 123, quotation marks, a carriage return, and a line feed.

Try one more example, as shown here:

```
String, please? a   ,   ,   ,  1  ,  2  ,  3

Doodle.One has 43 characters.
Doodle.Two has 45 characters.

Stuff from Doodle.One using LINE INPUT # :
a  ,   b  ,  c  ,  1  ,  2  ,  3

Stuff from Doodle.Two using LINE INPUT # :
"a  ,   b  ,  c  ,  1  ,  2  ,  3"

To do another, press a key.
```

Again, both files contain the same information, stored in the same way, except for the quotation marks supplied by the WRITE # statement in writing to Doodle.Two.

A Minor Modification

Edit the program so that the record to be put into both files is entered as two strings and written to each file as one record with two fields.
Change only this part of the program:

```
' Get data from keyboard. Put same data in two files in two ways.
CLS
LINE INPUT "String, please?"; strng$
PRINT #1, strng$
WRITE #2, strng$
```

Change the above to the following:

```
' Get data from keyboard. Put same data in two files in two ways.
CLS
INPUT "Firststring$, Secondstring$"; Firststring$, Secondstring$
PRINT #1, Firststring$, Secondstring$
WRITE #2, Firststring$, Secondstring$
```

After making these changes, Program 8-3 will write one record consisting of two fields to each file, then read each record exactly as it is stored by means of LINE INPUT # statements. Remember, LINE INPUT # reads an entire record (all fields) up to the carriage-return and line-feed characters that mark the end of the record.

Now run the modified program. Try this example:

```
Firststring$, Secondstring$? a,b

Doodle.One has 17 characters.
Doodle.Two has 9 characters.

Stuff from Doodle.One using LINE INPUT # :
a               b

Stuff from Doodle.Two using LINE INPUT # :
"a","b"
To do another, press a key.
```

This time, the length of Doodle.One is eight characters more than the length of Doodle.Two. The extra characters are spaces. These spaces are not included in Doodle.Two.

In writing the record to Doodle.Two, the WRITE # statement enclosed each string in quotation marks and inserted a comma between them as part of the record.

Here are three more examples:

```
Firststring$, Secondstring$? "a,b",c

Doodle.One has 17 characters.
Doodle.Two has 11 characters.

Stuff from Doodle.One using LINE INPUT # :
a,b             c

Stuff from Doodle.Two using LINE INPUT # :
"a,b","c"

To do another, press a key.

Firststring$, Secondstring$? 1234567890123,abc

Doodle.One has 19 characters.
Doodle.Two has 23 characters.

Stuff from Doodle.One using LINE INPUT # :
1234567890123 abc

Stuff from Doodle.Two using LINE INPUT # :
"1234567890123","abc"

To do another, press a key.

Firststring$, Secondstring$? 12345678901234,abc

Doodle.One has 33 characters.
Doodle.Two has 24 characters.

Stuff from Doodle.One using LINE INPUT # :
12345678901234          abc
```

```
Stuff from Doodle.Two using LINE INPUT # :
"12345678901234","abc"

To do another, press a key.
```

The last two examples illustrate the fact that the PRINT # statement, with commas between variable names, prints to a file in the same way as a PRINT statement prints to the screen. You can see this by changing the PRINT # statement to the following:

```
PRINT #1, Firststring$; Secondstring$
```

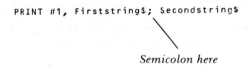

Semicolon here

Following this change, a sample run produced this:

```
Firststring$, Secondstring$? a,b

Doodle.One has 4 characters.
Doodle.Two has 9 characters.

Stuff from Doodle.One using LINE INPUT # :
ab

Stuff from Doodle.Two using LINE INPUT # :
"a","b"

To do another, press a key.
```

The next variation of Program 8-3 shows how numbers are written to and read from files. Change only the part of the program that gets information from the keyboard and writes it to the two files, as follows:

```
' Get data from keyboard.  Put same data in two files in two ways.
CLS
INPUT "Firstnumber, Secondnumber"; Firstnumber, Secondnumber
PRINT #1, Firstnumber, Secondnumber
WRITE #2, Firstnumber, Secondnumber
```

Then try this simple example:

```
Firstnumber, Secondnumber? 1,2

Doodle.One has 19 characters.
Doodle.Two has 5 characters.
```

```
Stuff from Doodle.One using LINE INPUT # :
 1             2

Stuff from Doodle.Two using LINE INPUT # :
 1,2

To do another, press a key.
```

In writing to Doodle.One, the PRINT # statement prints the two numbers in this way:

■ Prints the first number as space, digit, space.

■ Prints 11 spaces for a total of 14 character positions. This is the same as standard comma spacing for PRINT statements.

■ Prints the second number as space, digit, space.

■ Prints carriage-return and line-feed characters to mark the end of a record.

Add up the above and you will get a total of 19 characters.

In writing numbers to Doodle.Two, the WRITE # statement does not enclose each number in quotation marks. It does insert a comma between the two numbers.

In both cases, the numbers are stored in ASCII, one ASCII character for each digit.

Additional examples are shown below for your reading pleasure:

```
Firstnumber, Secondnumber? 1   ,   2

Doodle.One has 19 characters.
Doodle.Two has 5 characters.

Stuff from Doodle.One using LINE INPUT # :
 1             2

Stuff from Doodle.Two using LINE INPUT # :
 1,2

To do another, press a key.

Firstnumber, Secondnumber? 1234567,123

Doodle.One has 21 characters.
Doodle.Two has 13 characters.

Stuff from Doodle.One using LINE INPUT # :
 1234567       123

Stuff from Doodle.Two using LINE INPUT # :
 1234567,123
```

```
To do another, press a key.

Fistnumber, Secondnumber? 12345678,123

Doodle.One has 35 characters.
Doodle.Two has 18 characters.

Stuff from Doodle.One using LINE INPUT # :
   1.234568E+07                  123

Stuff from Doodle.Two using LINE INPUT # :
1.234568E+07,123

To do another, press a key.
```

Design your own experiments. Here are some suggestions. In the last variation, use semicolons for spacing in the PRINT # statement. For example:

```
PRINT #1, Firstnumber; Secondnumber
```

Instead of a record having two strings or two numbers, try one of each. For example:

```
' Get data from keyboard. Put some data in two files in two ways.
CLS
INPUT "String, Number"; Strng$, Number
PRINT #1, Strng$, Number
WRITE #2, Strng$, Number
```

Experiment with records that have three or more fields.

Review

This chapter discussed and demonstrated the use of structured sequential files using:

- OPEN # to open a file

- PRINT # and WRITE # to put information in a file

- INPUT #, INPUT$( ), and LINE INPUT # to read information from a file

■ LOF to find the length of a file

■ CLOSE # to close a file

You learned to create and scan sequential structured files composed of records with string fields and numeric fields, and records that combined strings and numbers in separate fields.

Two programs, STATES AND ABBREVIATIONS and FIND POSTAL ABBREVIATIONS, were used to demonstrate different ways to write to a sequential structured file and to read the data from the file.

The chapter concluded with a third program, FILE I/O EXPER-IMENTS, that allowed you to learn by experimenting with various ways to send (output) data to a file and read (input) data from a file.

9 Random-Access Files

You have learned a great deal about sequential files in the last two chapters. In this chapter, you will learn how to create, scan, print, and search random-access files.

You will learn to use the following statements or functions in random-access files.

OPEN #	Opening a file FOR RANDOM allows you to output to or input from a random-access file.
LEN =	A clause in an OPEN statement that specifies the record length of the file.
TYPE...END TYPE	A structure that defines variable types used in random-access files.
PUT #	Writes a record to a random-access file.
GET #	Reads a record from a random-access file.

CLOSE #   Closes specified random-access files. If no
                        file number is specified, all open files are
                        closed.

LOF   Returns the length of a file.

A Bit About Random-Access Files

As discussed in Chapter 7, records in random-access files are organized
differently from those in sequential files. Each random-access record
is defined with a fixed length. Each field within a record is also defined
with a fixed length. This fixed length determines where a record or a
field begins and ends. No commas separate fields or carriage-
return/line-feed characters between records.

Sequential files save a number as a sequence of ASCII characters,
each ASCII character representing one digit of the number. Random-
access files save numbers in a compressed binary format, thus saving
disk space and conversion time. Integers stored in random-access files
occupy two bytes, long integers and single-precision numbers occupy
four bytes, and double-precision numbers occupy eight bytes. Strings
are stored as a sequence of ASCII characters in both sequential files
and random-access files.

Creating a Random-Access File

Three steps are required in a program that creates a random-access
file. You must

1. Define the fields of each record.

2. Open the file in random-access mode and specify the length of each record.

3. Get data for a record and store the record in the file.

To create a random-access file, you will be modifying STATES AND ABBREVIATIONS, the sequential structured file used in Chapter 8. In that program you did not have to define the fields, as in step 1 above.

You can define a record with a TYPE...END TYPE statement, which allows you to mix string fields with numeric fields. You eliminate the need for functions that convert numeric data to strings, required in GW-BASIC and early versions of QuickBASIC.

Step 1 can be performed by the following lines:

```
      .
      .
      .
' Define the RecordType Structure
TYPE RecordType
   State AS STRING * 30
   Abbr AS STRING * 2
END TYPE
      .
      .
      .
```

This defines *State* as a string field that is 30 characters long and *Abbr* as a string field that is 2 characters long. Therefore, 1 record will have 32 characters.

Step 2 requires that the file be opened. In Program 8-1, the sequential structured file was opened with

```
OPEN "B:StateAbr.Dat" FOR OUTPUT AS #1
```

When you open a random-access file, your program should tell how long each record is to be. If you do not specify the length of the records, QuickBASIC will use the default length of 128 bytes. QuickBASIC will do the calculating for you if you declare a variable of the defined type. This can be done with a DIM, REDIM, COMMON, STATIC, or

SHARED statement. To specify the length, use the LEN = clause in the OPEN statement:

```
     .
     .
     .
' Declare StateRecord as the above type
DIM StateRecord AS RecordType

' Open random access file, specify length
OPEN "B:StateAbr.Dat" FOR RANDOM AS #1 LEN = LEN(StateRecord)
     .
     .
     .
```

Calculates the length of a record

Step 3 gets data for records and stores them in the random-access file. Program 8-1 used the following DO...LOOP to perform this step for a sequential structured file:

```
DO
   READ State$, Abbr$
   IF Abbr$ = "ZZ" THEN EXIT DO
   WRITE #1, State$, Abbr$
LOOP
```

Records of random-access files are assigned a number when they are written to the file. If a DO...LOOP is used in the random-access file to enter records and write them to the file, the record number must be initialized before the loop is entered. The number is incremented each time DO...LOOP is executed. A random-access file uses the PUT # statement instead of PRINT # or WRITE # to write records to a file. If the data has been defined by a TYPE...END TYPE statement, then a comparable DO...LOOP for a random-access file, along with the statement that initializes the record number, would be

```
     .
     .
     .
' Initialize the record number
RecordNumber = 0
```

```
DO
  READ StateRecord.State, StateRecord.Abbr
  IF StateRecord.Abbr = "ZZ" THEN EXIT DO
  RecordNumber = RecordNumber + 1
  PUT #1, RecordNumber, StateRecord
LOOP
     .
     .
     .
```

Records are read as individual fields:

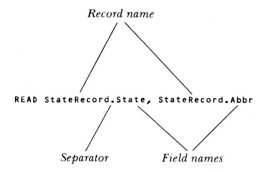

Record name

```
READ StateRecord.State, StateRecord.Abbr
```

Separator   *Field names*

In Program 8-1, the data file was first opened for output so that data could be written to the file. After writing to the file, Program 8-1 closed file number 1 because the file had to be reopened for input in order to read from the file.

```
     .
     .
     .
CLOSE #1                                    ◄——— In the main program
     .
     .
OPEN "B:StateAbr.Dat" FOR INPUT AS #1  ◄——— In the subprogram
```

A random-access file lets you write to or read from the file when it is opened. You don't need to close the file and reopen it in the subprogram. Therefore, delete the CLOSE #1 statement following the DO...LOOP in Program 8-1, as well as the subsequent OPEN statement in the ScanFile subprogram.

If you saved the STATES AND ABBREVIATIONS program from Chapter 8, you can use your editing skills to modify the main program to create a random-access file. So far, you have this portion of a random-access file program:

```
DECLARE SUB ScanFile ()
REM ** STATES AND APPREVIATIONS - RANDOM ACCESS **
' Program 9-1  9/1/87

REM ** CREATE THE FILE **
' Create StateAbr.Dat file with state names and abbreviations
' Random access file with two fields: State, Abbr

  ' Define the RecordType structure
  TYPE RecordType
    State AS STRING * 30              'string field of length 30
    Abbr AS STRING * 2               'string field of length 2
  END TYPE

  ' Declare StateRecord as the above type
  DIM StateRecord AS RecordType

  ' Open random access file, specifying length of one record
  ' as the length of the StateRecord variable
  OPEN "B:StateAbr.Dat" FOR RANDOM AS #1 LEN = LEN(StateRecord)

  ' Initialize record number
  RecordNumber = 0

  ' Read data and put it in file
  DO
    READ StateRecord.State, StateRecord.Abbr
    IF StateRecord.Abbr = "ZZ" THEN EXIT DO
    RecordNumber = RecordNumber + 1
    PUT #1, RecordNumber, StateRecord
  LOOP

  DATA  Alabama,AL,  Alaska,AK,  American Samoa,AS
  DATA  Arizona,AZ,  Arkansas,AR,  California,CA
  DATA  Colorado,CO,  Connecticut,CT,  Delaware,DE
  DATA  District of Columbia,DC,  Federated States of
        Micronesia,TT
  DATA  Florida,FL,  Georgia,GA,  Guam,GU
  DATA  Hawaii,HI,  Idaho,ID,  Illinois,IL
  DATA  Indiana,IN,  Iowa,IA,  Kansas,KS
  DATA  Kentucky,KY,  Louisiana,LA,  Maine,ME
```

```
DATA  Mariana Islands,CM,  Marshall Islands,TT,  Maryland,MD
DATA  Massachusetts,MA,  Michigan,MI,  Micronesia,TT
DATA  Minnesota,MN,  Mississippi,MS,  Missouri,MO
DATA  Montana,MT,  Nebraska,NE,  Nevada,NV
DATA  New Hampshire,NH,  New Jersey,NJ,  New Mexico,NM
DATA  New York,NY,  North Carolina,NC,  North Dakota,ND
DATA  Northern Mariana Islands,CM,  Ohio,OH,  Oklahoma,OK
DATA  Oregon,OR,  Palau,TT,  Pennsylvania,PA
DATA  Puerto Rico,PR,  Rhode Island,RI,  South Carolina,SC
DATA  South Dakota,SD,  Tennessee,TN,  Texas,TX
DATA  Utah,UT,  Vermont,VT,  Virgin Islands,VI
DATA  Virginia,VA,  Washingaton,WA,  West Virginia,WV
DATA  Wisconsin,WI,  Wyoming,WY
DATA  End of data, ZZ

REM ** SCAN THE FILE AND PROOF READ IT **
CALL ScanFile

END
```

Reading a Random-Access File

The STATES AND ABBREVIATIONS program of Chapter 8 called a subprogram to scan the sequential structured data file:

```
REM ** SCAN THE FILE AND PROOF READ IT **
CALL ScanFile
```

These two lines can also be used for a random-access file, but the name of the subprogram should be changed to avoid confusion. Call it ReadFile:

```
REM ** SCAN THE FILE AND PROOF READ IT **
CALL ReadFile
```

The subprogram used in STATES AND ABBREVIATIONS can be modified to fit a random-access file by changing a few lines. Be sure to change the subprogram's name to match the call from the main program:

```
SUB ReadFile STATIC
```

The OPEN statement of Program 8-1's subprogram can be deleted along with the remark preceding it. In the random-access subprogram the file is still open when the subprogram is called.

A user-defined type must be declared in a TYPE...END TYPE declaration before it can be used in a program. Although a user-defined type can only be declared in the module-level code, you may declare a variable (such as *StateRecord*) to be a user-defined type anywhere in the module, even in a SUB or FUNCTION. Use a DIM, REDIM, COMMON, STATIC, or SHARED statement to declare a variable to be a user-defined type.

A DIM statement is used in the subprogram to declare that *StateRecord* is defined in the same way as in the TYPE...END TYPE structure in the main program:

```
' Declare StateRecord as defined in main program
DIM StateRecord AS RecordType
```

STATES AND ABBREVIATIONS used the following DO... LOOP to read the sequential structured file records:

```
DO UNTIL EOF(1)
   LINE INPUT #1, record$
   PRINT record$
   PRINT
   nextkey$ = INPUT$(1)
   IF UCASE$(nextkey$) = "Q" THEN EXIT DO
LOOP
```

Random-access files use the GET # statement to read records. Therefore, the DO...LOOP must be changed to:

```
RecordNumber = 1
DO UNTIL EOF(1)
   GET #1, RecordNumber, StateRecord
   PRINT StateRecord.State; StateRecord.Abbr
   PRINT
   RecordNumber = RecordNumber + 1
   nextkey$ = INPUT$(1)
   IF UCASE$(nextkey$) = "Q" THEN EXIT DO
LOOP
```

These changes complete Program 9-1, STATES AND ABBREVIATIONS—RANDOM ACCESS.

```
DECLARE SUB ReadFile ()
REM ** STATES AND ABBREVIATIONS - RANDOM ACCESS **
' Program 9-1   9/1/87

REM ** CREATE THE FILE **
' Create StateAbr.Dat file with state names and abbreviations
' Random access file with two fields: State, Abbr

   ' Define the RecordType structure
   TYPE RecordType
      State AS STRING * 30            'string field of length 30
      Abbr AS STRING * 2             'string field of length 2
   END TYPE

   ' Declare StateRecord as the above type
   DIM StateRecord AS RecordType

   ' Open random access file, specifying length of one record
   ' as the length of the StateRecord variable
   OPEN "B:StateAbr.Dat" FOR RANDOM AS #1 LEN = LEN(StateRecord)

   ' Initialize record number
   RecordNumber = 0

   ' Read data and put it in file
   DO
      READ StateRecord.State, StateRecord.Abbr
      IF StateRecord.Abbr = "ZZ" THEN EXIT DO
      RecordNumber = RecordNumber + 1
      PUT #1, RecordNumber, StateRecord
   LOOP

   DATA  Alabama,AL,  Alaska,AK,  American Samoa,AS
   DATA  Arizona,AZ,  Arkansas,AR,  California,CA
   DATA  Colorado,CO,  Connecticut, CT,  Delaware,DE
   DATA  District of Columbia,DC,  Federated States of Micronesia,TT
   DATA  Florida,FL,  Georgia,GA,  Guam,GU
   DATA  Hawaii,HI,  Idaho,ID,  Illinois,IL
   DATA  Indiana,IN,  Iowa,IA,  Kansas,KS
   DATA  Kentucky,KY,  Louisiana,LA,  Maine,ME
   DATA  Mariana Islands,CM,  Marshall Islands,TT,  Maryland,MD
   DATA  Massachusetts,MA,  Michigan,MI,  Micronesia,TT
   DATA  Minnesota,MN,  Mississippi,MS,  Missouri,MO
   DATA  Montana,MT,  Nebraska,NE,  Nevada,NV
   DATA  New Hampshire,NH,  New Jersey,NJ,  New Mexico,NM
   DATA  New York,NY,  North Carolina,NC,  North Dakota,ND
   DATA  Northern Mariana Islands,CM,  Ohio,OH,  Oklahoma,OK
   DATA  Oregon,OR,  Palau,TT,  Pennsylvania,PA
   DATA  Puerto Rico,PR,  Rhode Island,RI,  South Carolina,SC
   DATA  South Dakota,SD,  Tennessee,TN,  Texas,TX
   DATA  Utah,UT,  Vermont,VT,  Virgin Islands,VI
   DATA  Virginia,VA,  Washington,WA,  West Virginia,WV
   DATA  Wisconsin,WI,  Wyoming,WY
   DATA  End of data,ZZ

REM ** SCAN THE FILE AND PROOF READ IT **
CALL ReadFile
END
```

Program 9-1. *STATES AND ABBREVIATIONS—RANDOM ACCESS*

```
SUB ReadFile STATIC
' Scan the StateAbr.Dat file, one record at a time.

   ' Put instructions in lines 21 to 25.
   Text$(1) = STRING$(74, 196)
   Text$(2) = "Scan the States & Abbreviations file, one record at a time."
   Text$(3) = "Put the data disk in drive B."
   Text$(4) = "Press a key to begin.  First record will open a viewport."
   Text$(5) = "Press space bar to get next record, Q to quit."
   CLS
   FOR row% = 1 TO 5
     LOCATE row% + 20, 3: PRINT Text$(row%);
   NEXT row%

   ' Define rows 1 to 20 as a viewport, used for scanning records.
   VIEW PRINT 1 TO 20

   ' Wait for a key press to begin.
   PRINT "Press a key to begin."
   anykey$ = INPUT$(1)
   CLS 2                                    'Clears only viewport

   ' Declare record type
   DIM StateRecord AS RecordType

   ' Read one record each time a key other than Q is pressed.
   RecordNumber = 1
   DO UNTIL EOF(1)
     GET #1, RecordNumber, StateRecord
     PRINT StateRecord.State; StateRecord.Abbr
     PRINT
     RecordNumber = RecordNumber + 1
     nextkey$ = INPUT$(1)
     IF UCASE$(nextkey$) = "Q" THEN EXIT DO
   LOOP

   ' Close the file and the subprogram
   VIEW PRINT 1 TO 25: CLS
   CLOSE #1

END SUB
```

Program 9-1. *STATES AND ABBREVIATIONS—RANDOM ACCESS*
(continued)

Figure 9-1 shows the screen output when the PRINT statement has a semicolon between the state and abbreviation fields, as shown here:

```
PRINT StateRecord.State; StateRecord.Abbr
```

The spacing appears exactly the way the data is stored in the random-access file. Thirty bytes are used to store the state and two bytes to store the abbreviation. Since the length of records and their fields are fixed, the computer is able to search the file for individual items.

```
American Samoa          AS

Arizona                 AZ

Arkansas                AR

California              CA

Colorado                CO

Connecticut             CT

Delaware                DE

District of Columbia    DC

Federated States of MicronesiaTT
_____

Scan the States & Abbreviations file, one record at a time.
Put the data disk in drive B.
Press a key to begin.  First record will open a viewport.
Press space bar to get next record, Q to quit.
```

Figure 9-1. *Output of Program 9-1 using semicolon spacing*

Figure 9-2 shows the screen output when the PRINT statement has a comma between the state and abbreviation fields, as shown here:

```
PRINT StateRecord.State, StateRecord.Abbr
```

The records are not stored on the disk in this format. The printed output is not as crowded because the comma spacing separates the two fields when printed to the screen.

Food and Nutrition

The next programming project is a random-access data file that includes the following.

```
American Samoa                          AS

Arizona                                 AZ

Arkansas                                AR

California                              CA

Colorado                                CO

Connecticut                             CT

Delaware                                DE

District of Columbia                    DC

Federated States of Micronesia          TT


Scan the States & Abbreviations file, one record at a time.
Put the data disk in drive B.
Press a key to begin.  First record will open a viewport.
Press space bar to get next record, Q to quit.
```

Figure 9-2.   *Output of Program 9-1 using comma spacing*

- A main program with a menu to select one item from a list

- A subprogram that adds records to the data file

- A subprogram that reads all the records in the data file

- A subprogram that reads selected records by record number from the data file

- A subprogram that does a key search for specific records

The data used in the file was taken from the *Handbook of the Nutritional Contents of Foods,* prepared for the United States Department of Agriculture by Dover Publications. Only a small portion of the database available in that publication is used in the file.

However, you will be able to add to the data file at any time. Information consists of the names of various foods, the types of food (raw, fresh, cooked, and so on), and the calorie count for a one-ounce portion. These categories are used as fields in the random-access data file records.

The program will be created in short modules. You can test each part before entering the next part. Enter the following program segment and run it. It requests the disk drive to be used to store the file and the name of the data file, and then combines the two to form the complete file name. This makes the program general so that it can be used with other data files.

```
REM ** NUTRITION FILE **
' Program 9-2  9/3/87

REM ** SELECT DISK DRIVE AND FILE NAME **
CLS
LOCATE 5, 5: INPUT "Which drive for file: "; drive$
drive$ = LEFT$(drive$, 1)
LOCATE 7, 5: INPUT "File name with extension: "; filename$
filename$ = drive$ + ":" + filename$

END
```

Typical prompts and responses to this part of the program are

```
Which drive for file: ?B

File name with extension: ?FoodFile.Dat
```

A section is now added to declare the record structure. This is done in the main program, not in a subprogram or function procedure. Put it just above the END statement of the first program segment.

```
REM ** DEFINE RECORD STRUCTURE **
TYPE FoodItem
  food AS STRING * 18
  kind AS STRING * 15
  calories AS INTEGER
END TYPE

END
```

This section defines a record with three fields. The total length of each record is 35 bytes, as follows:

Food is a string field 18 bytes long

Kind is a string field 15 bytes long

Calories is an integer 2 bytes long

A section that displays the menu is added to the previous portion of the program, just ahead of the END statement in the last program segment:

```
REM ** PRINT MENU **
DO
  LOCATE 5, 5: PRINT SPACE$(70); : LOCATE 7, 5: PRINT SPACE$(70);
  LOCATE 3, 23: PRINT STRING$(35, 220);
  LOCATE 19, 23: PRINT STRING$(35, 223);
  FOR row% = 4 TO 18
    LOCATE row%, 23: PRINT CHR$(221);
    LOCATE row%, 57: PRINT CHR$(222);
  NEXT row%
  LOCATE 5, 29: PRINT "RANDOM ACCESS FILE MENU";
  LOCATE 9, 29: PRINT "(A)dd records";
  LOCATE 11, 29: PRINT "(R)ead all records";
  LOCATE 13, 29: PRINT "(G)et specified records";
  LOCATE 15, 29: PRINT "(S)earch for records";
  LOCATE 17, 29: PRINT "(Q)uit";
END
```

Enter and run the program segment as it now exists. After you enter the disk drive and file name to be used, the menu is displayed, as shown in Figure 9-3.

The next section allows you to make a selection from the menu. SELECT CASE is used to implement the choice. An appropriate subprogram is called when you press a key. A beep sounds to remind you that an entry is required.

```
REM ** MAKE A CHOICE **
LOCATE 22, 3: PRINT SPACE$(70)
LOCATE 22, 3: PRINT "Type Menu Selection (A, R, G, S, or Q)";
DO
  BEEP: KeyChoice$ = UCASE$(INPUT$(1))
LOOP WHILE INSTR("ARGSQ", KeyChoice$) = 0
```

If you want to test the partial program that now exists, remember that the procedures called by SELECT CASE have not been written yet. For testing purposes, put PRINT statements in the SELECT CASE sections with the calls to subprograms enclosed in quotation marks.

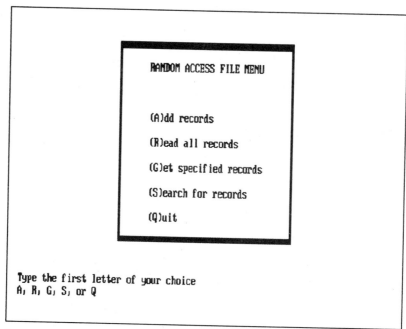

Figure 9-3. *Program 9-2 menu*

```
SELECT CASE KeyChoice$
CASE "A"
  PRINT "CALL AddRecords(filename$)"
CASE "R"
  PRINT "CALL ReadRecords(filename$)"
CASE "G"
  PRINT "CALL GetRecords(filename$)"
CASE "S"
  PRINT "CALL SearchRecords(filename$)"
```

Insert this section after the PRINT MENU block:

```
REM ** MAKE A CHOICE **
DO
  LOCATE 22, 3: PRINT SPACES$(70)
  LOCATE 22, 3: PRINT "Type Menu Selection (A, R, G, S, or Q)";
  DO
    BEEP: KeyChoice$ = UCASE$(LINPUT$(1))
  LOOP
```

```
SELECT CASE KeyChoice$
   CASE "A"
      PRINT "CALL AddRecords(filename$)"
   CASE "R"
      PRINT "CALL ReadRecords(filename$)"
   CASE "G"
      PRINT "CALL GetRecords(filename$)"
   CASE "S"
      PRINT "CALL SearchRecords(filename$)"
   CASE "Q"
      EXIT DO
END SELECT
CLS

LOOP

CLS: END
```

When the present program segment is run, the following prompts are again displayed:

```
Which drive for file: ?B
File name with extension: ?FoodFile.Dat
```

Press the key that corresponds to the first letter of any of the menu choices to test the SELECT CASE section. When the message that corresponds to your choice appears, press any key to display the menu for another choice.

The next task is to add the necessary procedures for the SELECT CASE choices. You will need procedures for

Case "A"	Subprogram AddRecords
Case "R"	Subprogram ReadRecords
Case "G"	Subprogram GetRecords
Case "S"	Subprogram SearchRecords

The AddRecords Subprogram

The AddRecords subprogram, entered with the New SUB... command from the Edit menu, may be used to create the original data file or to add records to an existing file. Use AddRecords as the name of the subprogram. When the name is entered, the opening and closing lines appear as follows:

```
SUB AddRecords_
END SUB
```

Add a CLS statement and then a DIM statement to declare a variable (*FoodRecord*), using the data type defined in the main program:

```
SUB AddRecords (filename$) STATIC
CLS

' Declare type for FoodRecord
  DIM FoodRecord AS FoodItem
```

The file is then opened:

```
' Open random access file
OPEN filename$ FOR RANDOM AS #1 LEN = LEN(FoodRecord)
```

Calculate the number of records already in the file, if any:

```
' Use LOF(1) to calculate records already in the file
RecordNumber = LOF(1)\LEN(FoodRecord)
```

The LOF(1) function calculates the total number of bytes in the file using integer division (\ ). If the data file is new, there are no records in it. In this case, LOF(1) returns a value of zero. LEN(*FoodRecord*) calculates the number of bytes in one record. Therefore:

$$\text{RecordNumber} = \frac{\text{Total bytes in file}}{\text{Bytes in one record}}$$

Since the records in a random-access file are all the same size, this formula can always be used to calculate the number of records in a file.

The next task is to provide for the entry of new records and to close the file when done. This is accomplished by the following program segment:

```
' Add new records
DO
  INPUT "Food name ?", FoodRecord.food
  INPUT "Food type ?", FoodRecord.type
```

```
    INPUT "Calories per oz. ?", FoodRecord.calories
    PUT #1, RecordNumber, FoodRecord
    INPUT "Any more (Y or N) ?", more$
    PRINT
  LOOP UNTIL UCASE$(more$) = "N"

  CLOSE #1

END SUB
```

Program 9-2, NUTRITION FILE, now contains a complete main program and one subprogram, AddRecords.

To test the subprogram entered under Case "A", go back to the main program. Remove the PRINT keyword and the beginning and ending quotation marks so that it reads

```
CASE "A"
  CALL AddRecords(filename$)
```

```
DECLARE SUB AddRecords (filename$)
REM ** NUTRITION FILE **
' Program 9-2  10/3/87

REM ** SELECT DISK DRIVE AND FILE NAME **
CLS
LOCATE 5, 5: INPUT "Which drive for file: "; drive$
drive$ = LEFT$(drive$, 1)
LOCATE 7, 5: INPUT "File name with extension: "; filename$
filename$ = drive$ + ":" + filename$

REM ** DEFINE RECORD STRUCTUTE **
TYPE FoodItem
   food AS STRING * 18
   kind AS STRING * 15
   calories AS INTEGER
END TYPE

REM ** PRINT MENU **
DO
  LOCATE 5, 5: PRINT SPACES$(70); : LOCATE 7, 5: PRINT SPACES$(70);
  LOCATE 3, 23: PRINT STRING$(35, 220);
  LOCATE 19, 23: PRINT STRING$(35, 223);
  FOR row% = 4 TO 18
     LOCATE row%, 23: PRINT CHR$(221);
     LOCATE row%, 57: PRINT CHR$(222);
  NEXT row%
```

Program 9-2. *NUTRITION FILE*

```
   LOCATE 5, 29: PRINT "RANDOM ACCESS FILE MENU";
   LOCATE 9, 29: PRINT "(A)dd records";
   LOCATE 11, 29: PRINT "(R)ead all records";
   LOCATE 13, 29: PRINT "(G)et specified records";
   LOCATE 15, 29: PRINT "(S)earch for records";
   LOCATE 17, 29: PRINT "(Q)uit";

   REM ** MAKE A CHOICE **
   LOCATE 22, 3: PRINT SPACE$(70);
   LOCATE 22, 3: PRINT "Type Menu Selection (A, R, G, S, or Q)";
   DO
     BEEP: KeyChoice$ = UCASE$(INPUT$(1))
   LOOP WHILE INSTR("ARGSQ", KeyChoice$) = 0

   SELECT CASE KeyChoice$
     CASE "A"
       CALL AddRecords(filename$)
     CASE "R"
       PRINT "CALL ReadRecords(filename$)"
     CASE "G"
       PRINT "CALL GetRecords(filename$)"
     CASE "S"
       PRINT "CALL SearchRecords(filename$)"
     CASE "Q"
       EXIT DO
   END SELECT
   CLS

LOOP

CLS : END

SUB AddRecords (filename$) STATIC
CLS

' Declare type for FoodRecord
  DIM FoodRecord AS FoodItem

  ' Open random access file
  OPEN filename$ FOR RANDOM AS #1 LEN = LEN(FoodRecord)

  ' Use LOF(1) to calculate record number
  RecordNumber = LOF(1) \ LEN(FoodRecord)

  ' Add records, then close file
  DO
    INPUT "Food name ?", FoodRecord.food
    INPUT "Food type ?", FoodRecord.kind
    INPUT "Calories per oz. ?", FoodRecord.calories
    RecordNumber = RecordNumber + 1
    PUT #1, RecordNumber, FoodRecord
    INPUT "Any more (Y or N) ? ", more$
    PRINT
  LOOP UNTIL UCASE$(more$) = "N"

  CLOSE #1

END SUB
```

Program 9-2. *NUTRITION FILE (continued)*

Run the program and select (A)dd Records from the menu by pressing A. The screen is cleared and the opening prompt appears:

```
Foodname ?
```

As the prompts appear, enter the data for three records, as shown in Figure 9-4. When you are finished, enter **N** at the prompt:

```
Any more (Y or N) ? n
```

This returns you to the menu shown in Figure 9-3. Select Q to quit and you are returned to the program in the View window.

The ReadRecords Subprogram

You have entered three records in the food data file. Now you need to have some way to read the records. The ReadRecords subprogram is similar to AddRecords. The type for FoodRecord is declared and the file is opened in the same way. LOF(1) is then used to calculate the total number of records in the file by

```
NumberOfRecords = LOF(1) \ LEN(FoodRecord)
```

A FOR . . . NEXT loop is used to read and print the records in this subprogram:

```
FOR RecordNumber = 1 TO NumberOfRecords
  GET #1, RecordNumber, FoodRecord
  PRINT FoodRecord.food; FoodRecord.kind; FoodRecord.calories
NEXT RecordNumber
```

The file is then closed and the subprogram ends as before. The subprogram looks like this:

```
SUB ReadRecords (filename$) STATIC
CLS

  ' Declare type for FoodRecord
  DIM FoodRecord AS FoodItem

  ' Open random access file
  OPEN filename$ FOR RANDOM AS #1 LEN = LEN(FoodRecord)
```

```
Food name ?Apple
Food type ?fresh
Calories per oz. ?15
Any more (Y or N) ? y

Food name ?Avocado
Food type ?fresh
Calories per oz. ?48
Any more (Y or N) ? y

Food name ?Banana
Food type ?fresh
Calories per oz. ?24
Any more (Y or N) ? n
```

Figure 9-4. *Three entries for food file*

```
' Calculate number of records
NumberOfRecords = LOF(1)\ LEN(FoodRecord)

' Read and print records
FOR RecordNumber = 1 to NumberOfRecords
  GET #1, RecordNumber, FoodRecord
  PRINT FoodRecord.food; FoodRecord.kind; FoodRecord.calories
NEXT RecordNumber

LOCATE 25, 1: PRINT "Press any key to continue";
waitkey$ = INPUT$(1)

CLOSE #1

END SUB
```

Enter the subprogram by the New SUB... command of the File menu, using the name ReadRecords.

Before you can test the ReadRecords subprogram, you must remove the **PRINT** keyword and the quotation marks from the **SELECT CASE** section of the main program:

```
SELECT CASE KeyChoice$
  CASE "A"
    CALL AddRecords(filename$)
  CASE "R"
    CALL ReadRecords(filename$)          ◄──────── PRINT and quotation
  CASE "G"                                           marks removed
    PRINT "CALL GetRecords(filename$)
  CASE "S"
    PRINT "CALL SearchRecords(filename$)
        •
        •
        •
```

Run Program 9-2 with this subprogram added, and choose (R)ead records from the program menu.

You entered three records when the data file was created earlier. Figure 9-5 shows these records displayed by the ReadRecord subprogram.

Getting Records by Record Number

Since random-access records are numbered by the PUT# statement, it is easy to retrieve a record from a data file using the GET# statement. The GetRecords subprogram shown below allows you to retrieve a specific record by entering its number.

```
SUB GetRecords (filename$) STATIC
CONST False = 0, True = NOT False
CLS

  ' Declare type for FoodRecord
  DIM FoodRecord AS FoodItem

  ' Open random access file
  OPEN filename$ FOR RANDOM AS #1 LEN = LEN(FoodRecord)

  ' Calculate number of records
  NumberOfRecords = LOF(1) \ LEN(FoodRecord)

  ' Get records requested
  GetMore = True

  DO
    PRINT "Enter record number desired ";
    INPUT "", RecordNumber
    IF RecordNumber > 0 AND RecordNumber <= NumberOfRecords THEN
      GET #1, RecordNumber, FoodRecord
      PRINT FoodRecord.food; FoodRecord.kind; FoodRecord.calories
    ELSEIF RecordNumber = 0 THEN
      GetMore = False
    ELSE
      PRINT "Input value out of range."
    END IF
```

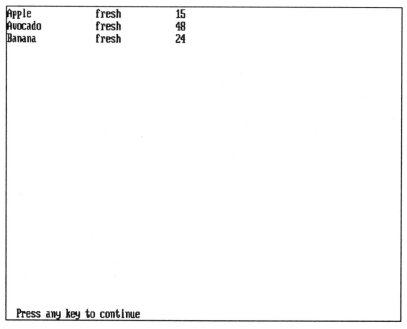

Figure 9-5. *Three-record output of food file*

```
    PRINT
LOOP WHILE GetMore

LOCATE 25, 1: PRINT "Press any key to continue";
waitkey$ = INPUT$(1)

CLOSE #1

END SUB
```

Two constants are declared at the beginning of the subprogram, *True* and *False*:

```
CONST False = 0, True = NOT False
```

A DO...LOOP is used to request a record number, get the record, and print the appropriate information. The variable *GetMore* is set to *True* before the loop is entered. When you enter the loop, you are prompted for a record number. The result of entering a record number is one of the following:

■ If the number is in the range of the number of records in the file, the record having the specified number is printed.

```
        .
        .
        .
IF RecordNumber > 0 AND RecordNumber <= NumberOfRecords THEN
    GET #1, RecordNumber, FoodRecord
    PRINT FoodRecord.food; FoodRecord.kind; FoodRecord.calories
        .
        .
        .
```

■ If the number is zero, the variable *GetMore* is set to *False*, which causes an exit from the loop.

```
        .
        .
        .
ELSEIF RecordNumber = 0 THEN
   GetMore = False
        .
        .
        .
LOOP WHILE Getmore   ◄───────── Loop if GetMore is true
```

■ If the number is greater than the number of records in the file or less than zero, an out-of-range message is printed, but you stay inside the loop for another entry.

```
        .
        .
        .
    ELSE
       PRINT "Input value out of range."
    END IF
  LOOP WHILE GetMore

END SUB
```

The subprogram ends when an exit is made from the loop. Enter **0** (zero) for the record number when you wish to exit.

Before trying the (G)et Records selection, run the program again and add the records shown in Table 9-1 using the AddRecords menu selection.

When the record for cottage cheese has been entered, answer **N** at the prompt:

```
Any more (Y or N) " N
```

Food	Type	Calories
Bass	sea — cooked	74
Beans	lima — cooked	32
Beef	chuck — cooked	93
Biscuits	homemade	105
Blueberries	fresh	18
Bread	whole wheat	69
Broccoli	cooked	7
Butter	salted	205
Cabbage	raw	7
Cake	angel food	77
Cake	devil's food	105
Carrots	raw	12
Chicken	roasted	83
Cottage cheese	creamed	30

Table 9-1. *Additional Nutritional Data*

The menu is then displayed again. You now have 17 records in the food file and can display the entire file. However, you must first remove the **PRINT** keyword and the quotation marks from the **SELECT CASE** section of the main program in order to use the GetRecords subprogram:

```
SELECT CASE KeyChoice$
   CASE "A"
      CALL AddRecords(filename$)
   CASE "R"
      CALL ReadRecords(filename$)
   CASE "G"
      CALL GetRecords(filename$)
   CASE "S"
      PRINT "CALL SearchRecords(filename$)
         .
         .
         .
```

Choose (R)ead Records and the screen shown in Figure 9-6 is displayed.

Press any key to return to the program menu. Then select (G)et Records from the menu. At the prompt, type the record number of the record you want to see and press ENTER. The requested record is

```
Apple           fresh          15
Avocado         fresh          48
Banana          fresh          24
Bass            sea-cooked     74
Beans           lima-cooked    32
Beef            chuck-cooked   93
Biscuits        home-made     105
Blueberries     fresh          18
Bread           whole wheat    69
Broccoli        cooked          7
Butter          salted        285
Cabbage         raw             7
Cake            angel food     77
Cake            devil's food  185
Carrots         raw            12
Chicken         roasted        83
Cottage cheese  creamed        38




Press any key to continue
```

Figure 9-6. *Food file output — 17 records*

displayed, along with the prompt for another record:

`Enter record number desired` ←————————— *No cursor shows*

Figure 9-7 shows typical responses to various entries.

Retrieving Records by Food Name

You will probably have trouble remembering the contents of a record by its number. You'll be glad to know you can search the records by the name of the food that you want to retrieve.

The SearchRecords subprogram allows you to display the complete record for any food that you name, as long as it is in the data file.

```
Enter record number desired 2
Avocado        fresh         48

Enter record number desired 4
Bass           sea-cooked    74

Enter record number desired 10
Broccoli       cooked        7

Enter record number desired 25
Input value out of range.

Enter record number desired 8
Blueberries    fresh         18

Enter record number desired 0




Press any key to continue
```

Figure 9-7.   *GetRecords output*

You do not have to enter the complete name of the food. The length of your entry is assigned to the variable *Length%*. The search is made for only that portion of the name entered.

```
' Get search key
INPUT "Enter name of food for search: "; item$
Length% = LEN(item$)
item$ = UCASE$(item$)
```

If you enter a single letter, all records of foods that begin with that letter will be displayed:

```
Enter name of food for search: ? a
Apple          fresh             15
Avocado        fresh             48
```

When you enter a search string, a search for a food whose leftmost letters match the search string starts from the first record number. The search proceeds through the file, one record at a time, until it reaches a food name that is greater than the search string — is beyond the search string alphabetically. For example:

```
' Print records from file that match
RecordNumber = 1: match% = 0
DO UNTIL EOF(1)
   GET #1, RecordNumber, FoodRecord
   look$ = UCASE$(LEFT$(FoodRecord.food, Length%))
   IF look$ = item$ THEN
     PRINT FoodRecord.food; FoodRecord.kind; FoodRecord.calories
     match% = 1
   ELSEIF look$ > item$ THEN
     EXIT DO
   END IF
   RecordNumber = RecordNumber + 1
LOOP
```

It is assumed that the data is arranged in alphabetical order by food name. If it is not, it should be sorted in that order. Sorting is discussed in the next chapter.

The variable *match%* is set to zero before the DO...LOOP is entered. As each match is found, the full food record is printed and *match%* is set equal to 1. This value serves as a flag, revealing that at least one match was found. An exit is made from the loop when the food name retrieved from the file is greater than the entry. If no match is found, *match%* is equal to zero and an appropriate message is printed. Here is an example:

```
IF match% = 0 THEN PRINT item$; " not found."

Example:  Enter name of food for search: ? donuts
          DONUTS not found.
```

After each search is completed, you are asked if you want to have another search. If you type the letter **Y** at the prompt, you are asked for a new search name. Otherwise, the file is closed and the subprogram ends. The SearchRecords subprogram follows. Enter it and test it with several search keys.

```
SUB SearchRecords (filename$) STATIC
CLS

   ' Declare FoodRecord type
   DIM FoodRecord AS FoodItem

   ' Open random access file
   OPEN filename$ FOR RANDOM AS #1 LEN = LEN(FoodRecord)

   ' Get search key
```

```
DO
  INPUT "Enter name of food for search: "; item$
  Length% = LEN(item$)
  item$ = UCASE$(item$)

  ' Print records from file that match
  RecordNumber = 1: match% = 0
  DO UNTIL EOF(1)
    GET #1, RecordNumber, FoodRecord
    Look$ = UCASE$(LEFT$(FoodRecord.food, Length%))
    IF Look$ = item$ THEN
      PRINT FoodRecord.food; FoodRecord.kind; FoodRecord.calories
      match% = 1
    ELSEIF Look$ > item$ THEN
      EXIT DO
    END IF
    RecordNumber = RecordNumber + 1
  LOOP
  IF match% = 0 THEN PRINT item$; " not found."
  PRINT : PRINT "Another search (Y or N) "
  Repeatkey$ = UCASE$(INPUT$(1))
  IF Repeatkey$ <> "Y" THEN EXIT DO
LOOP

LOCATE 25, 1: PRINT "Press any key to continue";
waitkey$ = INPUT$(1)

CLOSE #1

END SUB
```

Figure 9-8 shows the result of four searches.

The Case of the Faulty Choice

Everyone makes a mistake at the keyboard sooner or later. Therefore, you should provide for an attempted entry that is not on the menu. This is taken care of by a short DO...LOOP that gives a beep to signal when an entry is to be made. It also beeps if you make a wrong entry choice. It will accept only the keys A, R, G, S, or Q.

```
DO
  BEEP: KeyChoice$ = UCASE$(INPUT$(1))
LOOP WHILE INSTR("ARGSQ", KeyChoice$) = 0
```

You have put together the main program, four subprograms, and a function. This completes Program 9-2, NUTRITION FILE. You can add more records to the food file, read the entire file, read records selected by number, and search for records by name. Feel free to customize the program to fit your needs.

```
Enter name of food for search: ? cake
Cake            angel food      77
Cake            devil's food    185

Another search (Y or N)
Enter name of food for search: ? ca
Cabbage         raw             7
Cake            angel food      77
Cake            devil's food    185
Carrots         raw             12

Another search (Y or N)
Enter name of food for search: ? avoc
Avocado         fresh           48

Another search (Y or N)
Enter name of food for search: ? ba
Banana          fresh           24
Bass            sea-cooked      74

Another search (Y or N)



Press any key to continue
```

Figure 9-8. *Result of four searches*

Review

This chapter was devoted to random-access files. Files opened FOR RANDOM may be read from or written to. The length of random-access files is specified by the LEN clause in the OPEN statement. TYPE...END TYPE defines variable types to be used in a random-access file. Defining variable types in this way allows you to mix string and number fields in the same record. It also allows for automatic calculation of record length. PUT # is used to write a record to a random-access file, and GET # is used to read a record from a random-access file. The length of a random-access file is found by the LOF() function. The CLOSE # statement is used to close random-access files.

One program in this chapter reads data from DATA statements. The other uses keyboard entry of data. Menus are used for selecting the desired action from a list of several possibilities. File actions performed are to add records to the file, read all records in the file, read records in the file by specifying a number, and read records in the file specified by the name or part of a name.

10 **Massaging Files**

Data stored in files may become outdated as time passes. Such outdated information should be periodically updated. This chapter demonstrates several utilities that allow you to copy or alter files in one or more ways.

The first utility that is discussed and demonstrated allows you to copy and scan a sequential file. Then a more complex utility is presented, which allows you to append records, delete records, insert records, and scan a sequential file. The last utility covered in this chapter demonstrates how to sort records in a random-access file after they have been randomly scrambled.

Copying a Sequential File

One useful file utility makes a duplicate of your data file. This utility allows you to make backup copies or to copy a data file from one disk to another. MS-DOS has a copy utility program that you have probably used. For example:

```
A> COPY filename B:
```
← *Copies a file (file name) to the disk in drive B*

But sometimes you may want to copy a file as part of a QuickBASIC program without stopping and using the MS-DOS copy program. A program to copy a sequential file should include these steps:

1. Get the name of the old file to be copied and the disk drive where it is located.

2. Get the name of the new file (the copy) and the disk drive where it is located.

3. Use the information from steps 1 and 2 to form the file specifications used to access the two files.

4. Pause while disks are being placed in the proper drives.

5. Open the file to be copied for input and the file to receive the copy for output.

6. Read records from the old file and write them to the new file.

7. After all records have been read and copied, close both files.

8. Provide a message indicating that the original file has been copied.

9. Scan the file to see if it has been copied correctly.

Some of these steps may be omitted if copying a file is simply part of a larger program.

In writing a file copy program, you might begin with a skeleton program that contains a main program with subprograms that merely print the name of their function.

Program 10-1, COPY A SEQUENTIAL FILE, calls three subprograms:

```
CALL NameDrive(OldFile$, NewFile$)  ◄─────  To get disk drive and file names

CALL CopyFile(OldFile$, NewFile$)  ◄─────  To copy the file
CALL ScanFile(FileToScan$)  ◄─────  To scan the new file to verify
                                           a correct copy
```

Test the main program to make sure it works as expected. Enter Program 10-1 and run it.

```
DECLARE SUB NameDrive (OldFile$, NewFile$)
DECLARE SUB CopyFile (OldFile$, NewFile$)
DECLARE SUB ScanFile (FileToScan$)
REM ** COPY A SEQUENTIAL FILE **
' Program 10-1  9/12/87

CLS : PRINT "Program 10-1, COPY A SEQUENTIAL FILE"
PRINT

CALL NameDrive(OldFile$, NewFile$)

PRINT : PRINT "Press any key to continue."
startkey$ = INPUT$(1)

CALL CopyFile(OldFile$, NewFile$)

PRINT : PRINT "File copy is finished."
PRINT : PRINT "To scan new file, press S"
PRINT : PRINT "To quit, press any key except S"

ScanOrQuit$ = UCASE$(INPUT$(1))
IF ScanOrQuit$ = "S" THEN CALL ScanFile(NewFile$)

END
SUB CopyFile (OldFile$, NewFile$) STATIC
  PRINT : PRINT "CopyFile subprogram"
END SUB
SUB NameDrive (OldFile$, NewFile$) STATIC
  PRINT "NameDrive subprogram"
END SUB
SUB ScanFile (FileToScan$)
  PRINT : PRINT "ScanFile subprogram"
END SUB
```

Program 10-1. *COPY A SEQUENTIAL FILE*

Program 10-1 begins by clearing the screen and printing its name. It then calls the NameDrive subprogram. For now, this subprogram merely prints its name. A message is then printed and the program halts, waiting for you to press a key. The output at this point is

```
Program 10-1, COPY A SEQUENTIAL FILE

NameDrive subprogram

Press any key to continue.
```

When you press a key, the program calls the CopyFile subprogram. This subprogram prints its name. Then more messages are printed and the program halts again. The output is now

```
Program 10-1, COPY A SEQUENTIAL FILE
NameDrive subprogram
Press any key to continue.
CopyFile subprogram
File copy is finished.
To scan new file, press S
To quit, press any key except S
```

Press S and the ScanFile subprogram is called. It also prints its name. The final display is shown in Figure 10-1.

The program flow has now been checked. Add the subprograms, one at a time, so that they can be tested individually. Some of the subprograms will be used again, so they should be saved separately. You can then merge them with other programs as they are needed.

Adding the NameDrive Subprogram

From the File menu select New Program... and press ENTER. Enter this one line:

```
REM ** PRO10-2 NameDrive Subprogram - Use View Menu to see **
```

Then access the New SUB... command from the Edit menu. Type **NameDrive** in the dialog box and press ENTER. Then enter Program 10-2, NameDrive.

When you have entered the subprogram, use Save As... from the File menu to save the file (containing the one-line main program and the NameDrive subprogram) as NameDriv.Sub. This saves the subprogram as a separate file so that it can be merged with other programs, as well as with Program 10-1.

Next, reload Program 10-1. Access the View menu and select the SUBs... command. Press ENTER. Move the highlight down to the NameDrive subprogram. Use the TAB key to move to the DELETE

```
Program 10-1, COPY A SEQUENTIAL FILE

NameDrive subprogram

Press any key to continue,

CopyFile subprogram

File copy is finished,

To scan new file, press S

To quit, press any key except S

ScanFile subprogram




Press any key to continue
```

Figure 10-1. *Output of Program 10-1 before adding subprograms*

```
REM ** PRO10-2 NameDrive Subprogram - Use View Menu to see **

SUB NameDrive (OldFile$, NewFile$) STATIC

  CLS
  INPUT "Old File Name"; FromFile$
  INPUT "Old File Drive"; FromDrive$
  PRINT
  INPUT "New File Name"; ToFile$
  INPUT "New File Drive"; ToDrive$

  OldFile$ = LEFT$(FromDrive$, 1) + ":" + FromFile$
  NewFile$ = LEFT$(ToDrive$, 1) + ":" + ToFile$

END SUB
```

Program 10-2. *Name Drive*

button. Press ENTER and a dialog box asks if you want to delete the procedure from the main module. Since you want to delete the old three-line NameDrive subprogram, press ENTER while the OK button is highlighted. This deletes the old subprogram that merely printed the subprogram's name.

Access the main program and move the cursor to the beginning of it. To put the new subprogram in place, access the File menu. Then select the Merge... command and press ENTER. At the dialog box, enter the name of the file to be merged, which is

```
B:NameDriv.SUB
```

Press ENTER. Delete the REM statement that appears at the top of the main program. Then access the NameDrive subprogram from the View menu to make sure it was correctly merged. Make any necessary changes and save this new version of Program 10-1 as PRO10-1A.

Now you are ready to test the NameDrive subprogram. Run the new version of Program 10-1. The program name is printed as it was in the previous run. The NewDrive subprogram then produces the following display:

```
Old File Name? OldGold.BAS  ◄───    OldGold is the old file.
Old File Drive? A           ◄───    OldGold is on disk in drive A.

New File Name? NewLode.BAS   ◄───    NewLode is new file.
New File Drive? B           ◄───    Disk to accept NewLode is in drive B.

Press any key to continue.
```

This trial run shows that the NameDrive subprogram is working correctly.

Adding the CopyFile Subprogram

The CopyFile subprogram is added in the same way that you added the NameDrive subprogram. Enter the CopyFile subprogram as a separate file, just as you did with the NameDrive subprogram. Select New Program... from the File menu and enter the REM statement

```
REM ** PRO10-3 CopyFile Subprogram - Use View Menu to see **
```

Then access the New SUB. . . command from the Edit menu and enter the name **CopyFile**. Then press ENTER and enter Program 10-3, CopyFile.

When you have entered the subprogram, use Save As. . . from the File menu to save the file as CopyFile.Sub. This saves CopyFile as a separate file that can be merged with other programs.

Reload Program 10-1A and delete the old three-line CopyFile subprogram in the same way that you deleted the old three-line NameDrive subprogram.

When the old subprogram has been deleted, place the cursor at the beginning of the main program. Then access the File menu, select the Merge. . . command, and press ENTER. At the dialog box, enter the name of the new file to be merged:

```
B:CopyFile.SUB
```

Press ENTER. Once again, delete the REM statement that appears at the top of the main program. Access the CopyFile subprogram from the View menu to make sure it was merged correctly. Save this new version of the program as PRO10-1B.

```
REM ** PRO10-3 CopyFile Subprogram - Use View Menu to see **

SUB CopyFile (OldFile$, NewFile$) STATIC

   OPEN OldFile$ FOR INPUT AS #1
   OPEN NewFile$ FOR OUTPUT AS #2

   DO UNTIL EOF(1)
     LINE INPUT #1, record$
     PRINT #2, record$
   LOOP

   CLOSE #1, #2

END SUB
```

Program 10-3. *CopyFile*

You can test the CopyFile subprogram by creating a short file and using Program 10-1 to copy it. To create the file, select New Program... from the File menu and enter the following lines of text:

```
REM ** PROGRAM TO TEST COPYFILE SUBPROGRAM **
' Unnumbered Program
' For testing purposes
' Save as: REMFILE.BAS
```

Save the text as a file named RemFile.Bas on the same disk that contains the latest version of Program 10-1. Then put this disk into drive B. Load and run Program 10-1. The following dialog box is displayed.

```
Program 10-1 COPY A SEQUENTIAL FILE

Old File Name? REMFILE.BAS        ◄───── Be sure to enter the extension .BAS
Old File Drive? B

New File Name? TEMP.BAS           ◄───── Name with extension
New File Drive? B

Press any key to continue.
```

When you press any key, RemFile.Bas will be copied to the same disk (in drive B) with a new name: Temp.Bas. After the file has been copied the dialog continues.

```
     .
     .
     .
File copy is finished.

To scan new file, press S

To quit, press any key except S
```

Since the ScanFile subprogram has not been written yet, press a key other than S to quit.

You can look at the copied program by loading it using the Open Program... command from the Run menu. This is possible because RemFile.Bas was saved as a QuickBASIC program, even though technically it is a text file and not a program that can be executed.

Adding the ScanFile Subprogram

Select New Program... from the File menu and enter this line:

```
REM ** PRO10-4 ScanFile Subprogram - Use View Menu to see **
```

Then access New SUB... from the Edit menu. Enter the name **ScanFile** in the dialog box and press ENTER. Enter Program 10-4, ScanFile. Save it as ScanFile.Sub.

```
REM ** PRO10-4 ScanFile SUB - Use View Menu to see **
SUB ScanFile (FileToScan$) STATIC
' FileToScan$ includes drive designation
   ' Put instructions in lines 21 to 25.
   Text$(1) = STRING$(74, 196)
   Text$(2) = "Scan " + FileToScan$ + " file, one record at a time."
   Text$(3) = "Put the data disk in drive " + LEFT$(FileToScan$, 1) + "."
   Text$(4) = "Press a key to begin.  First record will appear on screen."
   Text$(5) = "Press space bar to get next record, Q to quit."
   CLS
   FOR row% = 1 TO 5
      LOCATE row% + 20, 3: PRINT Text$(row%);
   NEXT row%

   ' Define rows 1 to 20 as a viewport, used for scanning records.
   VIEW PRINT 1 TO 20

   ' Wait for a key press to begin.
   LOCATE 10, 28: PRINT "Press a key to begin."
   anykey$ = INPUT$(1)
   CLS 2                                 'Clears only viewport

   ' Open the file to scan for input as file #1.
   OPEN FileToScan$ FOR INPUT AS #1

   ' Read one record each time a key other than Q is pressed.
   DO UNTIL EOF(1)
      LINE INPUT #1, record$
      PRINT record$
      PRINT
      nextkey$ = INPUT$(1)
      IF UCASE$(nextkey$) = "Q" THEN EXIT DO
   LOOP

   PRINT : PRINT "End of file. Press any key to continue.";
   anykey$ = INPUT$(1)

   ' Close the file and end the subprogram
   VIEW PRINT 1 TO 25: CLS
   CLOSE #1

END SUB
```

Program 10-4. *Scan File*

Remove the old three-line ScanFile subprogram from Program 10-1 by selecting SUBs... from the View menu, highlighting the ScanFile subprogram in the dialog box, using TAB to move to the Delete button, and pressing the ENTER key. Then merge the new ScanFile subprogram with the Merge... command of the File menu.

When the subprogram has been merged, put the ScanFile subprogram in the View window to make sure it has been merged correctly.

Save the revised Program 10-1. You can now test the ScanFile subprogram. Use Program 10-1 to copy itself to a file named Temp.Bas. Then scan the copied program Temp.Bas. The following dialog is displayed

```
Program 10-1, COPY A SEQUENTIAL FILE

Old File Name? PRO10-1.BAS
Old File Drive? B

New File Name? TEMP.BAS
New File Drive? B

Press any key to continue.

File copy is finished.

To scan new file, press S

To quit, press any key except S
```

Press S to scan the Temp.Bas file. Figure 10-2 shows the scan of the copied file in progress. You may step through the entire file or press Q when you are satisfied the copy was made correctly.

The ScanFile subprogram reads each record with a LINE INPUT # statement. It prints a blank line between consecutive program lines so that the lines can be easily read. If you want to change the way records are read or the way they are printed to the screen, you can write individual subprograms to format the data as desired.

Here is a little program to create a file in which each record is a letter of the alphabet. Enter and run Program 10-5, CREATE FILE OF LETTERS FROM A TO Z. Then use Program 10-1 to copy the data file produced (Alphabet.Dat) to a temporary file (Temp.Dat). You will use Alphabet.Dat again later.

A scan of the Temp.Dat file is shown in Figure 10-3.

```
DECLARE SUB NameDrive (OldFile$, NewFile$)

DECLARE SUB CopyFile (OldFile$, NewFile$)

DECLARE SUB ScanFile (FileToScan$)

REM ** COPY A SEQUENTIAL FILE **

' Program 10-1  9/12/87



CLS : PRINT "Program 10-1, COPY A SEQUENTIAL FILE"

PRINT




_____

Scan the B:TEMP.BAS file, one record at a time.
Put the data disk in drive B.
Press a key to begin.  First record will open a viewport.
Press space bar to get next record, Q to quit.
```

Figure 10-2. *Scan of copied file in progress*

```
REM ** CREATE FILE OF LETTERS FROM A TO Z **
' Program 10-5  9/12/87

OPEN "B:Alphabet.Dat" FOR OUTPUT AS #1

FOR k% = 1 TO 26
  PRINT #1, CHR$(k% + 64)
NEXT k%

CLOSE #1

END
```

Program 10-5. *CREATE FILE OF LETTERS FROM A TO Z*

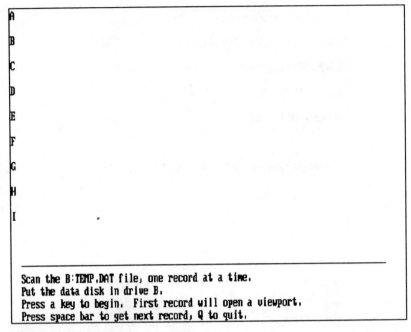

```
A
B
C
D
E
F
G
H
I
                                                          .

Scan the B:TEMP.DAT file, one record at a time.
Put the data disk in drive B.
Press a key to begin. First record will open a viewport.
Press space bar to get next record, Q to quit.
```

Figure 10-3. *Scan of Temp.Dat file*

Copying and Editing a Sequential File

So far, you have created, copied, and scanned a data file. If data in a file is to be changed, you need a utility program that lets you edit the information in a data file.

Program 10-6, COPY AND EDIT A SEQUENTIAL FILE, is a skeleton program that provides for subprograms to append data to a file, to delete data from a file, insert new data into a file, and to scan a file. The subprograms will be added and tested one at a time.

Enter the skeleton program and run it to see how the program flows. The main program provides displays similar to those of Program 10-1. The name of the program is printed. Then the NameDrive subprogram is called. At the present time, the subprogram merely prints its name.

```
DECLARE SUB NameDrive (OldFile$, NewFile$)
DECLARE SUB CopyEdit (OldFile$, NewFile$)
DECLARE SUB ScanFile (FileToScan$)
DECLARE SUB AppendFile (FileName$)
REM ** COPY & EDIT A SEQUENTIAL FILE **
' Program 10-6  9/12/87

CLS : PRINT "Program 10-6, COPY & EDIT A SEQUENTIAL FILE"
PRINT

CALL NameDrive(OldFile$, NewFile$)

PRINT : PRINT "Press any key to continue."
startkey$ = INPUT$(1)

CALL CopyEdit(OldFile$, NewFile$)

PRINT : PRINT "File copy & edit is finished."
PRINT : PRINT "Add additional records to "; NewFile$; " (Y or N)?"

DO
  BEEP: WhatToDo$ = UCASE$(INPUT$(1))
LOOP WHILE INSTR("YN", WhatToDo$) = 0

IF WhatToDo$ = "Y" THEN CALL AppendFile(NewFile$)

PRINT "To scan new file, press S"
PRINT : PRINT "To quit, press any key except S"

ScanOrQuit$ = UCASE$(INPUT$(1))
IF ScanOrQuit$ = "S" THEN CALL ScanFile(NewFile$)

END
SUB AppendFile (FileName$) STATIC
  PRINT : PRINT "AppendFile subprogram"
END SUB
SUB CopyEdit (OldFile$, NewFile$) STATIC
  PRINT : PRINT "CopyEdit subprogram"
END SUB
SUB NameDrive (OldFile$, NewFile$) STATIC
  PRINT "NameDrive subprogram"
END SUB
SUB ScanFile (FileToScan$)
  PRINT : PRINT "ScanFile subprogram"
END SUB
```

Program 10-6. *COPY AND EDIT A SEQUENTIAL FILE*

The program pauses after the NameDrive subprogram is executed. When you press a key at the message **Press any key to continue**, the CopyEdit subprogram is called. The name of the CopyEdit subprogram is printed.

Two messages are printed after the CopyEdit subprogram has been executed. They are

```
PRINT "File copy and edit is finished."
PRINT : PRINT "Add additional records to "; NewFile$; "(Y or N)?"
```

A DO...LOOP then beeps and waits for your response:

```
DO
  BEEP: WhatToDo$ = UCASE$(INPUT$(1))
LOOP WHILE INSTR("YN", WhatToDo$) = 0
```

If you respond by pressing Y, the AppendFile subprogram is called. It prints its name and returns to the main program where additional messages are printed. The dialog carried out so far looks like this:

```
Program 10-6, COPY & EDIT A SEQUENTIAL FILE

NameDrive subprogram

Press any key to continue.

CopyEdit subprogram

File copy & edit is finished.

Add additional records to  (Y or N)?

AppendFile subprogram
To scan new file, press S

To quit, press any key except S
```

If you respond with N, the AppendFile subprogram is not called. In this case, the dialog to this point is

```
Program 10-6, COPY & EDIT A SEQUENTIAL FILE

NameDrive subprogram

Press any key to continue.

CopyEdit subprogram

File copy & edit is finished.

Add additional records to  (Y or N)?
To scan new file, press S

To quit, press any key except S
```

The screen is then cleared. You are asked if you want to scan the file. If you do, press the letter S; if you do not, press any other key except S. This ends the program.

You can now add subprograms to replace the temporary subprograms in the skeleton program.

Adding the NameDrive and ScanFile Subprograms

Replace the temporary NameDrive subprogram with the subprogram of the same name used in Program 10-1. This allows you to enter the names and drives to be used.

Replace the temporary ScanFile subprogram with the subprogram of the same name used in Program 10-1. This allows you to scan the file after you have altered the file with the CopyEdit or AppendFile subprograms.

Adding the CopyEdit Subprogram

The CopyEdit subprogram has not been used before. Therefore, enter Program 10-7, CopyEdit, in just the way you entered previous subprograms in this chapter. Then delete the three-line subprogram used to print the subprogram's name. Merge the new subprogram into Program 10-3.

The CopyEdit subprogram allows you to execute one of four options:

- To read a record from an old file
- To copy a record on the screen to a new file
- To insert a new record before the one on the screen
- To quit a subprogram

When the CopyEdit subprogram is called, it prints a list of instructions at the bottom of the screen and opens two files. The file to be

```
REM ** PRO10-7 CopyEdit Subprogram - Use View Menu to see **

SUB CopyEdit (OldFile$, NewFile$) STATIC
  ' Print menu and open viewport
  CLS
  LOCATE 19, 3: PRINT STRING$(74, 196)
  LOCATE 20, 3: PRINT "Type Menu Instruction (R, C, I, or Q):"
  LOCATE 21, 3: PRINT "  (R)ead a record from "; OldFile$
  LOCATE 22, 3: PRINT "  (C)opy the record on the screen to "; NewFile$
  LOCATE 23, 3: PRINT "  (I)nsert a new record before the one on screen"
  LOCATE 24, 3: PRINT "  (Q)uit";
  VIEW PRINT 1 TO 18

  OPEN OldFile$ FOR INPUT AS #1
  OPEN NewFile$ FOR OUTPUT AS #2

  DO

    DO
      BEEP: WhatToDo$ = UCASE$(INPUT$(1))
      LOCATE 18, 1: PRINT STRING$(79, 32);
    LOOP WHILE INSTR("RCIQ", WhatToDo$) = 0

    SELECT CASE WhatToDo$
      CASE "R"
        IF NOT EOF(1) THEN
          LINE INPUT #1, OldRecord$
          CLS 2: PRINT OldRecord$
        ELSE
          LOCATE 18, 1: PRINT "All records have already been read.";
        END IF
      CASE "C"
        PRINT #2, OldRecord$
        LOCATE 18, 1: PRINT " Record on screen is copied to "; NewFile$;
      CASE "I"
        LOCATE 10, 1: PRINT "Type new record and press ENTER:"
        LINE INPUT NewRecord$
        PRINT #2, NewRecord$
        CLS 2: PRINT OldRecord$
      CASE "Q"
        EXIT DO
    END SELECT
  LOOP

  CLOSE #1, #2

END SUB
```

Program 10-7. *Copy Edit*

edited (OldFile$) is opened for input. The file resulting from the edit (NewFile$) is opened for output.

```
Type Menu Instruction (R, C, I, or Q):
  (R)ead a record from OldFile$
  (C)opy the record on the screen to NewFile$
  (I)nsert a new record before the one on the screen
  (Q)uit
```

The name of the file being edited and the new file that results are inserted in place of OldFile$ and NewFile$ in the list of instructions.

When one of the keys R, C, I, or Q is pressed, the appropriate case is selected from SELECT CASE.

Adding the AppendFile Subprogram

The last subprogram to be added is Program 10-8, AppendFile. Delete the three-line subprogram presently called AppendFile and merge Program 10-8 in its place, as you have done with other subprograms.

Instructions for AppendFile are printed at the bottom of the screen. A viewport is then used to display input prompts and records that you enter. These records are added to the end of the data file.

This subprogram completes Program 10-6. After you have entered the last subprogram, run the program.

Using Program 10-6, COPY AND EDIT A SEQUENTIAL FILE

A data file, Alphabet.Dat, was created by Program 10-5. Use it now to test Program 10-6. Figure 10-4 shows the opening dialog, which names the files and disk drives to be used. When the prompt **Press any key to continue** is displayed, put the disk containing Alphabet.Dat into drive **B.**

When you press any key, the CopyEdit subprogram is called. The instructions are printed at the bottom of the screen.

```
REM ** PRO10-8 AppendFile Subprogram - Use View Menu to see **

SUB AppendFile (FileName$) STATIC
' Append information to FileName$, which includes disk drive designation.

   ' Put instructions in lines 21 to 25
   text$(1) = STRING$(74, 196)
   text$(2) = "Append records to" + FileName$
   text$(3) = "Press ENTER to begin."
   text$(4) = "At the prompt (>), type one record and press the ENTER key."
   text$(5) = "To end the file, press ENTER without typing data."
   CLS
   FOR row% = 1 TO 5
     LOCATE row% + 20, 3: PRINT text$(row%);
   NEXT row%

   ' Define rows 1 to 20 as a viewport.  Used for appending records.
   VIEW PRINT 1 TO 20

   ' Wait for a key press to begin.
   LOCATE 10, 28: PRINT "Press a key to begin."
   anykey$ = INPUT$(1)
   CLS 2                                  'Clears only viewport

   ' Open the file for append as file #1.
   OPEN FileName$ FOR APPEND AS #1

   ' Enter records from keyboard and append to file.
   DO
     LINE INPUT "> "; record$
     PRINT
     IF record$ = "" THEN EXIT DO
     PRINT #1, record$
   LOOP

   ' Close the file and end the subprogram.
   CLOSE #1

END SUB
```

Program 10-8. *Append File*

```
Type Menu Instruction (R, C, I, or Q):
  (R)ead a record from b:alphabet.dat
  (C)opy the record on the screen to b:editalph.dat
  (I)nsert a new record before the one on the screen
  (Q)uit
```

Use the following steps to read the Alphabet. Dat file, copying only selected records:

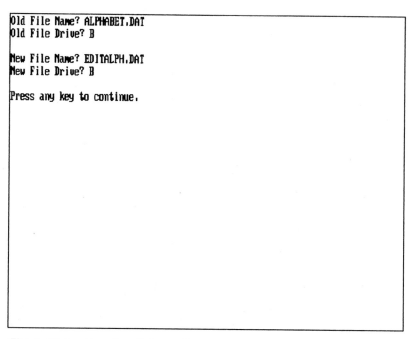

Figure 10-4.   *Opening dialog of Program 10-6*

1. Press R to read a record. A, the first record in Alphabet.Dat, is displayed in the viewport.

2. Do not copy the letter *A*. Press R again for another record. The letter *B* appears in the viewport.

3. Press C to copy the letter *B* into the EditAlph.Dat file. Record B is copied but remains on the screen. A message confirming the copy appears at the bottom of the viewport, just above the instructions, as shown in Figure 10-5.

4. Press R for the next record in Alphabet.Dat. The letter *C* appears, but do not copy it.

5. In the same manner, continue through the alphabet. Read in all records, A through Z, but copy only B, D, and F into the EditAlph.Dat file.

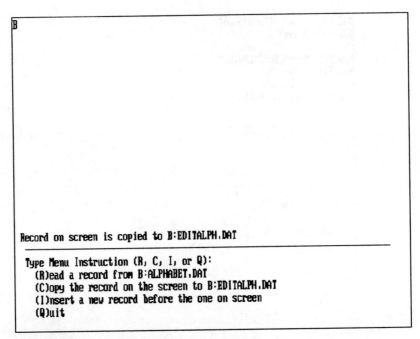

Figure 10-5. *Output confirming record copy*

When you have read the last record, any further attempts to read a record will display the message

`All records have already been read.`

Press Q to quit. A two-line message is printed and a beep sounds.

`File copy and edit is finished.`

`Add additional records to editalph.dat (Y or N)?`

Do not add any more records at this time. Press N and then ENTER. You are greeted by another two-line message:

`To scan a new file, press S`

`To quit, press any key except S`

Press S to scan the new file EditAlph.Dat. Press any key to see the first record, B. Press the SPACEBAR and the second record, D, appears. Press the SPACEBAR again, and the letter *F* appears. Press the SPACEBAR one more time and another message appears, which is

```
End of file. Press any key to continue.
```

Press any key to exit the ScanFile subprogram, and then press any key to end the program.

You have just created a new file, EditAlph.Dat, which contains three records, B, D, and F. The records were copied from the file Alphabet.Dat.

Now run Program 10-6 again. This time, enter EditAlph.Dat as the old file name and Edit2.Dat as the new file name. When the CopyEdit subprogram is called, read the first record of EditAlph.Dat. The letter *B* appears in the viewport.

Enter the letter *I* so that you can insert a record before the letter *B*. Press ENTER. Case I is selected from SELECT CASE. This message — **Type new record and press ENTER** — appears. Press A and then ENTER. This inserts the letter *A* as a record in the Edit2.Dat file before the record that holds the letter *B*. Record B stays on the screen so that you can choose what to do with it from the menu.

Press C to copy B into Edit2.Dat. The Edit2.Dat file now contains these two records:

A is record #1
B is record #2

In the same way, read the next record (D) from EditAlph.Dat and insert the letter *C* into Edit2.Dat. Then copy *D* into Edit2.Dat.

Do the same with the next record (F) from EditAlph.Dat. Insert the letter *E* and then copy the letter *F* into Edit2.Dat.

At this point, Edit2.Dat has six records:

#1   A
#2   B
#3   C
#4   D
#5   E
#6   F

If you attempt to read another record from EditAlph.Dat, you will see the message

```
File copy and edit is finished.
Add additional records to edit2.dat (Y or N)?
```

This time press Y. This calls the AppendFile subprogram. Press any key when the prompt **Press a key to begin** appears. At the prompt ($>$), type the next letter of the alphabet (G) and press ENTER. This appends G as a record at the end of the Edit2.Dat file. Continue in this manner until you have added as many records as you wish. Then press the ENTER key without entering any data. This causes an exit from the DO...LOOP in the AppendFile subprogram. The file is closed and the subprogram ends.

The main program prints the message

```
To scan new file, press S
To quit, press any key except S
```

You may scan the new file (Edit2.Dat) by pressing S or end the program by pressing any other key.

Shuffling and Sorting a Random-Access File

Records of random-access files can be more readily searched, retrieved, and sorted than sequential files. The records are numbered and have a fixed length.

Program 10-9, SHUFFLE AND SORT A RANDOM-ACCESS FILE, is a skeleton program that has four subprograms. The subprograms of the skeleton merely print their names and return to the main program. The program is written to use the food data file produced by Program 9-2. However, other subprograms can be substituted to accommodate other data files. You would also have to change the TYPE...END TYPE definitions in the main program to match the data file being used.

```
DECLARE SUB ReadRecords (NumberOfRecords%)
DECLARE SUB NameFile (FileName$)
DECLARE SUB ShuffleFile (FileName$, NumberOfRecords%)
DECLARE SUB SortFile (NumberOfRecords%)

REM ** SHUFFLE AND SORT RANDOM ACCESS FILE **
' Program 10-9  9/17/87
CLS
PRINT "Program to Shuffle and Sort a Random Access File"

REM ** DEFINE RECORD STRUCTURE **
TYPE FoodItem
   food AS STRING * 18
   kind AS STRING * 15
   calories AS INTEGER
END TYPE

CALL NameFile(FileName$)

CALL ShuffleFile(FileName$, NumberOfRecords%)

CALL ReadRecords(NumberOfRecords%)

CALL SortFile(NumberOfRecords%)

CALL ReadRecords(NumberOfRecords%)

CLOSE #1

END
SUB NameFile (FileName$) STATIC
   PRINT : PRINT "NameFile subprogram"
END SUB
SUB ReadRecords (NumberOfRecords%) STATIC
   PRINT : PRINT "ReadRecords subprogram"
END SUB
SUB ShuffleFile (FileName$, NumberOfRecords%) STATIC
   PRINT : PRINT "ShuffleFile subprogram"
END SUB
SUB SortFile (NumberOfRecords%) STATIC
   PRINT : PRINT "SortFile subprogram"
END SUB
```

Program 10-9. *SHUFFLE AND SORT A RANDOM-ACCESS FILE*

Enter the skeleton program and run it. The order in which the subprograms are called is

```
Program to Shuffle and Sort a Random Access File

NameFile subprogram

ShuffleFile subprogram
```

```
ReadRecords subprogram
SortFile subprogram
ReadRecords subprogram
```

You can see that the file is named first. Then the records are shuffled. The records are displayed in their random order by the ReadRecords subprogram. The file is then sorted alphabetically according to the food name that appears as the first field of each record.

Adding the NameFile Subprogram

The NameFile subprogram is similar to the NameDrive subprogram used in Programs 10-1 and 10-6. It is given a different name in this program to distinguish it from the NameDrive subprogram. If you save subprograms separately, this will help to avoid confusion when you want to merge one of the subprograms with a main program. Replace the temporary NameFile subprogram in Program 10-9 along with Program 10-10, NameFile.

The new subprogram prompts you for the file name and disk drive to be used and reminds you to put the appropriate disk in the drive. It then stops for a key press. When you press a key, control passes back to the main program. Test this part of the program to make sure it works correctly.

Adding the ShuffleFile Subprogram

The ShuffleFile subprogram declares FoodRecord and FoodTemp as FoodItem types by DIM statements:

```
DIM FoodRecord AS FoodItem
DIM FoodTemp AS FoodItem
```

File number 1 is then opened for random access and the number of records is calculated.

```
REM ** PRO10-10 NameFile Subprogram - Use View Menu to see **

SUB NameFile (FileName$) STATIC
   PRINT
   INPUT "File name with extension"; FileName$
   INPUT "Disk drive"; Drive$
   PRINT : PRINT "Put "; FileName$; " disk in drive "; Drive$
   FileName$ = LEFT$(Drive$, 1) + ":" + FileName$
   PRINT "Press any key to continue."
   anykey$ = INPUT$(1)

END SUB
```

Program 10-10. *Name File*

The random-number generator is seeded by the statement

```
RANDOMIZE TIMER
```

Thus, a new sequence of random numbers is generated each time the program is run, since the timer is continually changing when the computer is on.

A FOR...NEXT loop assigns increasing integer values (from 1 through the number of records in the file) to the value $k\%$. Each time $k\%$ changes, a new random number is assigned to the variable *rndindex%*. A GET statement reads FoodTemp:

```
GET #1, FoodTemp
```

Another GET statement reads FoodRecord from record number *rndindex%*. Therefore:

```
FoodTemp was read from record k%, and
FoodRecord was read from record rndindex%
```

PUT statements are used to put the records back in the file, but the positions of the records are changed.

```
PUT #1, k%, FoodRecord
PUT #1, rndindex%, FoodTemp
```

The loop is executed for as many times as there are records in the file. When an exit is made from the loop, the subprogram ends and control is passed back to the main program. Replace the temporary ShuffleFile subprogram with Program 10-11, ShuffleFile.

Adding the ReadRecords Subprogram

Program 10-12, ReadRecords, is a subprogram that reads and displays the records as they are presently stored in the file.

Replace the temporary ReadRecords subprogram with the new one. Now you can run Program 10-4 and test all three subprograms. Results of the test runs will vary as new random values are used in exchanging the records in the ShuffleFile subprogram. Figure 10-6 shows a typical output of the ReadRecords subprogram after the records have been scrambled.

```
REM ** PRO10-11 ShuffleFile Subprogram - Use View Menu to see **

SUB ShuffleFile (FileName$, NumberOfRecords%) STATIC

    DIM FoodRecord AS FoodItem
    DIM FoodTemp AS FoodItem

    OPEN FileName$ FOR RANDOM AS #1 LEN = LEN(FoodRecord)
    NumberOfRecords% = LOF(1) \ LEN(FoodRecord)

    RANDOMIZE TIMER
    FOR k% = 1 TO NumberOfRecords%
      rndindex% = INT(NumberOfRecords% * RND(1)) + 1
      GET #1, k%, FoodTemp
      GET #1, rndindex%, FoodRecord
      PUT #1, k%, FoodRecord
      PUT #1, rndindex%, FoodTemp
    NEXT k%
    CLS : PRINT "Records are now shuffled in the following order:"

END SUB
```

Program 10-11. *Shuffle File*

```
REM ** PRO10-12 ReadRecords Subprogram - Use View Menu to see **

SUB ReadRecords (NumberOfRecords%) STATIC

   DIM FoodRecord AS FoodItem

   FOR RecordNumber% = 1 TO NumberOfRecords%
     GET #1, RecordNumber%, FoodRecord
     PRINT FoodRecord.food; FoodRecord.kind; FoodRecord.calories
   NEXT RecordNumber%

   PRINT : PRINT "End of file. Press any key to continue."
   anykey$ = INPUT$(1)

END SUB
```

Program 10-12.   *Read Records*

```
Records are now shuffled in the following order:
Avocado        fresh         40
Cabbage        raw           7
Broccoli       cooked        7
Banana         fresh         24
Blueberries    fresh         18
Biscuits       home-made     105
Apple          fresh         15
Beans          lima-cooked   32
Beef           chuck-cooked  93
Bass           sea-cooked    74
Bread          whole wheat   69
Cake           angel food    77
Butter         salted        205

End of file. Press any key to continue.
```

Figure 10-6.   *Output of scrambled records*

```
REM ** PRO10-13 SortFile Subprogram - Use View Menu to see **

SUB SortFile (NumberOfRecords%) STATIC

   DIM FoodRecord AS FoodItem
   DIM FoodTemp AS FoodItem

   CLS : PRINT "Sorting file"

   top% = 1
   DO WHILE top% < NumberOfRecords%
     FOR here% = NumberOfRecords% TO top% + 1 STEP -1
       GET #1, here%, FoodTemp
       GET #1, here% - 1, FoodRecord
       A$ = FoodTemp.food: B$ = FoodRecord.food
       IF A$ < B$ THEN
          PUT #1, here%, FoodRecord
          PUT #1, here% - 1, FoodTemp
       END IF
     NEXT here%
     top% = top% + 1
   LOOP

   CLS : PRINT "Records are now sorted in the following order:"

END SUB
```

Program 10-13. *Sort File*

Adding the SortFile Subprogram

Program 10-13, SortFile, is a subprogram that uses PUT and GET statements to sort the scrambled file into alphabetical order by food names.

A DO...LOOP contains a simple bubble sort that reorders the array. GET statements are used to read adjoining records. If they are out of order, PUT statements are used to exchange their positions in the file.

Replace the temporary SortFile subprogram with the new one. Then you can test the complete program.

Figure 10-7 shows a typical shuffled file. Figure 10-8 shows the same file after it has been sorted.

```
Records are now shuffled in the following order:
Biscuits        home-made       105
Bread           whole wheat     69
Cabbage         raw             7
Banana          fresh           24
Beef            chuck-cooked    93
Broccoli        cooked          7
Avocado         fresh           48
Cake            angel food      77
Butter          salted          205
Bass            sea-cooked      74
Blueberries     fresh           18
Beans           lima-cooked     32
Apple           fresh           15

End of file, Press any key to continue,
```

Figure 10-7. *A shuffled file*

Review

This chapter has demonstrated various ways to create and manipulate data in sequential and random-access files. Subprograms were written as individual files and merged with a main program to form a complete program that performed several functions.

Program 10-1 contained subprograms to copy and scan a sequential file. Program 10-6 contained subprograms to append data to a sequential file, read data from a file, copy data from one file to another, insert data between records, and scan a sequential file. Program 10-9 scrambled records randomly and then sorted them in alphabetical order.

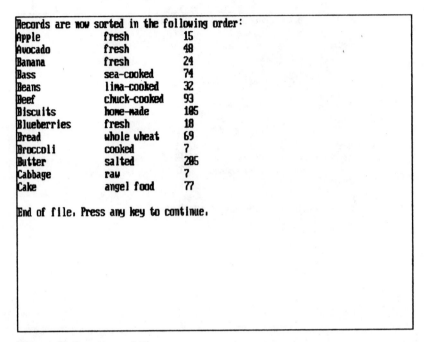

```
Records are now sorted in the following order:
Apple          fresh         15
Avocado        fresh         48
Banana         fresh         24
Bass           sea-cooked    74
Beans          lima-cooked   32
Beef           chuck-cooked  93
Biscuits       home-made     105
Blueberries    fresh         18
Bread          whole wheat   69
Broccoli       cooked        7
Butter         salted        205
Cabbage        raw           7
Cake           angel food    77

End of file. Press any key to continue.
```

Figure 10-8.   *A sorted file*

11 *Dynamic Debugging*

Bugs creep into programs just as they do into other places. Sometimes programs look good on paper but misbehave when they are run by the computer. A program "bug" causes the misbehavior. This chapter shows how to use QuickBASIC's debugging tools to prevent bugs, find bugs that prevent the proper running of a program, and find bugs that make programs misbehave.

If you have programmed in GW-BASIC, you have probably used tools such as STOP, PRINT, CONT, TRON, and TROFF statements to help find programming bugs. If you have programmed with a compiled version of BASIC, you may have debugged programs with a "symbolic debugger" that allows you to follow the flow of a program while watching what the program does.

QuickBASIC combines the easy-to-use debugging features of GW-BASIC with the powerful features of a symbolic debugger. QuickBASIC's debugging tools can be used while you are working on a QuickBASIC program.

In this chapter you will learn about

Tracing	A QuickBASIC feature that shows you which statement of your program is being executed. Tracing includes commands to run one statement at a time, to animate execution so that each statement is highlighted as it is executed, and to trace backward or forward through the last 20 statements that have been executed.
Watch expressions	Allow you to observe the value of variables or expressions in your program while the program is being run.
Watchpoints	Expressions that stop a program when the expression becomes true.
Breakpoints	Locations in your program where you want execution to stop temporarily to allow you to test parts of programs or examine a variable's value at specific points in the program.

The best way to develop bug-free programs is to reduce the number of possible points where bugs may enter. Bug prevention starts with program planning. Here are some preventive measures:

■ Design your program carefully before you sit down at the keyboard. List the tasks that you want the program to perform. Then write your programs as SUB or FUNCTION procedures. A short procedure is much easier to debug than a long program. Test the procedures individually.

■ Use the Immediate window at the bottom of the screen to isolate and test small pieces of your program. When you get the pieces working on their own, move them into the main body of your program.

■ Run each new part of your program several times within the context of the rest of the program. These checks help catch simple bugs that could be hard to track in a long, finished program.

■ Use the debugging tools described in this chapter.

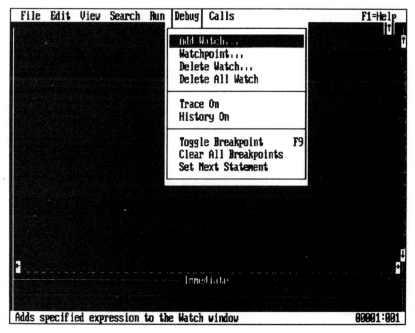

Figure 11-1.　*Debug menu*

The Debug Menu

Although other QuickBASIC menus contain commands that you often use when debugging, most of the debugging tools are implemented by commands from the Debug menu shown in Figure 11-1.

Tracing a Program

Tracing slows down the execution of a program to show you which statement of your program is being executed. QuickBASIC provides the following tracing features.

Single Step	Pressing the F8 key runs one statement of a program at a time.
Procedure Step	Works similarly to Single Step but treats procedures as one step.
Trace On	Provides "animated" execution so that each statement is highlighted when it is executed. The last 20 statements that were executed are recorded for review purposes.

Trace On

Enter Program 11-1, BAKER'S DOZEN SHUFFLE, and use it in the following sections to try out QuickBASIC's tracing features.

The main program creates an array with elements consisting of integers 1 through 13 in their natural order. The subprogram shuffles

---

```
DECLARE SUB Shuffle (array%())
REM ** BAKER'S DOZEN SHUFFLE **
' Program 11-1  9/10/87

' Dimension numbers as an integer array
DIM numbers%(1 TO 13)
CLS

' Create array and shuffle the elements
FOR k% = 1 TO 13
  numbers%(k%) = k%
NEXT k%

CALL Shuffle(numbers%())

END

SUB Shuffle (array%()) STATIC
  FOR k% = 1 TO 13
    rndindex% = INT(13 * RND(1)) + 1
    SWAP array%(k%), array%(rndindex%)
  NEXT k%

END SUB
```

Program 11-1. *BAKER'S DOZEN SHUFFLE*

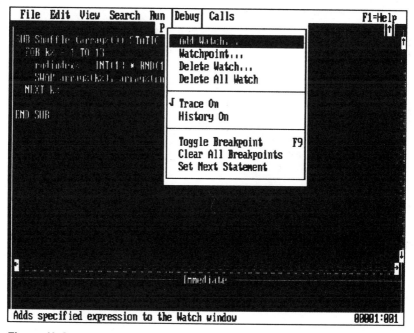

Figure 11-2. *Trace On checked*

the elements so that their order is random. A RANDOMIZE statement
was not used to reseed the random-number generator in this program
so that the sequence of random numbers would be the same for
demonstration purposes. If you want a new sequence of random
numbers each time the program is run, insert a RANDOMIZE
TIMER statement just ahead of the FOR . . . NEXT loop at the beginning of the subprogram.

When the program has been entered, go to the Debug menu. Move
the highlight down to Trace On and press ENTER. You are taken back
to the program in the View window. Access the Debug menu again.
Figure 11-2 shows a checkmark in front of Trace On, indicating that it
is activated. The checkmark is missing when Trace On is inactive.

Pressing the ENTER key when Trace On is highlighted toggles the
Trace On "switch," turning it on (checkmark present) or off (checkmark absent).

With Trace On active, run the program from the Run menu.

QuickBASIC single steps through the program. Each statement is highlighted as it is executed. This is called an animated trace. Keep your eyes on the screen as statements are executed in rapid succession. You can use Trace On to determine the general flow of your program to see whether or not the program is behaving as intended. Below is a review of what you will see when you run an animated trace of Program 11-1.

The trace quickly skips over any remarks and highlights the DIM statement:

```
DECLARE SUB Shuffle (array%())
REM ** BAKER'S DOZEN SHUFFLE **
' Program 11-1  9/10/87

' Dimension numbers as an integer array
DIM numbers%(1 TO 13)
    .
    .
    .
```

The CLS statement is highlighted next:

```
    .
    .
    .
DIM numbers%(1 TO 13)
CLS
    .
    .
    .
```

Then the FOR statement is highlighted:

```
    .
    .
    .
' Create array and shuffle the elements
FOR k% = 1 TO 13
    numbers%(k%) = k%
NEXT k%
    .
    .
    .
```

The highlight then cycles 13 times through the next 2 statements as the FOR...NEXT loop is executed, as shown next:

```
     .
     .
     .
  numbers%(k%) = k%          ◄──────────  First
NEXT k%
     .
     .
     .

     .
     .
     .
  numbers%(k%) = k%
NEXT k%                      ◄──────────  Then
```

The CALL statement is then highlighted and executed:

```
  .
  .
  .
CALL Shuffle(numbers%())

END
```

The computer then places the subprogram on the screen so that you can see the execution of the subprogram. The FOR statement is highlighted:

```
  .
  .
  .
SUB Shuffle (array%())
  FOR k% = 1 TO 13
     rndindex% = INT(13 * RND(1)) + 1
     SWAP array%(k%), array%(rndindex%)
  NEXT k%
```

As the FOR...NEXT loop is executed, the highlight cycles through the next three statements 13 times:

```
     .
     .
     .
  rndindex% = INT(13 * RND(1)) + 1     ◄──────  First step
     SWAP array%(k%), array%(rndindex%)            of cycle
  NEXT k%

END SUB
```

```
      .
      .
      .
   rndindex% = INT(13 * RND(1)) + 1
     SWAP array%(k%), array%(rndindex%)
   NEXT k%

END SUB
```

Second step
of cycle

```
      .
      .
      .
   rndindex% - INT(13 * RND(1)) + 1
     SWAP array%(k%), array%(rndindex%)
   NEXT k%

END SUB
```

Third step
of cycle

When the loop has been executed 13 times, the END SUB statement is highlighted as it is executed. Control then returns to the main program. The END statement is the last statement highlighted. Then the highlight is turned off.

You can tell if the program flow is correct by watching the program execute with Trace On, but you can slow things down even more with the Single Step debugging feature.

Single Step

You can completely control the program's execution with the Single Step debugging command. Use Program 11-1 again to experiment with the Single Step command. Do not start the program from the Run menu! Use Restart instead. This takes you to the beginning of the program.

Single Step is activated by the F8 key. It steps through one step of the program each time you press the F8 key.

The DIM statement is highlighted first. The highlighted statement is not executed until you press F8. Pressing F8 executes the highlighted statement and moves the highlight on to the next executable statement.

Continue pressing F8 and watch the highlight move through the program as it executes one statement at a time. This may seem tedious, but there will come a time when you will want to watch each individual step in order to find a program bug. Step through the entire program at least once.

If you have previously tested the procedures that are used in a program, there is a way to "step over" procedures. The Procedure Step command executes the procedure as one giant step—called stepping over the procedure.

Procedure Step

Procedure Step is activated by the F10 key. Its action is similar to single stepping, except that it treats each procedure as a single step. That is, the complete procedure is executed in its entirety, but the highlight action is treated as if the procedure were only one step. All the steps in the procedure are executed, but you only see the result of the procedure call.

Do not run the program from the Run menu! Use the F10 key to Procedure Step through Program 11-1.

The main program is single stepped by pressing the F10 key, just as the F8 key was used in the Single Step until you reach

```
        .
        .
        .
CALL Shuffle(numbers%())
END
```

When you press F10 this time, the subprogram is executed, and the highlight steps on to the END statement in the main program that follows the CALL statement. The program ends.

The Trace On toggle does not affect the Single Step or Procedure Step actions. If you want to turn off Trace On, access the Debug menu, highlight Trace On, and press the ENTER key. This toggles the Trace On command. If a checkmark is in front of Trace On, toggling it from the Debug menu removes it and deactivates the Trace On feature. If a checkmark is not in front of Trace On, toggling it from the Debug menu places a checkmark in front of Trace On and activates the Trace On feature.

Watching a Program

A Watch window opens at the top of the screen whenever you choose Add Watch... or Watchpoint... from the Debug menu. The name of each variable or expression that you choose to watch appears in the Watch window. As the program is executed, you can watch the values of the variables or expressions change.

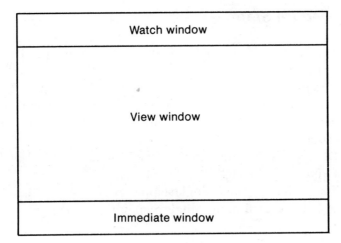

Use Program 11-1 again to experiment with the Watch commands of the Debug menu.

Add Watch...

When Program 11-1 was traced previously, the following statements (except remarks) were highlighted as they were executed:

```
' Dimension numbers as an integer array
DIM numbers%(1 TO 13)
CLS

' Create array and shuffle the elements
FOR k% = 1 TO 13
  numbers%(k%) = k%
NEXT k%
```

Add a subprogram to print the results of the next series of experiments. Put the CALL PrintFile statement between the CALL Shuffle and the END statement in the main program. The PrintFile subprogram will print the order of the array after the numbers are shuffled.

```
     .
     .
     .
CALL  Shuffle(numbers%())
CALL  PrintFile (numbers%())
END
```

It would be interesting to watch the variable *k%* and the array elements *numbers%(k%)* as they change while the main program is being executed. To put these variables in the Watch window, first place the main program in the View window, if it is not already there. Then access the Debug menu and select the Add Watch... command. When you press ENTER, the dialog box shown in Figure 11-3 appears.

Type **k%** as the expression to be added to the Watch window and press ENTER. You are returned to the View window. The variable **k%** appears in the Watch window at the top of the screen:

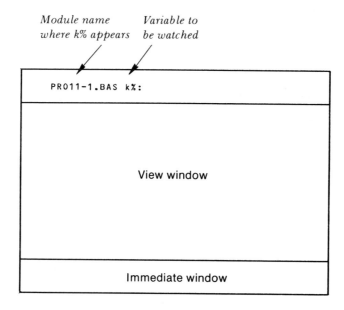

```
 File  Edit  View  Search  Run  Debug  Calls              F1=Help
                          PRO11-1.BAS                        ↑↓
DECLARE SUB PrintFile (numbers%())                            ↑
DECLARE SUB Shuffle (array%())
REM ** BAKER'S DOZEN SHUFFLE **
' Program 11 1  9/10/87

' Dimension
DIM numbers
CLS              Enter expression to be added to Watch window:

' Create ar
FOR k% = 1     ▄
  numbers%(
NEXT k%
                     ┌──────┐    ┌────────┐
CALL Shuffl          │  OK  │    │ Cancel │
                     └──────┘    └────────┘
CALL PrintFile(numbers%())                                   ↓
▓                                                          ▓
                          Immediate
Main: PRO11-1.BAS    Context: Program not running      00001:001
```

Figure 11-3.   *Add Watch . . . dialog box*

Again access the Add Watch. . . command dialog box shown in
Figure 11-3 from the Debug menu and enter **numbers%(k%)** as the
name of the expression to be added to the Watch window. The Watch
window now shows

```
PRO11-1.BAS k%:
PRO11-1.BAS numbers%(k%):
```

The executable statements in the Shuffle subprogram of Program
11-1 are

```
FOR k% = 1 TO 13
  rndindex% = INT(13 * RND(1)) + 1
  SWAP array%(k%), array%(rndindex%)
NEXT k%

END SUB
```

The variables to be watched in the Shuffle subprogram are $k\%$, *rndindex%*, and the elements of *array%( )*.

Put the subprogram in the View window. Then access the Add Watch... dialog box four times. Enter one of the following variables each time:

```
k%
rndindex%
array%(k%)
array%(rndindex%)
```

When all four variables have been added, the Watch window contains five variables to watch. They are

```
PRO11-1.BAS k%:
PRO11-1.BAS numbers%(k%):
Shuffle k%:
Shuffle rndindex%:
Shuffle array%(k%):
Shuffle array%(rndindex%):
```

Use the Single Step (F8) command to step through the main program. The four variables of the Shuffle subprogram display the message **<Not watchable>** because they lie outside the main program. Their values are unknown at this time.

The values of $k\%$ and *numbers%(k%)*, at the top of the Watch window, change as you step through the FOR...NEXT loop of the main program. As $k\%$ goes from 1 through 13, the value of *numbers%(k%)* is first zero (assigned when the array is dimensioned), then takes on the value of $k\%$ when the statement *numbers%(k%)* = $k\%$ is executed. When an exit is made from the FOR...NEXT loop, the CALL Shuffle(*numbers%( )*) statement is highlighted and the watch of the first two variables shows

```
PRO11-1.BAS k%:  14
PRO11-1.BAS numbers%(k%): Subscript out of range
```

Since the upper limit of the FOR...NEXT loop was 13, an exit was made from the loop.

Press F8 again to call the subprogram. The Watch window now shows

```
PRO11-1.BAS k%:<Not watchable>
PRO11-1.BAS numbers%(k%):<Not watchable>
Shuffle k%: 0
Shuffle rndindex%: 0
Shuffle array%(k%): Subscript out of range
Shuffle array%(rndindex%): Subscript out of range
```

The FOR statement is now highlighted. Since control has passed to the subprogram, the two variables in the main program now show the message **<Not watchable>**. The two variables $k\%$ and $rndindex\%$ in the subprogram equal zero. The subscripts of the array elements are out of range since $array\%(\ )$ was dimensioned 1 to 13.

As the FOR...NEXT loop is executed, the variable $rndindex\%$ is assigned a random integer (1 to 13). A swap is made between $array\%(k\%)$ and $array\%(rndindex\%)$. This swaps two elements of the number array. Then $k\%$ is incremented by 1 for another pass through the loop. A sample first pass through the loop displays the following variable watch:

```
when rndindex% = k% is executed:

SWAP array%(k%), array%(rndindex%) is highlighted
k% = 1
rndindex% = 10
array%(k%) = 1                the value 1 is assigned to array(1)
array%(rndindex%) = 10        the value 10 is assigned to array(10)

when SWAP array%(k%), array%(rndindex%) is executed:

NEXT k% is highlighted
k% = 1                        array%(k%) = array%(1)
rndindex% = 10                array%(rndindex%) = array%(10)
array%(k%) = 10               array%(1) and array%(10) were swapped
array%(rndindex%) = 1         array%(1) now holds the value 10
                             array%(10) now holds the value 1

k%       = 1   2   3   4   5   6   7   8   9   10   11   12   13

array(k%) = 10  2   3   4   5   6   7   8   9   1   11   12   13
```

These two were swapped

The random-number sequence generated for the variable $rndindex\%$ is 10, 13, 12, 5, 1, 2, 7, 10, 13, 5, 3, 7, 4. This same sequence

Array Positions

k	r	z	1	2	3	4	5	6	7	8	9	10	11	12	13
1	10	10	(10)	2	3	4	5	6	7	8	9	(1)	11	12	13
2	13	13	10	(13)	3	4	5	6	7	8	9	1	11	12	(2)
3	12	12	10	13	(12)	4	5	6	7	8	9	1	11	(3)	2
4	5	5	10	13	12	(5)	(4)	6	7	8	9	1	11	3	2
5	1	10	(4)	13	12	5	(10)	6	7	8	9	1	11	3	2
6	2	13	4	(6)	12	5	10	(13)	7	8	9	1	11	3	2
7	7	7	4	6	12	5	10	13	(7)	8	9	1	11	3	2
8	10	1	4	6	12	5	10	13	7	(1)	9	(8)	11	3	2
9	13	2	4	6	12	5	10	13	7	1	(2)	8	11	3	(9)
10	5	10	4	6	12	5	(8)	13	7	1	2	(10)	11	3	9
11	3	12	4	6	(11)	5	8	13	7	1	2	10	(12)	3	9
12	7	7	4	6	11	5	8	13	(3)	1	2	10	12	(7)	9
13	4	5	4	6	11	(9)	8	13	3	1	2	10	12	7	(5)

k = $k\%$

r = $rndindex\%$

a = $array\%(k\%)$

Table 11-1. *Results of Array Swaps*

will be generated each time Program 11-1 is run unless you insert a RANDOMIZE statement, as mentioned earlier.

Table 11-1 shows the values of $k\%$, $rndindex\%$, and $array\%(k\%)$. It also shows a complete list of the current elements of $array(k\%)$ after the SWAP statement has been executed for each pass through the loop. The array elements that were swapped are circled.

When an exit is made from the Shuffle subprogram, keep pressing the F8 key to execute the PrintFile subprogram that prints the final order of the array. When the program ends, press F4 to access the output screen. The elements are displayed in their final order:

```
4   6   11   9   8   13   3   1   2   10   12   7   5
```

You can also watch for expressions that will suspend program execution when the expressions become true. This is done with a debugging tool called Watchpoint.

Watchpoint...

Another subprogram, BubbleSort, has been added to Program 11-1. Call this revision Program 11-2, BAKER'S DOZEN SHUFFLE THEN SORT. The PrintFile subprogram is called again after the BubbleSort subprogram to show the sorted numbers.

It would take quite a bit of time to single step through this program since it is longer than Program 11-1. You can run the program from the Run menu with Trace On to make it execute without pressing the F8 or F10 key.

Use a Watchpoint to suspend the program when it gets to the BubbleSort subprogram. Then single step through BubbleSort while watching the swaps take place as the array of numbers is sorted.

Enter Program 11-2. Save it in text format as PRO11-2. Then access the Debug menu and move the highlight to Trace On. Press ENTER.

Put the BubbleSort subprogram in the View window from the View menu. Access the Debug menu again, move the highlight to Watchpoint..., and press ENTER. The dialog box appears, as shown in Figure 11-4.

Enter *top% = 1* as the Watchpoint... expression and press ENTER.

Access the Debug menu three more times and enter the following variables with the Add Watch... command:

```
here%
array%(here%)
array%(here% - 1)
```

You have selected

```
Trace On
Watchpoint: top% = 1
Watch Window: here%
              array%(here%)
              array%(here% - 1)
```

You are now ready to run the program. Access the Run menu. As the Start command is highlighted, press ENTER. Keep your eyes on the Watch window as the program runs. All expressions being watched show the message **<Not watchable>** until the BubbleSort subprogram is entered.

```
DECLARE SUB PrintFile (array%())
DECLARE SUB BubbleSort (array%())
DECLARE SUB Shuffle (array%())
REM ** BAKER'S DOZEN SHUFFLE THEN SORT **
' Program 11-2   9/10/87

' Dimension numbers as an integer array
DIM numbers%(1 TO 13)
CLS

' Create array and shuffle the elements
FOR k% = 1 TO 13
  numbers%(k%) = k%
NEXT k%

CALL Shuffle(numbers%())

CALL PrintFile(numbers%())

CALL BubbleSort(numbers%())

CALL PrintFile(numbers%())

END
SUB BubbleSort (array%()) STATIC
  top% = 1
  DO WHILE top% < 13
    FOR here% = 13 TO top% + 1 STEP -1
      IF array%(here%) < array%(here% - 1) THEN
        SWAP array%(here%), array%(here% - 1)
      END IF
    NEXT here%
    top% = top% + 1
  LOOP

END SUB
SUB PrintFile (array%()) STATIC
  FOR k% = 1 TO 13
    PRINT array%(k%);
  NEXT k%
  PRINT

END SUB
SUB Shuffle (array%()) STATIC
  FOR k% = 1 TO 13
    rndindex% = INT(13 * RND(1)) + 1
    SWAP array%(k%), array%(rndindex%)
  NEXT k%

END SUB
```

Program 11-2. *BAKER'S DOZEN SHUFFLE THEN SORT*

The program steps through each statement in the program until it executes the statement *top% = 1* in the BubbleSort subprogram. The execution of the program is suspended because the Watchpoint

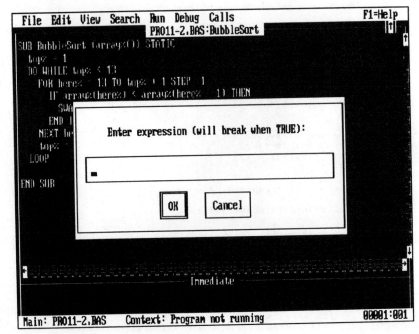

Figure 11-4. *Watchpoint... dialog box*

top% = 1 is now true, as shown in the Watch window:

```
BubbleSort topX = 1:   <TRUE>
```

The DO WHILE statement is highlighted. Now, use F8 to single step through the BubbleSort subprogram. Watch the array elements swap places when *array%(here%)* is less than (<) *array%(here% − 1)*. Single step through at least one cycle of the FOR...NEXT loop.

It takes a long time to single step through the BubbleSort subprogram. When you have seen enough, you can escape the DO...LOOP by setting *top%* to 12 in the Immediate window. Press F6 to move the cursor to the Immediate window. Then type **top% = 12**

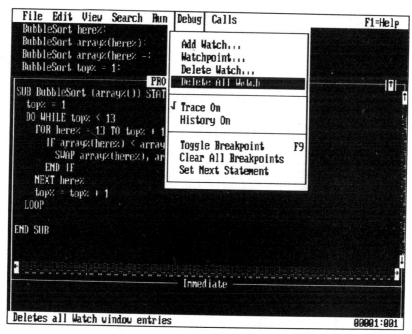

Figure 11-5. *Debug menu with Delete All Watch selected*

and press ENTER. Press F6 to move back to the View window. Press F8 a few times to complete the DO...LOOP and leave the subprogram.

When the FOR...NEXT loop of the PrintFile subprogram is entered, you can exit from that loop by entering **k% = 13** from the Immediate window in the same way you exited the DO...LOOP above.

A watchpoint allows you to pass quickly through the program until you reach a specified location. Then you can single step through that part of the program following the watchpoint to watch single statement results.

To turn off watchpoints and watch expressions, access the Debug menu, select the Delete All Watch, as shown in Figure 11-5, and press ENTER. Access the Debug menu again, move the highlight to Trace On, and press ENTER to toggle Trace Off.

Breakpoints and History On

A breakpoint is a location in your program that causes your program to stop execution. You set these locations from the Toggle Breakpoint command of the Debug menu or by pressing the F9 key, without going to the Debug menu.

Breakpoints can be used to test individual parts of programs. You can also insert breakpoints at strategic points to stop a program so that you can examine a variable's value at that point. This is a valuable tool that can be used to locate places where a program is misbehaving.

Another debugging tool that is useful in locating hard-to-find bugs is the History On command of the Debug menu. When the History On command has a checkmark in front of it, you may see the effect of the last 20 steps executed by using the History Back key combination, SHIFT+F8. Each time you press this combination, a step backward is made in the program. After stepping back through a sequence of statements, you may use the History Forward key combination, SHIFT+F10, to step forward through the same sequence. The program steps forward one statement for each press of SHIFT+F10.

The use of breakpoints and History On can be demonstrated by introducing a program bug into Program 11-2. Put the BubbleSort subprogram in the View window. Then move the cursor to this statement:

```
top% = top% + 1
```

Change the right side of the equation so that it reads

```
top% = top% + 2
```

Run Program 11-2 with this change and pretend you do not know you have made the error in entering the above statement. The numbers are shuffled and printed in the following order:

```
4  6  11  9  8  13  3  1  2  10  12  7  5
```

Then they are printed in their sorted order:

```
1  4  2  6  3  11  5  9  7  8  10  13  12
```

The numbers were not sorted in the proper order. Something must be wrong with the BubbleSort subprogram!

To look for a bug in this part of the program, place the BubbleSort subprogram in the View window. Then use the appropriate arrow key to move the cursor to the location where you want to set a breakpoint. For example, move it to the LOOP statement at the end of the DO...LOOP.

While the cursor is at this location, access the Debug menu and move the highlight to Toggle Breakpoint. Press ENTER. Now access the Debug menu and move the highlight to History On. Press ENTER.

When the subprogram is displayed in the View window, the LOOP statement changes background color.

You have set a breakpoint at the LOOP statement in the Bubble-Sort subprogram and turned History On to record the 20 statements executed before the LOOP statement is executed.

Run Program 11-2 again. This time the program stops at the end of the DO...LOOP with the LOOP statement highlighted.

Press SHIFT+F8 20 times and watch the cursor step backward through the loop. You will hear a beep if you try to step back more than 20 statements. Press SHIFT+F10 to step forward from this point, one step at a time. Notice that the flow of the program seems to be correct as you move through this part of the program. Therefore, the error is not in the order-of-statement operation.

You might wonder next about the values assigned to the variables as the BubbleSort subprogram is being executed. You can insert another breakpoint at the beginning of the FOR...NEXT loop to stop execution at that point. Then you can single step through the loop and watch the variables change in value.

Move the cursor to the FOR statement. Then access the Debug menu and toggle a breakpoint at this location.

Go back to the Debug menu two times and use Add Watch... to add *here%* and *top%* to the Watch window:

```
BubbleSort here%:
BubbleSort top%:
```

You can toggle the History On to the off position, if you wish, and run Program 11-2 again. This time the program stops at the FOR statement in the BubbleSort subprogram. Now single step through this loop with the Single Step key (F8). Watch the variables *here%* and *top%* in the Watch window.

top% is set equal to 1, and *here%* decreases by 1 from 13 down to 2 as you step through the FOR...NEXT loop. When the exit is made from the FOR...NEXT loop, the statement following the FOR... NEXT loop is highlighted.

```
top% = top% + 2
```

You may notice the error at this point, but suppose you do not. You are intently watching the Watch window. As you press F8 again, you suddenly notice that *top%* jumped from 1 to 3 as *here%* was reset to 13. Why did *top%* increase by two instead of one? If you don't see why, keep pressing the F8 key until another completion of the FOR... NEXT loop is made. This time *top%* jumps to 5. It is increasing by two each time the FOR...NEXT loop is completed.

By this time you have looked more closely at the variable *top%* in the program and have spotted the error. You correct the statement to read

```
top% = top% + 1
```

Rerun the program when this change is made. The program again stops at the breakpoint. Single step through this part of the program and you see that *top%* is now incremented correctly. You have killed the bug. You can now remove all the watch expressions, the breakpoint, and History On.

Breakpoints are removed by pressing ENTER with Toggle Breakpoint from the Debug menu or by pressing the F9 key. Watch expressions are removed individually with the Delete Watch... command or as a group with the Delete All Watch command of the Debug menu. History On is toggled off by pressing ENTER when History On is highlighted and a checkmark is in front of it.

You can use various combinations of the features discussed in this chapter to check program operations and to locate bugs. Without these tools, well-hidden bugs would be difficult to find.

Review

QuickBASIC has many built-in checks that find most obvious programming errors. The debugging tools discussed in this chapter are used to find well-hidden bugs. In this chapter, the debugging tools available from the Debug menu were discussed and demonstrated. You learned how to access and use Trace On with Single Step and Procedure Step keys, F8 and F10. You also learned to use watch expressions and watchpoints. The use of breakpoints was demonstrated, along with History On and its key combinations SHIFT+F8 to move History Back and SHIFT+F10 to move History Forward.

12 *Executable Files*

It is impossible to cover all the characteristics and capabilities of QuickBASIC in a single book. The basic aspects of QuickBASIC have been presented in previous chapters. This chapter takes a brief look at methods of creating QuickBASIC program files that can be run outside the QuickBASIC environment.

All QuickBASIC programs discussed in previous chapters have been created and saved to run from your QuickBASIC work disk. Once you have a program that runs within QuickBASIC, you can make a version that runs under MS-DOS directly from the MS-DOS command line. This version of a program is called an executable file.

Executable files do not require that QuickBASIC be in memory. They can be started simply and quickly; you do not have to load QuickBASIC. They run directly from MS-DOS. Executable files are optimized for speed and efficiency. Therefore, they perform floating-point arithmetic more quickly and more efficiently than the same program run in QuickBASIC.

Making Executable Files

An executable file has an .EXE extension. If you have a QuickBASIC program named PRO12-1.BAS, an executable file made from that program would logically be named PRO12-1.EXE. For example, suppose you had a disk containing an executable file (PRO12-1.EXE) in Drive B. From Drive A, you would access MS-DOS from your MS-DOS disk or from your QB work disk (if it contained COMMAND.COM). Then you would enter this command:

```
A>B:PRO12-1
```

If you have not added any files since Chapter 3, your QB work disk now contains these files:

COMMAND.COM   From MS-DOS
QB.EXE   From QuickBASIC
QB.HLP   From QuickBASIC

To create an executable file, make sure the proper files are available before you begin. If you don't have a hard disk with all QuickBASIC files on it and you are using 5 1/4-inch floppy disks, you must keep your files and other programs on several floppy disks.

Two different systems are being used to develop programs for this book. Neither system has a hard disk drive. One is a "bare-bones" system that is considered the minimum for using QuickBASIC. It has

384K of memory
Two 5 1/4-inch floppy disk drives (360K capacity per disk)

The second system is a little larger, somewhere between a minimum system and a hard disk system. It has

640K of memory
One 5 1/4-inch floppy disk drive (360K capacity)
One 3 1/2-inch drive (720K capacity)

A system with a hard disk can hold all QuickBASIC files on the hard disk, ready to be used. A system with a 720K 3 1/2-inch disk can hold the QuickBASIC files needed for almost any task. A system with only 5 1/4-inch floppy disks will have to use several disks and swap disks when necessary. The description that follows is for a minimum system with 5 1/4-inch floppy disk drives.

If QuickBASIC cannot find a file that it needs while making an executable file, it prompts you for a path name. When this happens, insert the correct disk and respond to the prompt. Your QuickBASIC work disk is fine if you are working with programs within Quick-BASIC. However, executable files require additional files.

There are many ways for the additional files to be organized on a floppy disk system. Your *Learning and Using Microsoft QuickBASIC* manual describes a recommended disk configuration for a two-floppy-disk system. However, you may use other configurations to suit your particular purpose. The configurations shown in Table 12-1 were used to create EXE files in this chapter.

Two 5 1/4-inch Floppy Disk System	3 1/2-inch and 5 1/4-inch Disk System
1. QB Work Disk	1. QB Work Disk (3 1/2-inch disk)

COMMAND.COM
   QB.EXE
   QB.HLP
	COMMAND.COM
	   QB.EXE
	   BC.EXE
	   LINK.EXE
	   BCOM40.LIB
	   BRUN40.LIB

2. QB Compile Disk	
BC.EXE LINK.EXE	
3. QB Library Disk	
BRUN40.LIB BCOM40.LIB	
4. QB Program Disk	2. QB Program Disk (5 1/4-inch disk)

BRUN40.EXE
   QB source files (.BAS)
   QB object files (.OBJ)
   QB executable files (.EXE)
	BRUN40.EXE
	   QB source files (.BAS)
	   QB object files (.OBJ)
	   QB executable files (.EXE)

Table 12-1. *Configurations for EXE Files*

Use your QB work disk as disk number 1. Use fresh, formatted disks to copy the necessary files to the new work disks. Copy BRUN40.EXE to several formatted disks. These disks will be used to store your QuickBASIC .BAS files, the object files (.OBJ) produced when creating EXE files, and the EXE files.

You now have three work disks. The one that you have been using, the QB work disk (disk number 1), is your main work disk. The other work disks, the QB compile work disk (disk number 2) and the QB library work disk (disk number 3), should be kept nearby when you are making EXE files.

When you create an executable file, QuickBASIC first uses BC.EXE (BASIC compiler) to compile your QuickBASIC program into an intermediate file known as an object file. The LINK.EXE file then joins all of the separately compiled modules of your program into a single executable file. LINK.EXE also combines the compiled object files created by BC.EXE with the supporting routines needed. The supporting routines are found in the run-time libraries BRUN40.LIB or BCOM.LIB. A simplified diagram of the operation is shown below.

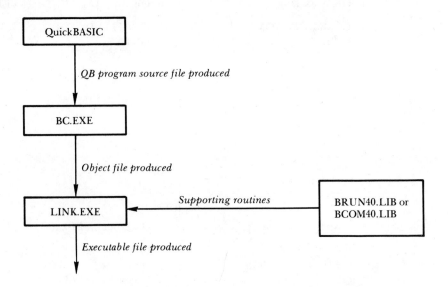

QuickBASIC can produce two types of executable files: EXE, requiring BRUN40.EXE, and Stand-Alone EXE. You make the choice when the QuickBASIC program is loaded and you choose the

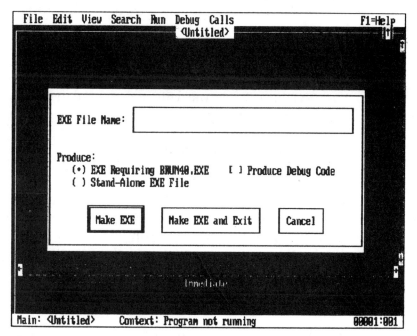

Figure 12-1. *Make EXE File... command*

Make EXE File... command from the Run menu. The entire process of creating an executable file will be discussed shortly. For now, access the Run menu and select the Make EXE File... command to study the dialog box shown in Figure 12-1.

Since no QuickBASIC program is in memory at this time, the EXE File Name text box remains blank except for the cursor. If a program was in memory, its base name plus an EXE extension would be displayed here.

Press the TAB key to move the cursor from the EXE File Name text box to the area headed by Produce:. Two choices appear below this heading. A dot is shown in the parentheses preceding the first choice, which indicates that the line "EXE Requiring BRUN40.EXE" is currently selected.

```
(•) EXE Requiring BRUN40.EXE
```

This choice requires a special file, BRUN40.EXE, when the EXE file you make is run.

Press the down arrow key to move the dot to the second choice, which is

```
(•) Stand-Alone EXE File
```

Your EXE file will now run without the special file (BRUN40.EXE) required by the first choice.

You can either use the arrow keys to move the dot between the two choices or press the X key (the *X* in **EXE** is printed in red to indicate that X activates this selection) or the A key (the *A* in Stand-Alone is printed in red to indicate that A activates this selection).

Press the TAB key again. The cursor moves inside the square brackets to the left of Produce Debug Code. Notice that the letter *D* is in red. Press the D key; an *X* appears inside the brackets. This indicates that the debug option has been selected. Press D again to turn the *X* off. The D key acts as a toggle for this selection.

```
[X] Produce Debug Code
```

If Produce Debug Code is selected, the code produced checks for the following at run time:

- Arithmetic overflow

- Array bounds

- Line location, so that run-time error messages can indicate the line number where the error occurred

- RETURN statements checked for matching GOSUB statements

- CTRL+BREAK, checked after executing each line to see if a CTRL+BREAK has occurred at the keyboard. If it has, execution is stopped

Three command buttons are displayed at the bottom of the dialog box. Press the TAB key to move from the Produce Debug Code option to the left command button, which is presently enclosed by a double-line box:

```
╔═════════════╗   ┌──────────────────────┐   ┌────────────┐
║  Make EXE   ║   │  Make EXE and Exit   │   │  Cancel    │
╚═════════════╝   └──────────────────────┘   └────────────┘
```

If this button is boxed when the ENTER key is pressed, it means that the file is compiled and the EXE file is created; you are returned to the QuickBASIC editor.

Press the TAB key again to move to the center command button. The center button now has the double-line box:

If this button is boxed with double lines when the ENTER key is pressed, it means that the file is compiled and the EXE file is created; the difference is that an exit from QuickBASIC is made.

Press the TAB key again to move to the far righthand command button. If you press the ENTER key while the Cancel button is boxed, the Make EXE File operation is cancelled and you are returned to the editor. You can also return to the editor and cancel the operation by pressing the ESC key while the dialog box is displayed. Do so now to return to the QuickBASIC editor.

Making an EXE File That Requires BRUN40.EXE

An EXE file requiring BRUN40.EXE is made when you choose the first option under Produce: from the Make EXE File... dialog box, which is

```
(•) EXE Requiring BRUN40.EXE
```

The BRUN40.EXE file must be available at the time a file of this type is run. BRUN40.EXE contains code needed to implement the Quick-BASIC language. Copy it to a fresh, formatted disk. Then the EXE files you create with this option can be saved and run from the same disk. One copy of BRUN40.EXE will serve all EXE files that are on the same disk.

EXE files that use BRUN40.EXE have the following advantages:

■ The EXE file produced is much smaller than if the Stand-Alone EXE option is used. If you want to save several EXE files on the same disk, more programs can be saved per disk.

■ Common variables and open files are preserved when CHAIN statements are used. This can be valuable in systems of programs that use shared data. Stand-alone programs do not preserve Common variables when CHAIN statements are used.

■ The BRUN40.EXE run-time module resides in memory, so it does not need to be reloaded for each program in a system of chained programs.

The following steps are suggested for creating an EXE file that uses BRUN40.EXE:

1. Have the required QuickBASIC files available.

2. Load a QuickBASIC program that has previously run successfully and save it to the disk that contains BRUN40.EXE.

3. With the disk containing BRUN40.EXE and your program in one disk drive, select Make EXE File... from the Run menu.

4. If you want to change the base name of the EXE file produced, type that name in the EXE File Name text box. Otherwise, leave the text box as it is and TAB to the Produce: area.

5. Choose EXE Requiring BRUN40.EXE. Then TAB to the Produce Debug Code area.

6. If you wish to produce a debug code, press the letter D. Otherwise, leave the square bracket blank. Choose the Produce Debug Code check box if you want your EXE file to include code that generates error-handling messages and reports error locations at run time. This option results in a larger and somewhat slower executable file.

7. Next, TAB to the command button desired. Choose either Make EXE or Make EXE and Exit. As previously discussed, the Make EXE command button creates the EXE file and then returns to Quick-BASIC. The Make EXE and Exit command button creates the EXE file and exits QuickBASIC.

The BAR GRAPH Program

To make your first EXE file, use Program 12-1, BAR GRAPH. The program is short—you can concentrate on creating the EXE file.

```
DECLARE SUB graph (income%())
DECLARE SUB label (month$())
REM ** BAR GRAPH **
' Program 12-1  9/18/87

DIM month$(12), income%(12)
CLS

' Read data to be graphed
FOR number% = 1 TO 12
   READ month$(number%), income%(number%)
NEXT number%
DATA Jan,84,  Feb,80,  Mar,74,  Apr,66
DATA May,72,  Jun,50,  Jul,54,  Aug,58
DATA Sep,64,  Oct,72,  Nov,88,  Dec,86

' draw graph and label
CALL graph(income%())
CALL label(month$())

COLOR 7

END

SUB graph (income%()) STATIC
  FOR number% = 1 TO 12
    COLOR number%
    blocks% = INT(income%(number%) / 10)
   .partblock = income%(number%) / 10 - blocks%

    LOCATE 16 - blocks%, 4 * number% + 12
    IF partblock > .3 AND partblock <= .7 THEN
      PRINT STRING$(2, 220);
    ELSEIF partblock > .7 THEN
      PRINT STRING$(2, 219);
    END IF
    FOR bar% = blocks% - 1 TO 0 STEP -1
      LOCATE 16 - bar%, 4 * number% + 12
      PRINT STRING$(2, 219);
    NEXT bar%
  NEXT number%

END SUB
SUB label (month$()) STATIC
  COLOR 11
  FOR row% = 1 TO 3
    FOR number% = 1 TO 12
      LOCATE row% + 17, 4 * number% + 12
      PRINT MID$(month$(number%), row%, 1);
    NEXT number%
  NEXT row%

  LOCATE 4, 32
  PRINT "Sales per Month";
  LOCATE 24, 1
  END SUB
```

Program 12-1. *BAR GRAPH*

Individual parts of the program can be easily modified or deleted and other functions can be added to customize it for your own purposes.

The main program reads a fictional company's monthly sales for a one-year period. Then two subprograms are called. One prints bars representing the income for each month. The other labels the bars with a vertical three-letter abbreviation of the month's name and prints a title.

The graph is drawn in the text mode using blocks formed by two adjacent ASCII character codes (219). Partial blocks are added by a pair of character codes (220). Graphs produced in the text mode do not provide much precision but can be used to show general trends.

The graph subprogram uses connected blocks and partial blocks to form a bar for each month.

```
blocks% = INT(income%(number%) / 1C)

partblock = income%(number%) / 10 - blocks%
```

The partial blocks and full blocks are connected to form the bars by the following section:

```
LOCATE 16 - blocks%, 4 * number% + 12
IF partblock > .3 AND partblock <= .7 THEN
   PRINT STRING$(2, 220);                    'Print a partblock
ELSEIF partblock > .7 THEN
   PRINT STRING$(2, 219);                    'Print a full block
END IF

FOR bar% = blocks% - 1 TO 0 STEP -1
   LOCATE 16 - bar%, 4 * number% + 12
   PRINT STRING$(2, 219);                    'Print a full block
NEXT bar%
```

The bars are drawn from the top downward and are two columns wide with two columns between bars. Table 12-2 shows examples of how the bars are calculated for two months.

The blocks are connected, as shown here:

January	April
number% = 1	number% = 4
income%(1) = 84	income% = 66
blocks% = INT (84/10) = 8	blocks% = INT(66/10) = 6
partblocks = 84/10 − 8 = 0.4	partblocks = 66/10 − 6 = 0.6
Draw a partblock since 0.4 is between 0.3 and 0.7	Draw a partblock since 0.6 is between 0.3 and 0.7
LOCATE partblock at 8,16 since 16 − 8 = 8 and 4 × 1 + 12 = 16	LOCATE partblock at 10,28 since 16 − 6 = 10 and 4 × 4 + 12 = 28
Calculate location of full blocks: FOR bar% = 7 TO 0 STEP −1	Calculate location of full blocks: FOR bar% = 5 TO 0 STEP −1
16 − 7, 16 = 9, 16	16 − 5, 28 = 11, 28
16 − 6, 16 = 10, 16	16 − 4, 28 = 12, 28
16 − 5, 16 = 11, 16	16 − 3, 28 = 13, 28
16 − 4, 16 = 12, 16	16 − 2, 28 = 14, 28
16 − 3, 16 = 13, 16	16 − 1, 28 = 15, 28
16 − 2, 16 = 14, 16	16 − 0, 28 = 16, 28
16 − 1, 16 = 15, 16	
16 − 0, 16 = 16, 16	

Table 12-2. *Blocks to Bars*

Each bar is printed in a different color by changing the foreground color each time a new month is referenced by number%.

```
    .
    .
    .
FOR number% = 1 TO 12
  COLOR number%
    .
    .
    .
```

The label program uses a similar locating scheme to print the three-letter abbreviation of each month below the appropriate bar. The title of the graph is then located and printed.

Notice that the main program resets the foreground to its original

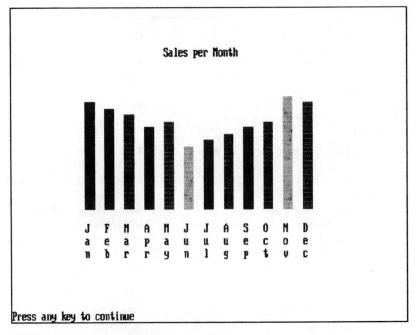

Figure 12-2.   *Output of PRO12-1.BAS*

color (white) before the program ends. If this is not done, any printing to the screen that you do after the program ends is in the last color specified by the program.

Figure 12-2 shows a run of Program 12-1.

Making the EXE File That Requires BRUN40.EXE

When you have entered and run Program 12-1 successfully, save it to a disk that contains BRUN40.EXE. That will complete Steps 1 and 2, listed previously. You are now ready for Steps 3 through 7, which may be summarized as follows:

3. Select Make EXE File... from the Run menu.

4. Leave the EXE file name as it is, which is

EXE File Name: | PRO12-1.EXE |

Press the TAB key to move to the Produce: area.

5. Choose EXE Requiring BRUN40.EXE. Then TAB to the brackets of the Produce Debug Code area.

6. This is your choice. Remember, a larger EXE file will be produced if you choose the Produce Debug Code option. Press D if you want Debug Code produced. An *X* will appear in the brackets. TAB to the command buttons.

7. Here again, you make the choice. Make EXE will return you to the QuickBASIC editor when the EXE file has been made. Make EXE and Exit will create the EXE file and then exit QuickBASIC.

Running the EXE File That Requires BRUN40.EXE

The details of running the EXE file will depend on the configuration of the system you are using. Suppose, typically, that you have a disk containing BRUN40.EXE and PRO12-1.EXE in Drive B and a disk containing MS-DOS is in Drive A.

Example 1 You enter

```
A>B:PRO12-1
```

Execution stops before the program is run and the display shows

```
A>B:PRO12-1
Input runtime module path:
```

The computer wants to know where to find the run-time module, BRUN40.EXE. Since it is on the disk in Drive B, type **B:** and press ENTER. The computer continues and PRO12-1.EXE is executed.

Example 2   This time Drive B: is accessed before the program name
is entered.

```
A>B:
```

Then the name is entered.

```
B:PRO12-1
```

The EXE file is executed with no interruptions.

Figure 12-3 shows the result of running the program from disk A,
as described in the first example. A run from disk B would be the same
except that the B> prompt would show in the lower lefthand corner.

Look at the directory of the disk drive containing your EXE
program. It contains BRUN40.EXE, the original QuickBASIC pro-

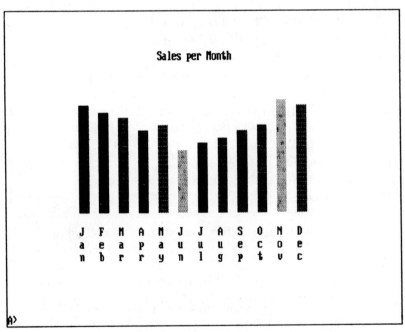

Figure 12-3.   *Output of EXE file PRO12-1.EXE*

gram, a corresponding object file, and the final EXE file. For example:

BRUN40.EXE   The run-time module using approximately 77K of memory

PRO12-1.BAS   The original QuickBASIC program using approximately 1.3K of memory

PRO12-1.OBJ   The object file using approximately 2.3K of memory

PRO12-1.EXE   The executable file using approximately 4.4K of memory

Each time you make a new executable file with this disk you will get a new QuickBASIC program, a new object file, and a new executable file. The amount of disk space used will depend on the lengths of these three files. BRUN40.EXE is only needed once. All EXE files on the same disk can use the same run-time module.

A Stand-Alone EXE File

Stand-alone programs are produced when you choose the Stand-Alone EXE File option from the Make EXE... dialog box. Files created with this option include the support routines found in BRUN40.EXE. Therefore, they require more disk space than those created with the EXE Requiring BRUN40.EXE option.

Stand-alone programs do not preserve variables listed in Common statements when a CHAIN statement transfers control to another program.

Files created with this option have these advantages:

■ You may save RAM space at run time if you have small, simple programs that do not require all the routines in the run-time module.

■ Execution of the program does not require that a run-time module be on the disk at run time. This is important if you write programs that others will copy, since others may not have a run-time module or know that it is needed.

Use the following steps to create a stand-alone EXE file:

1. Have the required QuickBASIC files available.

2. Load a QuickBASIC program that has previously run successfully.

3. Choose the Make EXE command from the Run menu.

4. If you want a different base name (file name without an extension), type it in the text box. Otherwise, leave the text box as it is.

5. Choose the Stand-Alone EXE File from the two options listed under Produce:.

6. TAB to the Debug area and press the letter D if you want to produce Debug Code.

7. Choose either Make EXE or Make EXE and Exit. The Make EXE command button creates the EXE file, and then returns you to Quick-BASIC. The Make EXE and Exit command button creates the EXE file and exits QuickBASIC.

If you decide not to make the EXE file while in the process of doing the above steps, press ESC or use the cancel button to cancel the operation.

The CIRCLE GRAPH Program

To demonstrate the creation of an executable file, use Program 12-2, CIRCLE GRAPH. Enter and run Program 12-2 to see how it works. The program dimensions several arrays used by subprograms. The rest of the main program consists of a DO...LOOP enclosing a call to the Menu subprogram and a SELECT CASE block used to call other subprograms.

When the program is run, the menu appears as shown in Figure 12-4. The first letter of each item on the menu is enclosed in paren-

```
DECLARE SUB Drawing ()
DECLARE SUB Info ()
DECLARE SUB Menu (KeyChoice$)
REM ** PIE GRAPH **
' Program 12-2  9/25/87

DIM percent(0 TO 12), amount(0 TO 12), angle(0 TO 12)
DIM col(0 TO 12) AS INTEGER, row(0 TO 12) AS INTEGER

DO
   CALL Menu(KeyChoice$)

   SELECT CASE KeyChoice$
     CASE "I"
       CALL Info
     CASE "P"
       CALL Drawing
     CASE "L"
       PRINT "CALL Label subprogram"
     CASE "Q"
       EXIT DO
   END SELECT
LOOP


END

SUB Drawing STATIC
   SHARED sec AS INTEGER, col AS INTEGER, row AS INTEGER, rad AS SINGLE
   SHARED ecc AS SINGLE, col() AS INTEGER, row() AS INTEGER

   SCREEN 1, 0: CLS
   CIRCLE (col, row), rad, 3, , , ecc
   FOR sector% = 1 TO sec
     LINE (col, row)-(col(sector%), row(sector%))
   NEXT sector%
   kolor = 1
   FOR sector% = 1 TO sec
     IF sector% = sec THEN
       last% = 1
       kolor = 3
     ELSE last% = sector% + 1
     END IF
     colpaint = (col(sector%) + col(last%) - 2 * col) / 4
     rowpaint = (row(sector%) + row(last%) - 2 * row) / 4
     PAINT (col + colpaint, row + rowpaint), kolor, 3
     kolor = kolor + 1
     IF kolor = 3 THEN kolor = 1
   NEXT sector%
   BEEP
   waitkey$ = INPUT$(1)
   SCREEN 0
   WIDTH 80

END SUB
```

Program 12-2. *CIRCLE GRAPH*

```
SUB Info STATIC

  SHARED sec AS INTEGER, col AS INTEGER, row AS INTEGER, rad AS SINGLE
  SHARED ecc AS SINGLE, col() AS INTEGER, row() AS INTEGER
  REDIM amount(0 TO 12) AS SINGLE
  REDIM percent(0 TO 12) AS SINGLE
  REDIM angle(0 TO 12) AS SINGLE

  CLS
  INPUT "Number of sections"; sec
  INPUT "Center of circle (col,row)"; col, row
  INPUT "Radius of circle"; rad
  INPUT "Ratio height/width"; ecc

  CLS : pi = 3.14159
  FOR sector% = 1 TO sec
    PRINT "Amount for item "; sector%;
    INPUT amount(sector%)
    amount(0) = amount(0) + amount(sector%)
  NEXT sector%

  FOR sector% = 1 TO sec
    angle(sector%) = percent(0) * pi / 50
    percent(sector%) = amount(sector%) * 100 / amount(0)
    percent(0) = percent(0) + percent(sector%)
    col(sector%) = col + rad * COS(angle(sector%))
    row(sector%) = row - rad * SIN(angle(sector%)) * ecc
  NEXT sector%

END SUB

SUB Menu (KeyChoice$) STATIC
  COLOR 4, 0, 12: CLS

  COLOR 9: LOCATE 5, 33: PRINT "PIE GRAPH MENU"
  LOCATE 10, 30: PRINT "("; : COLOR 4: PRINT "I";
  COLOR 9: PRINT ")nput Information"
  LOCATE 12, 30: PRINT "("; : COLOR 4: PRINT "P";
  COLOR 9: PRINT ")reliminary Drawing"
  LOCATE 14, 30: PRINT "("; : COLOR 4: PRINT "L";
  COLOR 9: PRINT ")abel Drawing"
  LOCATE 16, 30: PRINT "("; : COLOR 4: PRINT "Q";
  COLOR 9: PRINT ")uit"

  COLOR 27, 1
  LOCATE 22, 24: PRINT CHR$(219);
  COLOR 10: PRINT " PRESS A LETTER (I, P, L, or Q) ";
  COLOR 27: PRINT CHR$(219);

  COLOR 7, 0
  DO
    BEEP: KeyChoice$ = UCASE$(INPUT$(1))
  LOOP WHILE INSTR("IPLQ", KeyChoice$) = 0
  END SUB
```

Program 12-2.   *CIRCLE GRAPH (continued)*

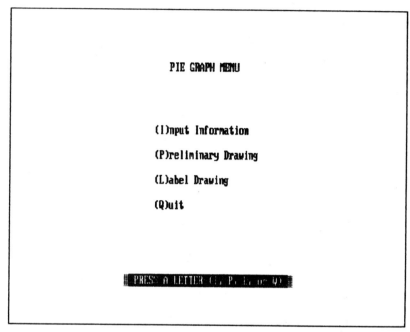

Figure 12-4. *Menu subprogram*

theses and highlighted in a different color than the rest of the item so that the key to be pressed stands out from the rest of the name.

First enter the information necessary to draw a circle graph (choice I on the menu). When this has been done, a return is made to the menu. Next draw the graph (choice D on the menu). When the graph is drawn, the program pauses to let you study the results. Press any key to return to the menu. The next step is to call the Label subprogram (choice L), where the graph can be labeled as you wish. This subroutine has been left for you to customize for the graph that you wish to produce. The choice in Program 12-2 merely prints its name. The last item on the menu (Quit, choice Q) allows you to exit the program.

If you don't like the first graph attempt, the data may be changed by entering the Info subprogram again from the menu. You would then have to enter all the information again. An alternative solution is

Number of sections? 5
Center of circle (x,y)? 160,100
Radius of circle? 70
Ratio height/width? .85

Figure 12-5. *Input Information subprogram showing circle parameters*

to write another subprogram that would allow you to choose which items you want to change.

The Info subprogram prompts you to enter the number of sections into which the circle is to be divided, where the circle's center is, how long the radius is, and the eccentricity to be used in drawing the circle. The default value for eccentricity is 1, but on most monitors an ellipse that is taller than it is wide will be displayed with this value. Usually, a number slightly smaller than 1 is required for a true circle. A value of 0.85 has been entered, as Figure 12-5 shows.

The subprogram also requests the information used to calculate the size of each sector of the circle. It calculates the size of each sector by totaling the items entered, then finding the percentage of the total for each item. A little trigonometry is applied to locate points on the circle that are used in the Drawing subprogram to divide the circle into sectors. Figure 12-6 shows the amounts entered for a five-sector circle graph.

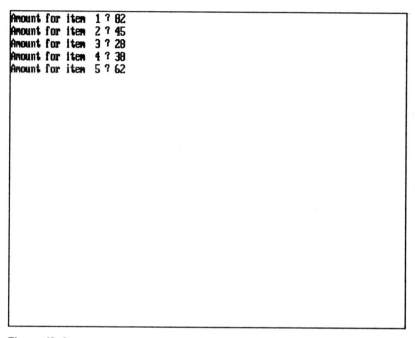

```
Amount for item  1 ? 82
Amount for item  2 ? 45
Amount for item  3 ? 28
Amount for item  4 ? 38
Amount for item  5 ? 62
```

Figure 12-6. *Input Information subprogram showing amounts for each sector*

A running total of the amounts entered (amount(0)) is calculated in the FOR...NEXT loop:

```
FOR sector% = 1 TO sec
  PRINT "Amount for item "; sector%;
  INPUT amount(sector%)
  amount(0) = amount(0) + amount(sector%)
NEXT sector%
```

As each pass through the FOR...NEXT loop is completed, the amounts and the running totals are

Sector%	Amount(sector%)	Amount(0)
1	82	82
2	45	127
3	28	155
4	38	193
5	62	255

A second FOR...NEXT loop calculates the percentage of the total for each sector, the angle of rotation for each sector, and the coordinates of the endpoints for each sector arc:

```
FOR sector% = 1 to sec
  angle(sector%) = percent(0) * pi / 50
  percent(sector%) = amount(sector%) * 100 / amount(0)
  percent(0) = percent(0) + percent(sector%)
  col(sector%) = col + rad * COS(angle(sector%))
  row(sector%) = row - rad * SIN(angle(sector%)) * ecc
NEXT sector%
```

Consider first the calculations for the percentage of each section and the running total of percentages.

```
percent(sector%) = amount(sector%) * 100 / amount(0)
percent(0) = percent(0) + percent(sector%)
```

The value of amount(0), which is the total of all amounts in the example being used, is 255. The percentage for each section and a running total of the sector percentages are

Sector%	Amount (sector%)	Total Before	Percent (sector%)	Total After
1	82	0	32.16	32.16
2	45	32.16	17.64	49.80
3	28	49.80	10.98	60.78
4	38	60.78	14.90	75.69
5	62	75.69	24.31	100

There are 2 * pi radians in a complete circle. Therefore, the angle in radians for any given percentage is

percent * 2 * pi / 100 or percent * pi / 50

The angle for the beginning of a given sector is

angle(sector%) = percent(0) * pi / 50

where percent(0) is the running total before the percentage for the current sector has been added.

The results calculated using the previous percentages are

Sector%	Percent(0) * pi / 50	Angle
1	0 * 3.14159 / 50	0
2	32.16 * 3.14159 / 50	2.02
3	49.80 * 3.14159 / 50	3.13
4	60.78 * 3.14159 / 50	3.82
5	75.69 * 3.14159 / 50	4.76

The angles are used to calculate the endpoints of the sectors (which lie on the circle), as shown here:

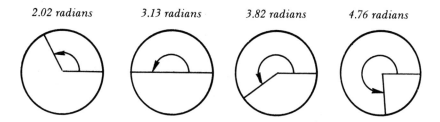

| 2.02 radians | 3.13 radians | 3.82 radians | 4.76 radians |

The calculations can be made more efficiently by dividing 3.14159 by 50 before the loop is entered. Then the result can be used to multiply each percent(0) inside the loop. This would substitute one division for the five divisions used inside the present loop.

After the angles are found, they are used to calculate the coordinates of the endpoints on the circle for each sector:

```
col(sectr%) = col + rad * COS(angle(sector%))
row(sector%) = row - rad * SIN(angle(sector%))
```

For any given point (column, row) on a circle, the mathematical relationship between the coordinates and the angle is

column = radius * COS(angle)
row = radius * SIN(angle)

The relationship between the coordinates and the angle is demonstrated on the next page.

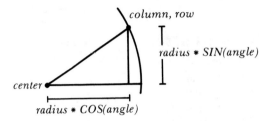

Since the row coordinates on the screen are measured from the top of the screen downward, the sign of the row coordinate must be negative to correspond to the mathematical relationship:

row = − radius * SIN(angle)

The eccentricity (ecc) is also used in the row coordinate calculation. The ecc variable is the ratio (height to width) that enables you to produce a true circle (one that looks round on the screen). You entered this value earlier in the Info subprogram. The QuickBASIC calculation of the coordinates is

```
col(sector%) = col + rad * COS(angle(sector%))
row(sector%) = row - rad * SIN(angle(sector%))
```

Using these equations, the coordinates in the example under consideration are

Sector%	Angle	COS	SIN	Coordinates
1	0	1.0	0	230, 100
2	2.02	−0.435	.401	130, 46
3	3.13	−1.0	.0123	90, 99
4	3.82	−0.779	−0.627	105, 137
5	4.76	.0431	−0.999	163, 159

Using these coordinates, the points are located on the circle as shown on the next page.

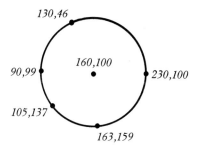

The Drawing subprogram uses a new statement: SHARED. This statement allows the subprogram to share variables between itself, the main program, and other procedures in the module without the need for passing them as parameters. The SHARED statements used in the Drawing subprogram are

```
SHARED sec AS INTEGER, col AS INTEGER, row AS INTEGER, rad AS INTEGER
SHARED ecc AS SINGLE, col() AS INTEGER, row() AS INTEGER
```

The circle is drawn by

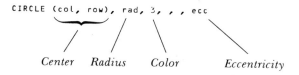

Lines are drawn to separate sectors of the circle by

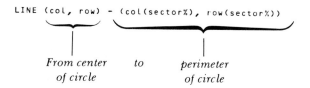

The values for the point on the perimeter (col(sector%), row(sector%)) are those calculated in the Info subprogram. They are shared between subprograms because of the SHARED statement. The lines

drawn result in the following circle sectors:

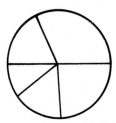

When the circle has been divided into sectors, the **PAINT** statement is used to color the interior of each sector by

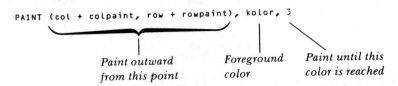

Careful consideration must be given to the coordinates of the point at which painting begins. This point must lie inside the correct sector, because painting is done from this point outward in all directions until the boundary color is reached. The steps that follow locate a point that lies inside the sector being painted.

1. Imagine a line radiating from the center of a circle that divides a sector into two equal parts.

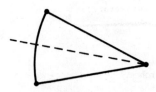

2. Now consider a point on the line of step 1 that is halfway between the endpoints of the sector's arc.

col(A) = (col(sector%) + col(last%)) / 2
row(A) = (row(sector%) + row(last%)) / 2

For example:

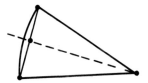

3. The point in step 2 looks satisfactory but is very close to the circle. It would be better to pick a point on the line that is closer to the center (but not too close). Pick a point halfway between the point in step 2 and the center of the circle.

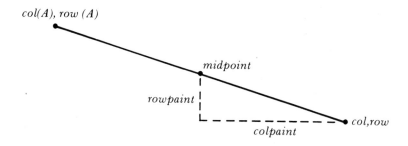

Using some algebraic manipulations, the distance from the center of the circle and the paint point can be calculated in QuickBASIC by

```
colpaint = (col(sector%) + col(last%) - 2 * col) / 4
rowpaint = (row(sector%) + row(last%) - 2 * row) / 4
```

Using results of the previous example, the paint point values to be added to the coordinates of the center of the circle are

Sector%	Col(sector%)	Col(last%)	Colpaint
1	230	130	10
2	130	90	−25
3	90	105	−31.25
4	105	163	−13
5	163	230	18.25

Sector%	Row(sector%)	Row(last%)	Rowpaint
1	100	46	−13.5
2	46	99	−13.75
3	99	137	9
4	137	159	24
5	159	100	14.75

When colpaint and rowpaint are added to the coordinates of the center of the circle (160,100), the result is the coordinate to use for painting the sector.

Sector%	Col(sector%)	Row(sector%)
1	170	86.5
2	90	72.5
3	77.5	118
4	114	148
5	176.5	129.5

Here is how the paint points are placed:

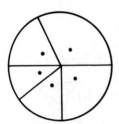

This method of locating the points from which to paint is an oversimplification that will not work for any sector that is greater than 50 percent of the circle. For example, consider a circle divided into three parts: 60 percent, 25 percent, and 35 percent. As calculated by Program 12-2, the paint point of the 60 percent sector lies outside the sector:

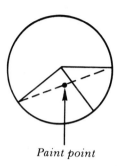

Paint point

The values of the variables *colpaint* and *rowpaint* in this case should be subtracted from the coordinates of the center of the circle, as follows:

PAINT (col − colpaint, row − rowpaint), kolor, 3

This gives the correct paint point:

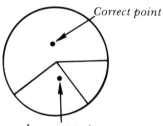

Incorrect point

You could use an IF...THEN...ELSE block to allow for sectors that are larger than 50 percent of the circle. The values of *colpaint* and *rowpaint* could be assigned negative quantities in such cases.

One other possibility arises. What if a sector is exactly 50 percent of the circle? This is left as a programming problem for you to solve.

The *kolor* variable changes for each sector. Only four foreground colors are available in the graphics mode being used (screen 1). Therefore, the same color will be repeated if there are more than four sectors.

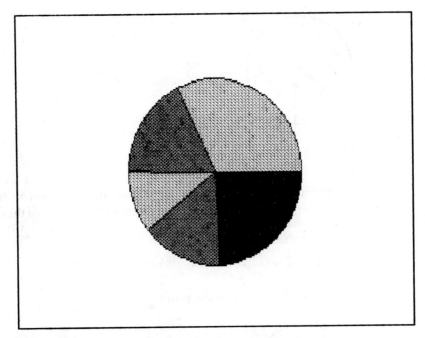

Figure 12-7.   *Circle graph*

When the circle is complete, a beep sounds and the program pauses for you to study the graph. Note any changes you want to make. Then press any key to return to the menu. A circle graph drawn with the data shown in Figure 12-6 is shown in Figure 12-7.

You can write your own subprogram for the Label subprogram so that your circle graph is labeled the way you want it to be. Text can be added to a graphics screen. In screen mode 1 (used in Program 12-2), text is printed in the same size as on a width 40 text-mode screen. Use LOCATE statements to place your labels where you want them.

As soon as Program 12-2 runs correctly, save the file as PRO12-2.BAS.

Making a Stand-Alone EXE File

A stand-alone EXE file is made in the same way as an EXE file that requires BRUN40.EXE, with one exception: the choice made in the Produce: area.

Access the Run menu and choose the Make EXE... command. The name of the EXE file to be created appears in the EXE File Name text box:

PRO12-2.EXE

If you want to have a different base name, type it in the box. Otherwise, leave the name as it is.

From the two options under Produce:, choose Stand-Alone EXE File by pressing the down arrow key. Then press TAB to move to Produce Debug Code.

If you want the debug options described earlier, choose the Produce Debug Code by pressing the D key. Otherwise, skip this option by pressing the TAB key.

Select the Make EXE or the Make EXE and Exit command button. The choice is yours. If you have more things to do in QuickBASIC after making the EXE file, choose Make EXE. If you want to go to MS-DOS after making the EXE file, choose Make EXE and Exit. In either case, press ENTER to make the EXE file.

Running Stand-Alone EXE File

Your stand-alone EXE file will run from MS-DOS in the same way as a file made from EXE File Requiring BRUN40.EXE. However, you do not need to have the BRUN40.EXE file available to run this type of EXE file. The result produced will be the same as that of PRO12-2.BAS run from QuickBASIC.

Files created using Stand-Alone EXE File include support routines found in BRUN40.EXE. Therefore, this type of file requires more disk space than those created with EXE Requiring BRUN40.EXE. If you examine the directory of your disk, you can see that the EXE file of Program 12-2 (PRO12-2.EXE.) is much larger than PRO12-1.EXE. Here is a comparison of the files produced by the two methods:

Stand-Alone EXE	EXE Requiring BRUN40.EXE
PRO12-2.BAS 2.9K	PRO12-1.BAS 1.3K
PRO12-2.OBJ 5.2K	PRO12-1.OBJ 2.3K
PRO12-2.EXE 52.3K	PRO12-1.EXE 4.4K
	BRUN40.EXE 76.7K

Each time another QuickBASIC program creates a new stand-alone EXE file, the EXE file produced will be quite large. That is, there will be one large EXE file for each QuickBASIC program.

In contrast, the large BRUN40.EXE file used with EXE Files Requiring BRUN40.EXE serves all such EXE files on the same disk. The BRUN40.EXE file resides only once on each disk containing this type of EXE file.

As mentioned before, other disk configurations can be used. The BRUN40.EXE file can be placed on one of your work disks instead of the program disk as long as it is available when the EXE file is run.

Review

This chapter discussed two methods of creating executable files that run directly from the MS-DOS command line. Executable files (.EXE) need the support of more QuickBASIC files than QuickBASIC programs (.BAS) that run within the QuickBASIC environment. Therefore, additional work disks must be made to create EXE files. The location of the support files on the work disks will depend on the disk configuration of your computer system.

The two types of files — Stand-Alone and EXE files that require BRUN40.EXE — are discussed and both types of EXE files are produced. A bar graph is created by one method. A circle graph is created by the other method.

This chapter concludes your introduction to using QuickBASIC, version 4.0. When discussing a programming environment with such a vast capability, it is impossible to cover all aspects of the system. It is hoped that some of the flavor of QuickBASIC has been conveyed by this book and that the book spurs you into discovering further capabilites on your own.

A

QuickBASIC Reserved Words

The following words are reserved in QuickBASIC. They may not be used as labels or as names of variables or procedures.

ABS	CALL	COM
ACCESS	CALLS	COMMAND$
ALIAS	CASE	COMMON
AND	CDBL	CONST
ANY	CDECL	COS
APPEND	CHAIN	CSNG
AS	CHDIR	CSRLIN
ASC	CHR$	CVD
ATN	CINT	CVDMBF
BASE	CIRCLE	CVI
BEEP	CLEAR	CVL
BINARY	CLNG	CVS
BLOAD	CLOSE	CVSMBF
BSAVE	CLS	DATA
BYVAL	COLOR	DATE$

DECLARE	HEX$	MKI$
DEF	IF	MKL$
DEFDBL	IMP	MKS$
DEFINT	INKEY$	MKSMBF$
DEFLNG	INP	MOD
DEFSNG	INPUT	NAME
DEFSTR	INPUT$	NEXT
DIM	INSTR	NOT
DO	INT	OCT$
DOUBLE	INTEGER	OFF
DRAW	IOCTL	ON
ELSE	IOCTL$	OPEN
ELSEIF	IS	OPTION
END	KEY	OR
ENDIF	KILL	OUT
ENVIRON	LBOUND	OUTPUT
ENVIRON$	LCASE$	PAINT
EOF	LEFT$	PALETTE
EQV	LEN	PCOPY
ERASE	LET	PEEK
ERDEV	LINE	PEN
ERDEV$	LIST	PLAY
ERL	LOC	PMAP
ERR	LOCAL	POINT
ERROR	LOCATE	POKE
EXIT	LOCK	POS
EXP	LOF	PRESET
FIELD	LOG	PRINT
FILEATTR	LONG	PSET
FILES	LOOP	PUT
FIX	LPOS	RANDOM
FOR	LPRINT	RANDOMIZE
FRE	LSET	READ
FREEFILE	LTRIM$	REDIM
FUNCTION	MID$	REM
GET	MKD$	RESET
GOSUB	MKDIR	RESTORE
GOTO	MKDMBF$	RESUME

RETURN	SPACE$	TRON
RIGHT$	SPC	TYPE
RMDIR	SQR	UBOUND
RND	STATIC	UCASE$
RSET	STEP	UNLOCK
RTRIM$	STICK	UNTIL
RUN	STOP	USING
SADD	STR$	VAL
SCREEN	STRIG	VARPTR
SEEK	STRING	VARPTR$
SEG	STRING$	VARSEG
SELECT	SUB	VIEW
SETMEM	SWAP	WAIT
SGN	SYSTEM	WEND
SHARED	TAB	WHILE
SHELL	TAN	WIDTH
SIGNAL	THEN	WINDOW
SIN	TIME$	WRITE
SINGLE	TIMER	XOR
SLEEP	TO	
SOUND	TROFF	

B ASCII Codes for the IBM PC

Decimal Value	Hexadecimal Value	Control Character	Character
0	00	NUL	Null
1	01	SOH	☺
2	02	STX	☻
3	03	ETX	♥
4	04	EOT	♦
5	05	ENQ	♣
6	06	ACK	♠
7	07	BEL	Beep
8	08	BS	◘
9	09	HT	Tab
10	0A	LF	Line-feed
11	0B	VT	Cursor home
12	0C	FF	Form-feed
13	0D	CR	Enter

Table B-2. *ASCII Codes for the PC*

Decimal Value	Hexadecimal Value	Control Character	Character
14	0E	SO	
15	0F	SI	
16	10	DLE	
17	11	DC1	
18	12	DC2	
19	13	DC3	
20	14	DC4	
21	15	NAK	
22	16	SYN	
23	17	ETB	
24	18	CAN	↑
25	19	EM	↓
26	1A	SUB	→
27	1B	ESC	←
28	1C	FS	Cursor right
29	1D	GS	Cursor left
30	1E	RS	Cursor up
31	1F	US	Cursor down
32	20	SP	Space
33	21		!
34	22		,,
35	23		#
36	24		$
37	25		%
38	26		&
39	27		'
40	28		(
41	29		)
42	2A		*
43	2B		+
44	2C		,
45	2D		-
46	2E		.
47	2F		/
48	30		0
49	31		1
50	32		2
51	33		3
52	34		4

Table B-2.   *ASCII Codes for the PC (continued)*

Decimal Value	Hexadecimal Value	Control Character	Character
53	35		5
54	36		6
55	37		7
56	38		8
57	39		9
58	3A		:
59	3B		;
60	3C		<
61	3D		=
62	3E		>
63	3F		?
64	40		@
65	41		A
66	42		B
67	43		C
68	44		D
69	45		E
70	46		F
71	47		G
72	48		H
73	49		I
74	4A		J
75	4B		K
76	4C		L
77	4D		M
78	4E		N
79	4F		O
80	50		P
81	51		Q
82	52		R
83	53		S
84	54		T
85	55		U
86	56		V
87	57		W
88	58		X
89	59		Y
90	5A		Z
91	5B		[

Table B-2.   *ASCII Codes for the PC (continued)*

Decimal Value	Hexadecimal Value	Control Character	Character
92	5C		\
93	5D		]
94	5E		^
95	5F		—
96	60		'
97	61		a
98	62		b
99	63		c
100	64		d
101	65		e
102	66		f
103	67		g
104	68		h
105	69		i
106	6A		j
107	6B		k
108	6C		l
109	6D		m
110	6E		n
111	6F		o
112	70		p
113	71		q
114	72		r
115	73		s
116	74		t
117	75		u
118	76		v
119	77		w
120	78		x
121	79		y
122	7A		z
123	7B		{
124	7C		¦
125	7D		}
126	7E		~
127	7F	DEL	⌂
128	80		Ç
129	81		ü
130	82		é

Table B-2. *ASCII Codes for the PC (continued)*

Decimal Value	Hexadecimal Value	Control Character	Character
131	83		â
132	84		ä
133	85		à
134	86		å
135	87		ç
136	88		ê
137	89		ë
138	8A		è
139	8B		ï
140	8C		î
141	8D		ì
142	8E		Ä
143	8F		Å
144	90		É
145	91		æ
146	92		Æ
147	93		ô
148	94		ö
149	95		ó
150	96		û
151	97		ù
152	98		ÿ
153	99		Ö
154	9A		Ü
155	9B		¢
156	9C		£
157	9D		¥
158	9E		Pt
159	9F		ƒ
160	A0		á
161	A1		í
162	A2		ó
163	A3		ú
164	A4		ñ
165	A5		Ñ
166	A6		a̲
167	A7		o̲
168	A8		¿
169	A9		⌐

Table B-2. *ASCII Codes for the PC (continued)*

Decimal Value	Hexadecimal Value	Control Character	Character
170	AA		¬
171	AB		½
172	AC		¼
173	AD		¡
174	AE		«
175	AF		»
176	B0		░
177	B1		▒
178	B2		▓
179	B3		│
180	B4		┤
181	B5		╡
182	B6		╢
183	B7		╖
184	B8		╕
185	B9		╣
186	BA		║
187	BB		╗
188	BC		╝
189	BD		╜
190	BE		╛
191	BF		┐
192	C0		└
193	C1		┴
194	C2		┬
195	C3		├
196	C4		─
197	C5		┼
198	C6		╞
199	C7		╟
200	C8		╚
201	C9		╔
202	CA		╩
203	CB		╦
204	CC		╠
205	CD		═
206	CE		╬
207	CF		╧
208	D0		╨

Table B-2. *ASCII Codes for the PC (continued)*

Decimal Value	Hexadecimal Value	Control Character	Character
209	D1		╤
210	D2		╥
211	D3		╙
212	D4		╘
213	D5		╒
214	D6		╓
215	D7		╫
216	D8		╪
217	D9		┘
218	DA		┌
219	DB		█
220	DC		▄
221	DD		▌
222	DE		▐
223	DF		▀
224	E0		α
225	E1		β
226	E2		Γ
227	E3		π
228	E4		Σ
229	E5		σ
230	E6		μ
231	E7		τ
232	E8		Φ
233	E9		θ
234	EA		Ω
235	EB		δ
236	EC		∞
237	ED		$\emptyset$
238	EE		ϵ
239	EF		$\cap$
240	F0		$\equiv$
241	F1		$\pm$
242	F2		$\geq$
243	F3		$\leq$
244	F4		$\lceil$
245	F5		$\rfloor$
246	F6		$\div$
247	F7		$\approx$

Table B-2. *ASCII Codes for the PC (continued)*

Decimal Value	Hexadecimal Value	Control Character	Character
248	F8		$^{\circ}$
249	F9		$\bullet$
250	FA		$\cdot$
251	FB		$\sqrt{}$
252	FC		^{n}
253	FD		^{2}
254	FE		$\blacksquare$
255	FF		(blank)

Table B-2.   *ASCII Codes for the PC (continued)*

C *Error Messages*

During the development of a BASIC program using the QuickBASIC compiler, four kinds of errors can occur:

- Invocation errors
- Compile-time errors
- Link-time errors
- Run-time errors

Invocation errors can occur when you invoke QuickBASIC from the MS-DOS command line, using the QB or BC commands.

Compile-time errors occur when the program is compiled.

Run-time errors occur when the program is being run or executed.

Link-time errors occur only when you use the link command to link object files created with BC or other language compilers. This feature of QuickBASIC is not covered in this book.

When run-time errors occur in programs that are compiled and run from within the QuickBASIC environment, the line at which the error occurred appears in green and the error message is displayed. In stand-alone executable programs (that is, programs that are executed by entering the base name of the executable file at the system prompt), the run-time system prints the error messages followed by an address, unless the /d), /e, or (/w) option is specified on the BC command line. In those cases, the error message is followed by the number of the line in which the error occurred. The standard forms of this type of error message are

Error X in module *module-name* at address *segment:offset.*

and

Error X in line *linenumber* of module *module-name* at address *segment:offset.*

An ERR code is listed for some errors. If an error occurs, the ERR variable is set to the appropriate code when an error-trapping sub-routine is entered. (Error-trapping routines are entered via the ON ERROR GOTO line statement.) The ERR variable remains at this value until a RESUME statement returns control to the main program. See the *QuickBASIC Language Reference Manual* for detailed information.

Run-time error codes are shown in Table C-1.

Descriptions of Error Messages

The *QuickBASIC Language Reference Manual* has more than 40 pages describing error messages. Here are condensed compile-time, run-time, invocation errors, and messages.

Advanced feature unavailable   Compile-time or run-time error. You are attempting to use a feature of QuickBASIC that is not available. May also occur if you are using DOS version 2.1 and trying to use a feature supported only in later versions. ERR code 73.

Argument-count mismatch   Compile-time or run-time error. Incorrect number of arguments used with a subprogram or function.

Code Description	Code Description
3 RETURN without GOSUB	55 File already open
4 Out of DATA	56 FIELD statement active
5 Illegal function call	57 Device I/O error
6 Overflow	58 File already exists
7 Out of memory	59 Bad record length
9 Subscript out of range	61 Disk full
11 Division by zero	62 Input past end of file
14 Out of string space	63 Bad record number
16 String formula too complex	64 Bad file name
19 No RESUME	67 Too many files
20 RESUME without error	68 Device unavailable
24 Device timeout	69 Communication-buffer overflow
25 Device fault	70 Permission denied
27 Out of paper	71 Disk not ready
39 CASE ELSE expected	72 Disk-media error
40 Variable required	73 Advanced feature unavailable
50 FIELD overflow	74 Rename across disks
51 Internal error	75 Path/File access error
52 Bad file name or number	76 Path not found
53 File not found	
54 Bad file mode	

Table C-1. *Run-Time Error Codes*

Array already dimensioned Compile-time error. (1) More than one DIM statement for the same static array. (2) A DIM statement after initial use of array; static arrays must be deallocated with an ERASE statement before they can be redimensioned; dynamic arrays are redimensioned with the REDIM statement. (3) An OPTION BASE statement occurs after an array is dimensioned.

Array not dimensioned Compile-time error. An array is referenced but not dimensioned.

Array too big Compile-time error. There is not enough user data space to accommodate the array declaration. Reduce the size of the array or use the $DYNAMIC metacommand.

Array undefined Compile-time error. An array that has been referenced has not been defined.

AS clause required Compile-time error. A variable declared with an AS clause is referenced without one. If the first declaration of a variable has an AS clause, every subsequent DIM, REDIM, SHARED, and COMMON statement that references that variable must have an AS clause.

AS clause required on first declaration Compile-time error. A variable that has not been declared using an AS clause is being referenced with an AS clause.

AS missing Compile-time error. The compiler expects an AS keyword, as in OPEN "FILENAME" FOR INPUT AS #1.

Asterisk missing Compile-time error. Asterisk is missing from a string definition in a user type.

Bad file mode Run-time error. (1) The program is trying to use PUT or GET with a sequential file or to execute an OPEN with a file mode other than I, O, or R; or (2) the program is trying to read from a file open for OUTPUT or APPEND; or (3) QuickBASIC is trying to compile and run an include file that has been saved in compressed format. Include files must be saved in text format. Reload the include file, save it in text format, then try to run the program again. ERR code 54.

Bad file name   Run-time error. An illegal form is used for the file name with LOAD, SAVE, KILL, or OPEN, for example, a file name with too many characters. ERR code 64.

Bad file name or number   Run-time error. A statement or command references a file with a file name or number that is not specified in the OPEN statement or is out of the range of file numbers specified at initialization. ERR code 52.

Bad record length   Run-time error. A GET or PUT statement was executed that specified a record variable whose length did not match the record length specified in the corresponding OPEN statement. ERR code 59.

BASE missing   Compile-time error. The compiler expected the keyword BASE here, as in OPTION BASE.

Binary source file   Compile-time error. The file you have attempted to compile is not an ASCII file. All source files saved by BASICA should be saved with the ,A option.

Block IF without END IF   Compile-time error. There is no corresponding END IF in a Block IF structure.

Buffer size expected after /C: BC invocation error. You must specify a buffer size after the /C option.

BYVAL allowed only with numeric arguments   Compile-time error. BYVAL does not accept string or record arguments.

Cannot continue   Compile-time error. While debugging, you have made a change that will prevent execution from continuing.

Cannot find file (filename). Input path: QB invocation error. Occurs when QuickBASIC cannot find a Quick library or stand-alone library required by the program. Enter the correct pathname or press CTRL+C to return to the DOS prompt.

Cannot start with FN   Compile-time error. You used FN as the first two letters of a subprogram or variable name. FN can only be used as the first two letters when calling a DEF FN function.

CASE ELSE expected   Run-time error. No matching case was found for an expression in a SELECT CASE statement. ERR code 39.

CASE without SELECT   Compile-time error. The first part of a SELECT CASE statement is missing or misspelled.

/C: buffer size too large   BC invocation error. The maximum size of the communications buffer is 32767 bytes.

Choose New from Edit menu to create new SUB or function   Compile-time error. You are attempting to enter a procedure in a module-level window.

Colon expected after /C   BC invocation error. A colon is required between the option and the buffer-size argument.

Comma missing   Compile-time error. The compiler expects a comma.

COMMON in Quick library too small   Compile-time error. More common variables are specified in the module than in the currently loaded Quick library.

COMMON must precede executable statements   Compile-time error. A COMMON statement is misplaced. COMMON declarations must appear before any executable statements. All BASIC statements are executable except for COMMON, DEF type, DIM (for static arrays), OPTION BASE, REM, all metacommands.

COMMON name illegal   Compile-time error. The compiler encountered an illegal */blockname/* specification (for example, a *blockname* that is a BASIC reserved word) in a named COMMON.

Communication-buffer overflow   Run-time error. During remote communications, the receive buffer overflowed. The size of the receive buffer is set by the /c command-line option. Try checking the buffer more frequently (with the LOC function) or emptying it more often (with the INPUT$ function). ERR code 69.

Data-memory overflow   Compile-time error. The program data is too big to fit in memory. Often caused by too many constants or too much static array data.

DECLARE required   Compile-time error. An implicit subprogram or function procedure call appears before the procedure definition. (An implicit call does not use the CALL statement.) All procedures must be defined or declared before they are called implicitly.

DEF without END DEF   Compile-time error. There is no corresponding END DEF in a multiline function definition.

DEFtype character specification illegal   Compile-time error. A DEF*type* statement is entered incorrectly. DEF can only be followed by LNG, DBL, INT, SNG, STR or for user-defined functions, a blank space.

Device fault   Run-time error. A device has returned a hardware error. If this message occurs while data is being transmitted to a communications file, it indicates that the signals being tested with the OPEN COM statement were not found in the specified period of time. ERR code 25.

Device I/O error   Run-time error. An I/O error occurred on a device I/O operation. The operating system cannot recover from the error. ERR code 57.

Device timeout   Run-time error. The program did not receive information from an I/O device within a predetermined amount of time. Retry the operation. ERR code 24.

Device unavailable   Run-time error. The device you are attempting to access is not on line or does not exist. ERR code 68.

Disk full   Run-time error. There is not enough room on the disk for the compiler to write out an .OBJ or .EXE file. ERR code 61.

Disk-media error   Run-time error. Disk-drive hardware has detected a physical flaw on the disk. ERR code 72.

Disk not ready   Run-time error. Disk-drive door is open or no disk is in drive. ERR code 71.

Division by zero   Compile-time error. This message results from division by zero, division of the integer −32,768 by 1 or −1, or MODing of the integer −32,768 by 1 or −1.

Division by zero   Run-time error. A division by zero is encountered in an expression or the operation of involution results in zero being raised to a negative power. This also occurs if the integer −32,768 is divided by 1 or −1, or if −32,768 is MODed by 1 or −1. ERR code 11.

DO without LOOP   Compile-time error. The terminating LOOP clause is missing from a DO...LOOP statement.

Duplicate definition   Compile-time or run-time error. You are using an identifier that has already been defined. For example, you are attempting to use the same name in a CONST statement and as a variable definition, or you have a SUB or FUNCTION procedure with the same name as a variable. This error also occurs if you attempt to dimension the same static array twice.

Duplicate label   Compile-time error. Two program lines are assigned the same number or label. Each line number or label must be unique.

Dynamic array element illegal   Compile-time error. Dynamic array elements are not allowed with VARPTR$.

Element not defined   Compile-time error. A user-defined type element is referenced but not defined.

ELSE without IF   Compile-time error. An ELSE clause appears without a corresponding IF. Sometimes this is caused by incorrectly nested IF statements.

END DEF without DEF   Compile-time error. An END DEF statement has no corresponding DEF statement.

END IF without Block IF   Compile-time error. The beginning of an IF Block is missing.

END SELECT without SELECT   Compile-time error. The end of a SELECT CASE statement appears without a beginning SELECT CASE. The beginning of the SELECT CASE statement may be missing or misspelled.

END SUB or END FUNCTION must be last line in window Compile-time error. You are attempting to add a code after a procedure. You must either return to the main module or open another module.

END SUB/FUNCTION without SUB/FUNCTION   Compile-time error. You deleted the SUB or FUNCTION statement.

END TYPE without TYPE   Compile-time error. An END TYPE statement is used outside a TYPE declaration.

Equal sign missing   Compile-time error. The compiler expects an equal sign.

Error during QuickBASIC initialization   QB invocation error. Several conditions can cause this error. It is most commonly caused when there is not enough memory in the machine to load QuickBASIC.

Error in loading file (file) — Cannot find file   QB invocation error. This error occurs when redirecting input to QuickBASIC from a file. The input file is not at the location specified on the command line.

Error in loading file (file)—Disk I/O error   QB invocation error. Caused by physical problems in accessing the disk, for example, if the drive door containing the file is open.

Error in loading file (file)—DOS memory-arena error   Run-time error. The area of memory used by DOS has been written to, either by an assembly language routine or with the POKE statement.

Error in loading file (file)—Invalid format   QB invocation error. You are attempting to load a Quick library that is not in the proper format.

Error in loading file (file)—Out of memory   Run-time error. More memory is required than is available. ERR code 7.

EXIT DO not within DO...LOOP   Compile-time error. An EXIT DO statement is used outside of a DO...LOOP statement.

EXIT not within FOR...NEXT   Compile-time error. An EXIT FOR statement is used outside of a FOR...NEXT statement.

Expected: item   Compile-time error. This is a syntax error. The cursor is positioned at the unexpected item.

Expression too complex   Compile-time error. This error is caused when certain internal limitations are exceeded. For example, during expression evaluation, strings that are not associated with variables are assigned temporary locations by the compiler. A large number of such strings can cause this error to occur. Try simplifying expressions and assigning strings to variables.

Extra file name ignored   QB invocation error. You specified too many files on the command line; the last file on the name is ignored.

FIELD overflow   Run-time error. A FIELD statement is attempting to allocate more bytes than were specified for the record length of a random file. ERR code 50.

FIELD statement active   Run-time error. A GET or PUT statement was executed that specified a record variable on a file for which FIELD statements had also been executed. GET or PUT with a record variable argument may only be used on files where no FIELD statements have been executed. ERR code 56.

File already exists   Run-time error. The file name specified in a NAME statement is identical to a file name already in use on the disk. ERR code 58.

File already open   Run-time error. The sequential output mode OPEN is issued for a file that is already open, or a KILL is given for a file that is open. ERR code 55.

File not found   Run-time error. A KILL, NAME, FILES, or OPEN statement references a file that does not exist at the specified location. ERR code 53.

File previously loaded   Compile-time error. You are attempting to load a file that is already in memory.

Fixed-length string illegal   Compile-time error. You are attempting to use a fixed-length string as a formal parameter.

FOR index variable already in use   Compile-time error. This error occurs when an index variable is used more than once in nested FOR loops.

FOR index variable illegal   Compile-time error. Usually caused when an incorrect variable type is used in a FOR-loop index. A FOR-loop index variable must be a simple numeric variable.

Formal parameters not unique   Compile-time error. A function or subprogram declaration contains duplicate parameters, as in SUB (A, B, C, A) STATIC.

Formal parameter specification illegal   Compile-time error. There is an error in a function or subprogram parameter list.

FOR without NEXT   Compile-time error. Each FOR statement must have a matching NEXT statement.

FUNCTION already defined   Compile-time error. Occurs when a previously defined function is redefined.

Function name illegal   Compile-time error. A BASIC reserved word is used as a user-defined function name.

Function not defined   Compile-time error. Functions must be declared or defined before they are used.

GOSUB missing   Compile-time error. The GOSUB is missing from an ON *event* GOSUB statement.

GOTO missing   Compile-time error. The GOTO is missing from an ON ERROR GOTO statement.

GOTO or GOSUB expected   Compile-time error. The compiler expects a GOTO or GOSUB statement.

Identifier cannot end with %, &, !, #, or $ Compile-time error. The above suffixes are not allowed in type identifiers or named COMMON names.

Identifier cannot include period   Compile-time error. Scalar variable, array, user-type identifier, and record element names cannot contain periods. The period should only be used as a record-variable separator.

Identifier expected   Compile-time error. Attempt to use a number or a BASIC reserved word where an identifier is expected.

Identifier too long   Compile-time error. Identifiers must not be longer than 40 characters.

Illegal function call   Run-time error. A parameter that is out of range is passed to a math or string function. A function call error can also occur for these reasons: (1) negative or unreasonably large subscript; (2) negative number raised to a noninteger power; (3) negative record number with GET or PUT; (4) strings are catenated to create a string that is longer than 32,767 characters. ERR code 5.

Illegal in direct mode   Compile-time error. This statement is only valid within a program and cannot be used in the Immediate window.

Illegal in procedure or DEF FN   Compile-time error. This statement is not allowed inside a procedure.

Illegal number   Compile-time error. The format of the number does not correspond to the number format defined in the *QuickBASIC Language Reference*.

Illegal outside of SUB/FUNCTION   Compile-time error. The STATIC, EXIT SUB, and EXIT FUNCTION statements are not allowed in module-level code.

Illegal outside of TYPE block   Compile-time error. The *element* AS *type* clause is permitted only within a TYPE...END TYPE block.

Illegal type character in numeric constant   Compile-time error. A numeric constant contains an inappropriate type-declaration character.

$INCLUDE-file access error   Compile-time error. The include file named in the $INCLUDE metacommand cannot be located.

INPUT missing Compile-time error. The compiler expects the keyword INPUT.

Input past end of file Run-time error. An INPUT statement reads from a null (empty) file or from a file in which all data has already been read. To avoid this error, use the EOF function to detect the end-of-file character. ERR code 62.

Input runtime module path: Run-time error. This prompt appears if the run-time module is not found. Enter the correct path specification. This error is severe and cannot be trapped.

Integer between 1 and 32767 required Compile-time error. The statement requires an integer argument.

Internal error Run-time error. An internal malfunction occurred in the QuickBASIC compiler.

Invalid character Compile-time error. The compiler found an invalid character, such as a control character, in the source file.

Invalid constant Compile-time error. An invalid expression is used to assign a value to a constant.

Invalid DECLARE for BASIC procedure Compile-time error. You are attempting to use the DECLARE statement's CDECL or BYVAL keywords with a BASIC procedure. CDECL and BYVAL can only be used with non-BASIC procedures.

Label not defined Compile-time error. A line label is referenced (in a GOTO statement, for example), but does not occur in the program.

Label not defined: label Compile-time error. A GOTO *linelabel* statement refers to a nonexistent line label.

Left parenthesis missing Compile-time error. The compiler expects a left parenthesis.

Line invalid. Start again BC invocation error. An invalid file name character was used following the path characters \ or : .

Line number or label missing Compile-time error. There is a line-number or label missing from a statement that requires one, for example GOTO.

Line too long Compile-time error. Lines are limited to 255 characters.

LOOP without DO Compile-time error. The DO starting a DO...LOOP statement is missing or misspelled.

Lower bound exceeds upper bound Compile-time error. The lower bound exceeds the upper bound defined in a DIM statement.

Math overflow Compile-time error. The result of a calculation is too large to be represented in BASIC number format.

Warning: $Metacommand error Compile-time warning. A meta-command is incorrect.

Minus sign missing Compile-time error. The operand is missing from a subtraction operation.

Missing Event Trapping (/W) or Checking Between Statements (/V) option Compile-time error. The program contains an ON *event* statement requiring one of these options.

Missing On Error (/E) option   Compile-time error. When compiling with the BC command, programs that contain ON ERROR GOTO statements must be compiled with the On Error (/e) option.

Missing Resume Next (/X) option   Compile-time error. When compiling with the BC command, programs that contain RESUME, RESUME NEXT, and RESUME zero 0 statements must be compiled with the Resume Next (/x) option.

Must be first statement on the line   Compile-time error. In Block IF...THEN...ELSE constructs, ELSE, ELSEIF, and END IF can only be preceded by a line number or label.

Name of subprogram illegal   Compile-time error. Caused when a subprogram name is a BASIC reserved word or a subprogram name is used twice.

Nested function definition   Compile-time error. A function definition appears inside another function definition or inside an IF...THEN...ELSE clause.

NEXT missing for variable: Compile-time error. A FOR statement is missing a corresponding NEXT statement. The *variable* is the FOR-loop index variable.

NEXT without FOR   Compile-time error. Each NEXT statement must have a matching FOR statement.

No line number in module-name at address segment: offset   Run-time error. Occurs when the error address cannot be found in the linenumber table during error trapping. This error is severe and cannot be trapped.

No main module. Choose Set Main Module from the Run menu to select one   Compile-time error. You are attempting to run the program after you have unloaded the main module. Every program must have a main module.

No RESUME   Run-time error. The end of the program was encountered while the program was in an error-handling routine. A RESUME statement is needed to remedy this situation. ERR code 19.

Numeric array illegal   Compile-time error. Numeric arrays are not allowed as arguments to VARPTR$. Only simple variables and string array elements are permitted.

Only simple variables allowed   Compile-time error. User-defined types and arrays are not permitted in READ and INPUT statements. (Array elements that are not a user-defined type are permitted.)

Operation requires disk   Compile-time error. Attempt to load from or save to a nondisk device such as the printer or keyboard.

Option unknown   BC invocation error. You have given an illegal option.

Out of DATA   Run-time error. A READ statement is executed when there are no DATA statements with unread data remaining in the program. ERR code 4.

Out of memory   Run-time error. More memory is required than is available. For example, there may not be enough memory to allocate a file buffer. ERR code 7.

Out of memory   Compile-time error. The compiler needs more memory than is available.

Out of memory   BC invocation error. There is not enough memory available to run the compiler.

Out of paper   Run-time error. The printer is out of paper or is not turned on. ERR code 27.

Out of stack space   Run-time error. Can occur when a recursive function nests too deeply or if there are too many active subroutine, subprogram, and function calls.

Out of string space Run-time error. String variables exceed the allocated amount of string space. ERR code 14.

Overflow Run-time error. The result of a calculation is too large to be represented within the range allowed for floating-point numbers. ERR code 6.

Overflow in numeric constant Compile-time error. The numeric constant is too large.

Parameter type mismatch Compile-time error. A subprogram parameter type does not match the DECLARE statement argument or the calling argument.

Path not found Run-time error. During an OPEN, MKDIR, CHDIR, or RMDIR operation, DOS was unable to find the path specified. The operation is not completed. ERR code 76.

Path/File access error Run-time error. During an OPEN, MKDIR, CHDIR, or RMDIR operation, the operating system was unable to make a correct path-to-filename connection. The operation is not completed. ERR code 75.

Permission denied Run-time error. An attempt was made to write to a write-protected disk. ERR code 70.

Procedure already defined in Quick library Compile-time error. A procedure in the Quick library has the same name as a procedure in your program.

Program-memory overflow Compile-time error. You are attempting to compile a program whose code segment is larger than 64K. Try splitting the program into separate modules and placing them in the Quick library, or use the CHAIN statement.

Read error on standard input BC invocation error. A system error occurred while reading in the source file.

Redo from start Run-time error. You have responded to an INPUT prompt with the wrong number or type of items.

Rename across disks Run-time error. An attempt was made to rename a file with a new drive designation. This is not allowed. ERR code 74.

Requires DOS 2.10 or later QB invocation error. You are attempting to use QuickBASIC with an incorrect version of DOS.

Requires DOS 2.10 or later Run-time error. You are attempting to use QuickBASIC with an incorrect version of DOS.

RESUME without error Run-time error. A RESUME statement is encountered before an error-trapping routine is entered. ERR code 20.

RETURN without GOSUB Run-time error. A RETURN statement is encountered for which there is no previous, unmatched GOSUB statement. ERR code 3.

Right parenthesis missing Compile-time error. The compiler expects a right (closing) parenthesis.

SEG or BYVAL not allowed in CALLS Compile-time error. BYVAL and SEG are permitted only in a CALL statement.

SELECT without END SELECT Compile-time error. The end of a SELECT CASE statement is missing or misspelled.

Semicolon missing Compile-time error. The compiler expects a semicolon.

Separator illegal   Compile-time error. There is an illegal delimiting character in a PRINT USING or WRITE statement. Use a semicolon or a comma as a delimiter.

Simple or array variable expected   Compile-time error. The compiler is expecting a variable argument.

Statement cannot precede SUB/FUNCTION definition   Compile-time error. The only statements allowed before a procedure definition are REM and DEF*type*.

Warning: Statement ignored   Compile-time warning. You are using the BC command to compile a program that contains TRON and TROFF statements without using the /d option.

Statement illegal in $INCLUDE file   Compile-time error. SUB... END SUB and FUNCTION...END FUNCTION statement blocks are not permitted in include files. Use the Merge command from the File menu to insert the include file into the current module or load the include file as a separate module.

Statement illegal in TYPE block   Compile-time error. The only statements allowed between the TYPE and END TYPE statements are REM and *element* AS *typename*.

Statements or labels illegal between SELECT CASE and CASE   Compile-time error. Statements and line labels are not permitted between SELECT CASE and the first CASE statement.

Statement unrecognizable   Compile-time error. You have probably mistyped a BASIC statement.

STOP statement executed   Run-time error. A STOP statement was encountered in the program.

String assignment required   Compile-time error. The string assignment is missing from an LSET or RSET statement.

String constant required for ALIAS Compile-time error. The DECLARE statement ALIAS keyword requires a string constant argument.

String expression required Compile-time error. The statement requires a string expression argument.

String space corrupt Run-time error. This error occurs when an invalid string in string space is being deleted during heap compaction. The probable cause of this error is that: (1) a string descriptor or string back pointer has been improperly modified; (2) out-of-range array subscripts are used and string space is inadvertently modified; or (3) the POKE or DEF SEG statement has been used incorrectly.

String variable required Compile-time error. The statement requires a string variable argument.

Subscript out of range Run-time error. An array element was referenced with a subscript that was outside the dimensions of the array or an element of an undimensioned dynamic array was accessed. ERR code 9.

Subscript syntax illegal Compile-time error. An array subscript contains a syntax error, for example, both string and integer data types.

SUB or FUNCTION missing Compile-time error. A DECLARE statement has no corresponding procedure.

SUB/FUNCTION without END SUB/FUNCTION Compile-time error. The terminating statement is missing from a procedure.

Subprogram error Compile-time error. This is a subprogram definition error and is usually caused by one of the following: (1) the subprogram is already defined; (2) the program contains incorrectly nested SUB...END SUB statements; or (3) the subprogram or function does not end with an END SUB or END FUNCTION statement.

Subprograms not allowed in control statements Compile-time error. Subprogram definitions are not permitted inside control constructs such as IF...THEN...ELSE and SELECT CASE.

Subprogram not defined Compile-time error. A subprogram is called but never defined.

Syntax error Compile-time error. Several conditions can cause this error. The most common cause is a mistyped BASIC keyword or argument.

Syntax error in numeric constant Compile-time or run-time error. A numeric constant is not properly formed.

THEN missing Compile-time error. The compiler expects a THEN keyword.

TO missing Compile-time error. The compiler expects a TO keyword.

Too many arguments in function call Compile-time error. Function calls are limited to 60 arguments.

Too many dimensions Compile-time error. Arrays are limited to 60 dimensions.

Too many files Compile-time or run-time error. The 255-file directory maximum is exceeded by an attempt to create a new file with a SAVE or OPEN statement. ERR code 67.

Too many labels Compile-time error. The number of lines in the line list following an ON...GOTO/GOSUB statement exceeds 255.

Too many named COMMON blocks Compile-time error. The maximum number of named COMMON blocks permitted is 126.

Too many TYPE definitions Compile-time error. The maximum number of user-defined types permitted is 240.

Too many variables for INPUT   Compile-time error. An INPUT statement is limited to 60 variables.

Too many variables for LINE INPUT   Compile-time error. Only one variable is allowed in a LINE INPUT statement.

Type mismatch   Compile-time or run-time error. The variable is not the required type. For example, you are trying to use the SWAP statement with a string variable and a numeric variable.

TYPE missing   Compile-time error. The TYPE keyword is missing from an END TYPE statement.

Type more than 65535 bytes   Compile-time error. A user-defined type cannot exceed 64K.

Type not defined   Compile-time error. The *usertype* argument to the TYPE statement is not defined.

TYPE statement improperly nested   Compile-time error. User-defined type definitions are not allowed in subprograms.

TYPE without END TYPE   Compile-time error. There is no END TYPE statement associated with a TYPE statement.

Typed variable not allowed in expression   Compile-time error. Variables that are user-defined types are not permitted in expressions such as CALL ALPHA ((X)), where X is a user-defined type.

Unprintable error   Run-time error. An error message is not available for the error condition that exists. This may be caused by an ERROR statement that doesn't have a defined error code.

Valid options: [/RUN] file /AH /B /C:buf /G /H /L [lib] /MBF /CMD string   QB invocation error. This message appears when you invoke QuickBASIC with an invalid option.

Variable-length string required Compile-time error. Only variable-length strings are permitted in a FIELD statement.

Variable name not unique Compile-time error. You are attempting to define x as a user-defined type after x.y has been used.

Variable required Compile-time error. The compile encountered an INPUT, LET, READ, or SHARED statement without a variable argument.

Variable required Compile-time error. A GET or PUT statement didn't specify a variable when operation on a file opened in BINARY mode. ERR code 40.

WEND without WHILE Compile-time error. This error is caused when a WEND statement has no corresponding WHILE statement.

WHILE without WEND Compile-time error. This error is caused when a WHILE statement has no corresponding WEND statement.

Wrong number of dimensions Compile-time error. An array reference contains the wrong number of dimensions.

Trademarks

Apple II®	Apple Computer, Inc.
Apple II+™	Apple Computer, Inc.
Apple IIc™	Apple Computer, Inc.
Apple IIe™	Apple Computer, Inc.
Apple IIGS™	Apple Computer, Inc.
AppleSoft™	Apple Computer, Inc.
Atari®	Atari, Inc.
GW-BASIC®	Microsoft Corporation
Hewlett-Packard®	Hewlett-Packard Company
HP™	Hewlett-Packard Company
IBM®	International Business Machines Corporation
Microsoft®	Microsoft Corporation
Microsoft BASIC®	Microsoft Corporation
Tandy 1000™	Tandy Corporation

The manuscript for this book was prepared and submitted
to Osborne/McGraw-Hill in electronic form. The
acquisitions editor for this project was Jeffrey Pepper and
the technical reviewer was Seth Pratt.

Text set in Baskerville and display in Megaron. Cover art by
Bay Graphics Design Associates. Color separation by Colour
Image. Cover supplier, Phoenix Color Corp. Book printed
and bound by R.R. Donnelley & Sons Company,
Crawfordsville, Indiana.

Index